NOTORIOUS & NOTABLE
New Englanders

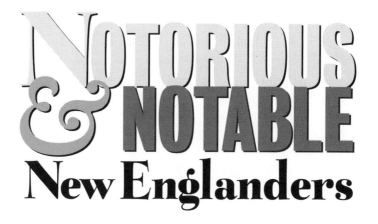

NOTORIOUS & NOTABLE New Englanders

By

Peter F. Stevens

DOWN EAST BOOKS

Copyright © 1997 by Peter F. Stevens
ISBN 0-89272-397-1
Book design by Eugenie S. Delaney
Printed and bound at BookCrafters, Inc., Chelsea, Mich.

9   8   7   6   5   4   3   2   1

Down East Books / Camden, Maine
Book Orders: 800-766-1670

Library of Congress Cataloging-in-Publication Data
Stevens, Peter F.
     Notorious and notable New Englanders / by Peter F. Stevens.
          p.   cm.
     Includes bibliographical references and index.
     ISBN 0-89272-397-1 (softcover)
     1. New England—Biography.   I. Title
CT247.5.S74   1997
920.074—dc21   96-52201
                                                              CIP

Contents

Acknowledgments

$\backsim$

All authors must enlist the help of numerous people. I'd like to thank Peg Stevens for her unflagging support and help with the manuscript, Greg Stevens for his computer expertise when a hard-drive glitch erupted in the middle of the project, and Paula and Karen Stevens. I also want to thank Mary Clark and Linda Beeler, librarians of the Thomas Crane Public Library, in Quincy, Massachusetts; as with all my books and articles, Mary and Linda aided me in countless aspects of research.

To Tom Fernald, publisher of Down East Books; Karin Womer, my editor; and Alice Devine, I am grateful for their support of this book and for their patience and effort on its behalf.

SINNERS

AMONG

THE

SAINTS

Murder in the New World

∽

Trouble arrived quickly in John Winthrop's Boston. Standing before Governor Winthrop inside the rude pine walls of Boston's first meetinghouse in the late fall of 1630 was a man with ample reason to dread Winthrop's anger. Even today, Winthrop's portrait, that of a stern-eyed man with a barbed beard, can intimidate viewers. The object of the governor's scrutiny, as well as that of seven other leaders of the fledgling Massachusetts Bay Colony, had reminded fellow Puritans that they could not escape in the New World the basest human instincts of the Old World. Walter Palmer, a man who had stepped ashore with Winthrop and the other settlers of Boston scant months ago, stood accused of murder—the murder of another Puritan.

The gravity of Palmer's predicament could not be overstated: he would hang for manslaughter if convicted, the first Puritan so punished. He had already achieved a dubious honor, that of appearing as the defendant in the first case brought before a Puritan court in America.

If Palmer knew that one colonist, a Pilgrim named John Billington, had been hanged at Plymouth Plantation less than a month before, in September 1630, he had reason to break into a cold sweat at the prospect of sharing Billington's fate. But Palmer, unlike the Pilgrim, had not murdered a man in cold blood, but in self-defense. The dilemma of the accused Puritan lay in convincing his jury and the judges of that fact. In the General Court, from which lawyers were banned, Palmer stood alone, armed only with his version of the spat that had ended in a fatal fistfight. As the survivor of the fray opened his defense, his hands still bruised for all to see, he could not deny that he had thrashed Austen Bratcher to death; his chances of convincing the jury of his innocence appeared tenuous at best.

Walter Palmer claimed that Bratcher had provoked the fracas, first with insults and oaths and then with a sudden flurry of punches. Unfortunately, Winthrop's journal never cataloged the reasons behind the quarrel, but court records reveal that Austen Bratcher died as a result of "strookes [strokes] given by Walter Palmer."[1] That Palmer had given better than he had got had saved his life from Bratcher's fists and feet. Against the magistrates' pondering of Palmer's entreaties, his fistic prowess could avail him little. Words now constituted Palmer's only weapon.

Palmer finished his testimony and stood braced against the prisoner's bar while a stream of neighbors—men in tall brimmed hats, in woolen doublets or leather jerkins, in breeches, stockings, and buckled shoes; and women in prim bonnets, capes, and layered petticoats to ward off fall gusts—testified before the court. Eyewitnesses to the brawl were split over who had instigated it. Finally, after the witnesses in the Puritans' first trial had painted their varying verbal renditions of *Palmer v. Bratcher,* the jury huddled to deliberate the evidence and, most important, their gut feelings about Palmer's veracity.

Palmer had to worry most about Winthrop, for the taciturn leader of the Massachusetts Bay Colony had hoped that the Puritans—*his* Puritans—would live free of sin as God's chosen people, the latter-day Israelites. "The Lord will make our name a praise and glory," Winthrop had proclaimed at the settlement's founding, "so that men shall say of succeeding plantations: 'The Lord make it like that of New England. . . . We shall be like a City upon a Hill; the eyes of all people are on us.' "[2]

The telltale moment loomed: Would Palmer twist beneath a rope or would he live among Winthrop's saints? Across the benches and within the rough-hewn walls of the first meetinghouse, the jury's verdict echoed: "Innocent by balance of evidence."

Walter Palmer had dodged the hangman. But if Winthrop and company still hoped that their small settlement on the Shawmut Peninsula would prove a haven from mayhem, disillusionment lurked. Throughout Puritan New England the Ten Commandments would

3

take a beating, and colonists would commit astonishing transgressions not found in the original commandments or in any code of law the Puritans would devise.

Duel in the Sun

〜

I n a tree-shrouded clearing on June 18, 1621, two young men eyed one another. Each one brandished a sword in his right hand, a dagger in his left. Moving in a slowly tightening circle, each waited for the other to lunge or parry.

These were not feuding sons of European nobility. Nor did the ground on which they paced and parried lie outside a castle. The pair hailed from Plymouth Plantation. To the scandal and ire of William Bradford and Myles Standish, among others, the first recorded duel in the thirteen colonies had erupted in their foothold in the New World. According to a later chronicler, one of the village's "few marriageable girls"[1] may have ignited the feud.

The duelists, Edward Dotey and Edward Leister, had trudged up the gangplank of the *Mayflower* in July 1620 as the indentured servants of Stephen Hopkins, a fiery thirty-five-year-old self-made clerk from Gloucestershire. Both manservants had signed standard indentures, bonding themselves to Hopkins for a term of years. Each had little but brutal labor awaiting him in the New World until his contract expired.

For men such as Dotey and Leister, both in their early twenties and "lusty," fractious sorts from the slums of London, bonded servitude was virtual slavery.[2] Their masters, legally required to furnish only food, clothing, and shelter, could buy, sell, or rent servants on a whim. Nine other bonded young men shuffled onto the *Mayflower* with Dotey and Leister. Jostling each other for scant space in the hold of the vessel, they braced themselves for the stormy, scurvy-wracked Atlantic crossing.

Their youthful resilience served Dotey and Leister well, as they choked down brackish water and rancid salt pork during the passage; in late November 1620, they first glimpsed the wooded New England shoreline in relatively good health. But their state of mind—along with that of many of the free but lesser Pilgrims, "the goodmen"—concerned William Bradford, John Carver, Myles Standish, and the rest of the expedition's leaders.[3] At worst, mutiny simmered among the men; at best, dissension. It was rumored that "when they [disgruntled goodmen] came ashore, they would use their own libertie, for none had the power to command then, the patente they had," according to *Mayflower* malcontents, "giving Bradford and other notables no power to command their lessers."[4]

With the first New England winter, uncertain relations with the Indians, and the selection of a fitting site for settlement all confronting the Pilgrims, dissension in the social pecking order threatened the band's very survival. To defuse "the discontented and mutinous speeches"[5] permeating the ship from forecastle to afterdeck, on November 11, 1620, Bradford and others drew up the Mayflower Compact, in which the signers agreed to honor "Laws, Ordinances, Acts, Constitutions and offices . . . as shall be thought most meet and convenient for the general good of the Colony, unto which we promise all due submission and obedience."[6] The last two men invited, or compelled, to make their mark on the pact were Edward Dotey and Edward Leister.

On December 6, 1620, Dotey clambered over the gunwales of the *Mayflower* and joined Hopkins, Bradford, Standish, and fourteen other men in the vessel's shallot. They rowed the squat, one-masted vessel toward the shore to scout favorable spots for settlement. Hopkins left his other servant, Leister, aboard the *Mayflower*.

Dotey and the others in the shallow-draft boat huddled against frigid salt spray that made the men's cloaks, linen shirts, jerkins, and breeches cling "as if they had been glazed with ice" and bailed water that splashed incessantly over the gunwales.[7] Two of the explorers fainted from exposure. After several days spent rowing, beaching the shallot, stumbling across sand and through gnarled woods and nights spent crouching behind makeshift barracks of pine boughs, the shore party took soundings of the bay at "Thievish Harbor"[8] (dubbed Plymouth several years earlier by explorer John Smith), found it deep enough for large ships, and on December 11, 1620, selected the adjoining landfall as their foothold in the New World, a site of "diverse cornfields, a little running brook, a place fit for situation."[9]

Along with the other *Mayflower* passengers, Dotey and Leister began their new lives, the two indentured servants shouldering their fair share—and then some—of the on-shore labors. The duo, cooped up too long with few outlets for their high-spirited natures, hauled boulders, chopped firewood, sawed and lugged logs for the settlers' common house, and, shivering and wet in the struggle to erect the house against winter's winds and snow, helped raise the twenty-foot-square walls of the structure. With bulrushes hacked and gathered along ice-encrusted Town Brook, the servants and freemen, such as a tall young man named John Alden, thatched the roof and wattled and daubed the timbers to keep out Atlantic gusts.

Dotey and Leister not only added their muscle to the community tasks, but also labored on the main chore their master had appointed: the construction of a sturdy home for the Hopkins family. When they were not drafted for such jobs as hauling five cannons up a hill and mounting them atop a wooden platform, they managed to complete part of the thatched cottage by early March, their feat a minor miracle given its backdrop against the Pilgrims' "starving time," the winter of 1620.[10]

Dotey and Leister required every ounce of their youthful strength to survive New England's snow, ice, and winds. "Half of their [the Pilgrim's] company died," Bradford wrote, "especially in January and February, being the depth of winter, and wanting houses and other comforts; being infected with the scurvy and other diseases which this long voyage had brought upon them, so as there died sometimes two or three a day. Of 100 and odd persons, scarce fifty remained."[11] Sprawled across the floor of the common house, many of the men languished from illness, exposure, and exhaustion; aboard the *Mayflower*, the women and children also suffered cold and disease. Those men still able to stand hacked unmarked graves in frozen turf, praying that the Indians would not realize how many settlers had perished, how weak the rest were.

Finally, in early March 1620, the first signs of spring's thaw heartened the survivors, whose ranks included the Hopkins family and their two manservants. As soon as the ground softened, Stephen Hopkins sent his gaunt bondsmen to the acreage granted him, and Dotey and Leister cleared the soil of trees, rocks, and brush and sowed seed-corn and beans. The duo's mistress, Elizabeth Hopkins, planted carrots, radishes, and cabbages in the plot behind her unfinished cottage.

Stephen Hopkins, sweating in the fields alongside his servants, did not typify the traditional master. A self-made man who began his career as an impoverished clerk, Hopkins worked his servants hard, but treated them decently—too decently, in the opinions of the Pilgrim Fathers, who would reproach him for allowing too much familiarity with his "inferiours" and would fine him for "allowing servants and such to sit in his house drinking and playing shovelboard."[12] His neighbors' arched eyebrows notwithstanding, Hopkins never lost his common touch, refusing to embrace fellow leaders' autocratic attitudes even during his stint as Plymouth's lieutenant governor.

With Dotey and Leister, the former a particularly hot-headed young man, Hopkins's informality would temporarily haunt him. Although both servants had labored unstintingly in Hopkins's fields and had done their enforced part to build seven private homes and four common houses along Plymouth's main road in the spring and summer of 1621, long hours of toil did not quell all the energies of youth. According to Hopkins's biographer Margaret Hodges, the lack of marriageable young women in Plymouth may have frustrated the two servants. Neither Leister, whose term of indenture would expire in 1622, nor Dotey, whose contract ran for several more years, offered much in the way of prospects to potential brides. And to the likes of pretty Priscilla Mullins, attracting the attentions of Myles Standish (whose wife, Rose, had perished of fever aboard the *Mayflower* in the winter of 1620–21) and the handsome John Alden was more important than winning the affections of Dotey and Leister, ruffians from London's nether neighborhoods. Their lowly status notwithstanding, Hodges speculates, both servants had located a prospective wife. A pretty settler bridging the distance from girl to young woman, she was Constance Hopkins, the teenaged daughter of Stephen Hopkins and his deceased first wife.

Whether a quarrel over Constance Hopkins—Hodges is the only one to offer this "romantic" theory—or some other impetuous slight ignited the feud between Dotey and Leister is not known, but tensions erupted on June 18, 1621. Hopkins was away from the settlement; he often went on diplomatic missions to Indian villages with other Pilgrim leaders, leaving his servants to tend his field and watch out for the Hopkins women. Dotey and Leister walked from Plymouth Plantation and into the woods, clutching daggers and swords. One brash servant or the other had issued a challenge at single combat; the challenge was readily accepted.

The pair halted in a clearing away from the notice of neighbors, who would have seized them if they had possessed any inkling of the impending clash. They squared off on their field of honor, fingers clenching the hilts of their daggers and swords, ready to break English—and now colonial—laws that banned dueling.

The ring and scrape of steel upon steel pealed above the clearing. No Pilgrim witnessed which duelist had lunged first, but at least two thrusts amid the flurry of feints and parries found their mark. Dotey walked back to Plymouth with one hand slashed and bloodied. His foe limped along the main street with a sliced thigh. In the words of a later Pilgrim historian, "honor was satisfied; but not so with justice."[13]

When Stephen Hopkins returned home a short time after the duel, he found his servants wounded and manacled. The men's flagrant disregard for the community's laws had infuriated Bradford, Standish, and the other leaders. And equally important, Plymouth needed every able-bodied man; the injury the bondservants had caused the community in impaired labor was no less alarming than the wounds they had inflicted upon each other.

The Pilgrim Fathers convened a tribunal before the townspeople, and the duelists, groaning from their wounds, were judged for a crime for which they offered no reasonable defense. No notions of chivalry or honor among servants excused the offense. Not even Myles Standish, the red-bearded career soldier with the hair-trigger temper, a man of action himself, condoned the melee. The tribunal's guilty verdict was a foregone conclusion, as would have been the case in a London courtroom. The only question remaining for the judges lay in the proper punishment. A London magistrate could have rendered a stiff jail sentence—or worse. But Bradford and his fellow masters grappled with the very issue that had made the crime seem worse: a tiny settlement heavily outnumbered by Indians required every available man for defense, as well as manual labor. Thus Dotey and Leister's muscle dictated some measure of mercy from the tribunal.

The tribunal struck a compromise: the wounded miscreants would not be jailed or flogged, but were "adjudged by the whole company to have their head and feet tied together, and so to lie for twenty-four hours, without meat or drink."[14]

On the appointed date of punishment, the Pilgrims assembled in Plymouth's main road—men, women, and children alike forming a loose circle. Back in London, at the infamous Smithfield and Tyburn Prisons, crowds swilling street-vendors' liquors would sing, laugh, hiss, and cheer as sentences ranging from floggings to hangings were carried out. No such holiday air engulfed the Pilgrims. Although the duelists were mere indentured servants, they had suffered alongside their loftier

Mayflower passengers the past winter and had not shirked their chores. The imminent punishment offered neither sport nor entertainment to the onlookers.

Dotey and Leister were led out to the main road and trussed from head to foot. Their muscles grew taut, slowly began to ache, and eventually throbbed with bone-searing agony. Beneath a hot sun, many "hog-tied" prisoners were soon drenched with sweat and swooned. Some lapsed into unconsciousness, or, in extreme cases, a coma.

Whether out of concern for Dotey and Leister's welfare or for their value as property, Hopkins appealed to Standish, Governor Bradford, and others for the pair's release. "Within an hour" of the instant the bonds first bit into the prisoners' skin and the agonies of their wounds combined with the "great Pains" of their punishment, Dotey and Leister added their own "humble request" for mercy.[15]

The thirty-two-year-old Bradford—entrusted with the governor's post in early April 1621, after John Carver complained "greatly in his head" while hoeing a field and died two days later—mulled over the entreaties.[16] "A commone blessing and father to them all [the Pilgrims],"[17] Bradford elicited the prisoners' "Promise of better Carriage [conduct]."[18] Then, with Hopkins's assurances that the two servants would honor their oath, Bradford released them to their master's watchful charge.

Dotey and Leister kept their word through the term of their indentures, slowly regaining their community's wary trust. Both men were allowed to eat and to drink their fill at the first Thanksgiving, several months after the notorious duel. Aside from the plantation's bountiful harvest that would save the settlers during the upcoming winter, the two servants had ample reason for thanks: a harsher leader than Bradford might easily have let them suffer their full punishment regardless of their wounds.

When Edward Leister's indenture expired, he wasted little time in boarding a ship for the Virginia colony, having found neither a wife nor a stake among the Pilgrims. Of his path once he last saw the thatched and frame dwellings and the hilltop fort of Plymouth, history records only that "after he was at liberty, [he] went to Virginia, & there dyed," possibly killed in battle against Indians in 1622 at Jamestown.[19]

Edward Dotey finished his service to Stephen Hopkins, remained with the band who had trussed him in public, and, in one of New England's first rags-to-riches sagas, parlayed his share of Plymouth's crops, and later his real-estate "empire," into a sizable estate of 140 pounds. But despite his success, the hot temper that had prodded Dotey into America's first recorded duel continued to land him in court for a range of verbal and physical assaults upon his neighbors. Typical of his ongoing legal woes was a case in which he had swindled a neighbor "about a flitch of bacon"[20] and had publicly denounced the aggrieved customer as "a rogue."[21] The court fined Dotey fifty shillings. The plaintiff was fortunate to have increased his purse at Dotey's expense— and to have eluded the erstwhile duelist's fists.

In 1633 or 1634, those fists pounded and bloodied a man named Josias Cooke. The court fined Dotey six shillings for fighting and forced him to pay damages for three shillings, four pence to his victim.

Dotey resorted to his fists again in January 1638, when he "broke the King's Peace" by flailing away at George Clarke.[22] This time, the court fined the Plymouth pugilist ten shillings. But court records indicate that two months later, he assaulted Clark a second time. A magistrate pried another ten shillings from Dotey's purse.

Edward Dotey died at Yarmouth, Massachusetts, in 1655, having married twice and fathered nine children. The lowliest of passengers aboard the *Mayflower*, he had risen farther in Plymouth's financial scene than most of the Pilgrim Fathers.

Despite Dotey's belligerent success in business and his temper-fueled dates in court, Bradford, Standish, and the other Pilgrim leaders had curbed him in one respect: he never fought another duel. No other colonist in Plymouth ever followed America's first duelist onto the field of honor.

Out of Order:
Thomas Lechford, Esq.

He spelled his name Lechford, but pronounced it *Leech*ford. In the collective opinion of John Winthrop and other proper Puritans of Boston in 1639, the syllable "Leech" proved fitting, for Thomas Lechford, flaunting his "silver-laced coate and a gold-wrought cap,"[1] quaffing beer, and puffing clay pipeloads of choice Spanish tobacco imported or pirated from Venezuela, cut a controversial figure not only for conspicuous consumption, but for his profession of "lawyering for a fee."[2]

To Puritan magistrates straining to keep lawyers out of Massachusetts Bay Colony courts and to preserve the theocratic nature of Boston, their "City upon a Hill,"[3] Lechford, the first to "lawyer" for a price, proved a threat. His outbursts against the Puritans' Congregationalist meetinghouses infuriated Boston's leaders even more.

In September 1639, Lechford's foes, the powerful Reverend John Cotton foremost among them, seized an opportunity to chasten the solicitor and scrivener and ruin his flourishing practice: the Boston quarter court charged him with "jury embracing," the colonial version of jury tampering.[4] For the first time in the history of the thirteen colonies, a solicitor faced disbarment.

Although Lechford had landed in Boston less than a year earlier, his legal career tattered in England's courts, he had never been summoned to appear before a King's Bench judge to battle for the very right to continue "lawyering." In the Bay Colony he had no powerful friends to whom he could appeal for help. As he usually did, however, Lechford devised an effective defense, one his foes did not anticipate.

Thomas Lechford's early life has long puzzled historians, some speculating that he was descended from nobility, the Lechfords of Surrey, England. No ironclad proof of this blue-blooded lineage has emerged, however.

What is known is that in the 1630s he studied law at St. Clement's Inn, one of the British legal system's nine Inns of Chancery under the aegis of the four Inns of Court, which controlled the selection of aspiring barristers. In Lechford's day, unless a law student had an influential patron or a noble name, his chance of becoming a barrister and gaining entry to a prestigious Inn of Court was slight. The Inns of Chancery, such as St. Clement's, were the training grounds for second-tier lawyering—attorneys, court clerks, and solicitors, all of whom were barred from pleading cases.

Despite the barriers, the law still offered ambitious young men a chance to rise from modest origins to wealth and influence in London. Lechford seethed with ambition during his late twenties and early thirties as he built a practice from St. Clement's as a solicitor and scrivener, a drafter of legal documents. A deeply religious adherent to the Anglican Church, he nonetheless loathed bishops and other church leaders who abused their power by interfering in civil matters. His ambition and his religious fervor soon landed him in a rancorous controversy between church and court.

In 1635, Lechford served as the solicitor for Ferdinando Adams, a Puritan churchwarden embroiled in a suit against Henry Dade, an Anglican lackey of William Laud, the formidable archbishop of Canterbury. The case soon drew him into a morass of politics and religion. When Dade, at the behest of Laud, ordered Adams to remove seats from St. Mary-at-Tower, in Ipswich, Suffolk, and to replace them with a conference table, Adams had vandalized Dade's chair with a message aimed clearly at Dade's boss, the controversial and high-living Laud: "My house shall be called the house of prayer; but ye have made it a den of thieves."

Dade excommunicated Adams. The enraged churchwarden retained barrister William Prynne to sue Laud's surrogate, and to an eager man named Thomas Lechford fell the task of soliciting "the cause [of Adams] for Mr. Prynne," who would two years later face charges of seditious libel for "witnessing" against Laud and other bishops.[5]

By the time—in 1636 or 1637—that Laud, Justice Jones, and George Croke of the King's Bench gutted Adams's suit and harangued the Puritan churchwarden for "lending his [Laud's] name in such a scandalous cause,"[6] Lechford not only saw his dreams of a London legal career dissolving in the archbishop's courtroom counterattacks, but also was hauled off by constables to a cell on the order of Justice Jones and languished there until Adams withdrew his case. Lechford was imprisoned for contempt of court, but his true sin was soliciting the case of a Puritan bold enough to challenge Archbishop Laud. Of his ordeal in one of London's fetid, damp jails Lechford would write: "I suffered imprisonment . . . for some acts construed to oppose, as tending to subvert Episcopacy, and the settled Ecclesiastical government of England."[7]

William Prynne, Lechford's boss in the case, viewed his solicitor's plight as something far less than legal martyrdom: Prynne "blamed Lechford for deserting the suit," which was easy for Prynne to charge since he, unlike Lechford, was not sitting in a cell.[8]

The source of Lechford's misery, Adams, slipped aboard a vessel bound for Boston and eventually turned up in Dedham, Massachusetts, branded a liar by the archbishop but embraced and "admitted free" by the Puritan reformers for his stand against the Church of England's bishops.[9] Lechford, still a staunch member of the church despite his suffering at Laud's hands, faced the backlash of his advocacy of the Adams case even after the plaintiff's flight and his own release from jail.

The chief repercussion proved a blackballing of Lechford from even the work of "a common solicitor of causes"[10] in England, as he described himself. Although Laud's animosity and the stint in jail choked off any hope that Lechford would recover his reputation and climb up London's proverbial legal ladder, he refused to abandon a career in law but realized he must seek a practice far from home. He later claimed that he had received an offer from the court of Prince

George Rakoczy, of Transylvania, and that "the Lords of Providence [Rhode Island] offered me place of preferment with them which I will not name."[11]

Lechford's letters indicate that in his enforced search for a new situation, he turned to two notable acquaintances. Various scholars speculate that in the fallout of the Adams case, Lechford traveled to Ireland to seek out "my Lord Deputy Wentworth now Lord Lieutenant-general" and "to follow my old profession . . . there at least."[12]

The second luminary to whom the lawyer wrote was the Reverend Hugh Peters, who lived in Boston and, like Lechford, was a man who had bucked the Church of England. But unlike the chastened solicitor, Peters had confronted the bishops on grounds of religious ideology. A leading light of Boston's pulpits and its burgeoning fishing, shipbuilding, and mercantile concerns, he had far more in common with Adams than with the solicitor, who, scholars contend, had heard Peters preach his famed fiery sermons at St. Sepulcher's Church, in London. Though an Anglican, Lechford hoped to convince Peters to win him admission to Boston's church and to introduce him to John Winthrop, the Reverend John Cotton, and other Massachusetts Bay power brokers. The beleaguered solicitor had decided to open a fresh practice in the Puritans' City upon a Hill. To Peters, Lechford wrote, "[I was] thrown out of my station in England . . . banished out of this good Land."[13]

On June 27, 1638, a Wednesday, from the gunwales of a ship sliding into Boston's harbor, Thomas Lechford first saw the hilly peninsula with its rugged "crown," the Trimountain, whose "beacon sett on the sentry hill at Boston, to give notice to the country of any danger," would inspire the name Beacon Hill.[14]

Unknown to Lechford, many eminent Bostonians deemed his profession a threat to the colony. The Reverend Nathaniel Ward asserted that, in the Massachusetts courts, no man should be allowed "fee or reward" for representing another person's case—this from a man who had won admission to England's bar in 1615.[15] John Winthrop, also a

15

former barrister, looked down on "common solicitors" and the "multitude of Atturnies . . . [who] take out processe against their neighbors upon very light occasions."[16]

From his pulpit in the First Church, the Reverend Cotton railed against "unconscionable Advocates" who argue a "bad case by quirks of wit, and tricks and quillets of Law" and who "use their tongues as weapons of unrighteousness . . . to plead in corrupt causes."[17]

Leery of shysters and their verbal chicanery, striving to keep justice in the hands of Puritan magistrates, many of Boston's leaders acknowledged the citizens' right to legal representation, but "felt no compulsion to recruit it."[18] As one legal scholar would later write, Lechford, from the moment he opened a practice in Boston, "was the proverbial Cyclops in the land of the blind," and some in his new home would attempt to blind the Cyclops—figuratively, of course.

As Lechford strolled through Boston, passing frame houses covered with clapboards and flanked by fences and tidy vegetable gardens, he soon found that Great Street (now State Street) comprised the town's political and commercial nerve center, the very spot to solicit clients who needed everything from deeds and wills to written pleadings in civil cases. On the future site of Boston's Old State House, Great Street stretched 113 feet wide to accommodate an open-air market clotted daily with Puritans, townspeople, farmers, sailors, and Indians. Perched at the front corner of the market was a long, low-ceilinged wood-frame building. Lechford intended to be a frequent visitor there, for that building, the meetinghouse, was the site of the General Court.

For Lechford, accustomed to the ornate trappings of London's King's Bench—though only its fringes—the rude, diminutive meetinghouse posed one more culture shock. Yet despite the muddy paths the colonists dubbed roads, despite the absence in 1639 of grand homes, Lechford and other newcomers to Boston discovered comforting vestiges of their homeland. The town's Puritan settlers who hailed from London, writes Professor Bernard Bailyn, "sought to recreate the life they had known at home . . . in the towns around

Boston Bay . . . they saw many of the same people with whom they had pushed through the crowds of Cheapside a few years earlier. From the first, they called the main thoroughfare of Boston 'Cornhill', and along it and the intersecting King Street, which led to the wharf, many established their residences. The list of property owners on Cornhill between Milk and Dock Streets . . . reads like the roster of expatriated tradesmen and shopkeepers of the old business district. . . The settling together of old friends and the use of old street names were fragments of the settlers' never-ending attempts to make the wilderness of America familiarly English."[19]

The settlers of the growing commercial town needed someone to draw up business letters, promissory notes, affidavits, and a broad range of other legal documents, and Lechford soon discovered he had chosen a propitious time to land in Boston. Once he had stowed his belongings in a home rented for five pounds a year, tradesmen, farmers, merchants, and even Puritan leaders retained the solicitor's services, flooding him with a workload few lawyers then or now could juggle. Somehow, Lechford did just that, churning out an average of three detailed documents every four days, six days a week, unable to afford "even the luxury of illness" to keep him from the papers heaped atop his writing table.[20]

The solicitor had little time to acclimate himself during his first few months in Boston; in summer, ships from England lay moored in the harbor, and Puritan merchants scrambled to load their goods and write bills of lading, business letters, and letters of attorney for the vessels' return trips.

Lechford's first commission in Boston required him to draft a mortgage agreement regarding a house and yard "next Mr. Cottons."[21] Though he did not yet know it, Lechford would find Cotton to be one of the town's sternest foes of solicitors.

Lechford harbored far grander dreams of legal renown and civic influence than the lot of a mere legal draftsman. He chafed at making "my living by writing petty things," for he craved to make "pleadings" before the colonial court and establish himself as a force there.[22]

Notable justices and clerics preferred that the scrivener constrain his practice to business documents, wills, and "real property," the colonial version of real estate law. But his expertise in property law should have tipped off any leader scrutinizing Lechford's work in his first year in Boston to his real intent, for in England that field was the realm of the barrister, not a mere solicitor or scrivener. Legal historian Thomas G. Barnes would later compare Lechford's skills to those of the members of London's lofty Inner Temple.

The solicitor's frustration with his petty cases notwithstanding, those commissions allowed him to live high, always a suspicious development to proper Puritans. His success also supported his wife, Elizabeth, in style. No one knows whether he married her in New England or Old England, but by 1639 she had joined her spouse in his rented home. In a town where ministers extolled modesty in behavior, fashion, and home life, Elizabeth Lechford disdained the prim Puritan petticoat for a costly "tuft holland" waistcoat and new gowns.[23] Elizabeth and her husband, in his "silver-laced" coat and his gold-trimmed cap, were bound to stand out in any Boston crowd.

The Lechfords also enjoyed household amenities beyond the means of most of their neighbors. Many colonists had to satisfy their sweet tooth with molasses or local honey, but the Lechfords dipped spoons into the "best sugar."[24] For many Boston men desiring to wash away the dust of a hard day's work with a refreshing tankard of ale, a trip to a waterfront inn was necessary; Lechford sipped his private stash in the comfort of his home. And whenever the time arrived to clear his table of tankards or to cover the sugar bowl, whenever the floorboards needed sweeping or a simmering pot required stirring, Lechford and his wife summoned their maid.

Despite his financial success, Thomas Lechford found his career path blocked by a weighty obstacle: his Church of England membership. He could not vote or hold a public office—such as court magistrate—unless the Congregational leaders in Boston accepted him. Any attempt the Reverend Hugh Peters made on Lechford's behalf fell short. Lechford's profession and his Anglican background made him a suspicious character to such Massachusetts Bay ministers as John Cotton and Nathaniel Ward. As Puritans also took stock of the solicitor's flashy clothes, Lechford's hopes of civic prominence in his new home floundered.

As distressing to Lechford as his checked ambitions was his denied access to a meetinghouse. Every Sabbath, while his clients donned their Sunday best and worshipped God, Lechford was compelled to pray at home. A deeply religious man, he anguished over his neighbors' denying him the Sacrament: "Once I stood without one of the doors [of a meetinghouse], and looked in, and saw the administration."[25] But he was not allowed inside. To a friend in England, Lechford wrote: "Never since I saw you have I received the Sacrament of the Lord's supper. . . . Yet blessed be the Lord, to my better satisfaction at the last."[26]

As the months passed, and Lechford proved his usefulness to the court's magistrates, he was allowed to expand his practice from petty documents to pleadings on behalf of plaintiffs and defendants. By the summer of 1639, he employed "a terseness and straightforwardness in common-law pleading" better suited to life in frontier New England than to the conventions of his training ground, British courts.[27] Lechford would "draw pleadings" in thirty-five New England cases, all but five on behalf of the plaintiff.

One of those cases, an innocuous civil matter involving one William Cole and his wife, provided Lechford's detractors an opportunity to silence his pleadings permanently. In the September 3, 1639, session of the quarter court, clerks and court officials alike lined up against him. As the flamboyant solicitor faced his soberly clad accusers, he was forced to summon every scrap of his pleading skills. The magistrates had already decided to disbar him: "Mr. Thomas Lechford," the court record intoned, "for going to the jury & pleading with them out of Court, is debarred from pleading any man's cause hearafter, unless his owne, & admonished not to presume to meddle beyond what he shall be called to by the Court."[28]

The words rendered within the wood-frame walls of the meetinghouse threatened to limit Lechford's practice to only "petty things." Lechford would not submit without a rebuttal. Standing in front of the magistrates so eager to muzzle him, the solicitor conceded that the Coles had "retained" him and that he "did offend in speaking to the Jury without leave," which was "not to be done by the law of England."[29] But then, just as his foes felt certain not only of their victory but also of this outsider's humiliation, Lechford argued that his misdeed "was not Embracery for he had no reward so to do."[30] Resorting to an argument of "extenuating circumstances," he invoked "one or two seeming approbations of the like which he hath observed on other Causes here."[31] He argued that his accusers were unethically holding him to a standard they did not levy upon themselves.

In his legal *coup de grâce* he countered: "Some speeches of mine, specially some involuntary and of sudden [nature] . . . and zeal of speaking for my matters, may seem to offend such as have not been accustomed much to public pleadings of advocates."[32]

Cloaked in a deferential tone, Lechford's words nonetheless revealed a challenge: What right did the magistrates—still bound by *English* law—have to deny freeborn Englishmen their right to "public pleadings of advocates?" The court's desire to run proceedings free of advocates, Lechford hinted, had fueled his disbarment—not his having approached a jury "without leave."[33] Lechford then quickly concluded his defense with contrition. "Notwithstanding [the double standard of the court]," he was "heartily sorry for his offense."[34]

Although his subtle challenge threatened to overwhelm his apology and ruin any chance of his disbarment's repeal, Lechford had proven true to his self-image: "I speak according to my light and dare do no otherwise."[35]

The magistrates relented. The solicitor continued to plead for clients. In the same court session as his disbarment hearing, Lechford, acting as a defense counsel, comported himself in a "brilliant" manner, "one worthy of the ablest barrister."[36] And his pleadings, along with his writing of legal documents, continued to earn him a fine living despite his complaints to a friend that "the practice scarce finds me bread."[37] One glance at Lechford's *Note-Book* (housed at the American Antiquarian Society) reveals in his own hand that his financial gripes were, at best, disingenuous. He averaged 28 pounds, 14 shillings a year, charging approximately two-and-a-half shillings per document. His income stacked up favorably against that of skilled solicitors and attorneys in England and did not include the payments he took "in truck"—produce and various other goods from clients' gardens and shops. In September 1640, Lechford reached into his purse and paid cash for a house and garden. A lawyer would later point out that Lechford's ledger belied the old legal adage: "if there are two lawyers in town, they are both millionaires, if one, he is a pauper."[38]

The reasons Lechford cried poor mouth rested with his religious and social frustration. In September 1640, almost a year to the day that he was temporarily disbarred, he openly challenged Boston's ministers on a range of Congregationalist policies, sparked in part by church elders' refusal to allow him the Sacrament.

Lechford was ordered once again to appear before the quarter court, this time the December 1640 session, to answer for his indiscretions. He would describe the furor, during which he was threatened with banishment from Boston: "I never intended openly to oppose the godly here in any thing I thought they mistooke, but I was lately taken at advantage, and brought before the Magistrates, before whom, giving a quiet and peaceable answer, I was dismissed with favor, and respect promised me by some of the chiefe for the future."[39]

Once again, having spoken his mind and enraged Puritan leaders, Lechford found that a well-worded apology and a humble demeanor over a "misunderstanding" mollified enough magistrates to earn him a second chance. The elders warned him, however, to refrain from religious criticism and "to attend his calling."[40] That calling was what had disturbed many Puritans in the first place.

Lechford did attend to his practice, but shortly after the magistrates rebuked him in December 1640, he wrote an English friend a letter complaining not only that Puritan ministers had barred him from the church, but also that his opponents had banned him from holding the office of notary public and from attaining "all place of preferment in the Common-wealth."[41]

Dismayed by the strictures shackling his ambition and believing that the Puritan magistrates and ministers were leading the colony to chaos by meshing religion and the law, Lechford wrote a letter to the General Court urging that all its proceedings be assiduously compiled to ensure that all citizens would know "what is the Law, and what right they may look for at the mouthes of their Judges."[42] How much weight the General Court gave Lechford's appeal is unknown, but shortly after his proposal, the magistrates began to keep records of all cases and their verdicts.

Lechford's proposal also contained new criticism of the Puritans' Massachusetts Bay theocracy. He accused the town leaders of "pride and dangerous improvidence. . . . upon pretense that the Word of God is sufficient to rule."[43] Then, in a stinging harangue of the Boston church and a proud endorsement of the legal profession, Lechford wrote: "But take heede my brethren, despise not learning, nor the worthy Lawyers . . . lest you repent too late."[44]

Lechford was not worried about the possible repercussions of his missive, for he had decided to close his practice and return to England. Civil war was brewing there between Oliver Cromwell's Puritan Roundheads and the Royalists of King Charles I, supported by the Church of England. Having chafed beneath Puritan rule in New England, Lechford would number himself a Royalist.

On August 3, 1641, a little more than three years after his first glimpse of Trimountain and the City upon a Hill, Thomas Lechford walked up the gangplank of a vessel headed for England. He did so without his wife. Whether Elizabeth refused to go or intended to join him later, no one knows. John Winthrop, John Cotton, and the others the frustrated Lechford had deemed prideful and improvident would never see the solicitor or his "silver-laced" coat and gold-trimmed hat again. By November 1641, Lechford was entrenched once more at St. Clement's Inn and tormented Boston's Puritans from afar in 1642 with his publication of *Plain Dealing: or, News from New England,* a treatise decrying the colony's opposition to the Crown and to the bishops of the Episcopal Church. The solicitor, however, also offered faint praise to the Massachusetts Puritans who had banned him from their church and from public office: "I think that wiser men than they, going into a wildernesse to set up another strange government differing from the setled government here, might have falne [fallen] into greater errors than they have done."[45]

Not long after the publication of *Plain Dealing,* Lechford died of an undisclosed ailment. When news of his death reached Boston, the Reverend John Cotton penned a malicious obituary, the cleric railing that he saw "the wise hand of God disappointing his [Lechford's] ends; when he came to England, the Bishops were falling, so that he lost his friends, and hopes both in Old-England and New. . . .yet put out his Book [*Plain Dealing*] and died."[46]

Some three years after Lechford's death, his widow remarried, her new spouse a Boston merchant. Her first husband's name slipped from the Puritans' memory.

Although Lechford's name faded, his legacy forever changed New England. America's first disbarred solicitor and the first practicing lawyer in Massachusetts not only kept the earliest records of the colony's courts, but also paved the way for future attorneys in Massachusetts. By 1650, the colonists' demand for advocates such as Lechford forced the General Court to accede to the inevitable—practicing lawyers. Many legal scholars also believe that Lechford's appeal for a body of precedents forced Massachusetts not only to catalog its court cases, but also to codify the colony's laws.

Despite the ignominy of America's first (albeit temporary) disbarment, despite the Reverend Cotton's pronouncement that "Divine wrath" had claimed the solicitor, Thomas Lechford opened New England to worthy and unworthy lawyers alike.

The Maine
Murderess

⟨⟩

From the depths of the York River in 1644, settlers pulled up a grisly catch—the corpse of an Agamenticus man named Cornish. "His head bruised and a pole sticking in his side, he had been sunk in "his canoe laden with clay."[1] The finger of suspicion pointed at the victim's wife and one of her local lovers.

That Mrs. Cornish, her first name absent from the records of the era, had emerged under "strong suspicion" as a murderess in Maine did not surprise a lofty Boston Puritan like John Winthrop, for he had seen and heard Cornish in action. According to his journal, the young woman, a "bawd"[2] "dwelling for some time in Weymouth,"[3] Massachusetts, had distinguished herself among her prim and proper neighbors as "a lewd woman"[4] who specialized in adultery.

So sordidly did the "common Baud" strut her stuff amid Boston's environs that, in 1638, the colony's Court of Assistants rebuked her for her chronic "suspitious incontinency [promiscuity]," and she "was seriously admonished to take heed."[5]

Rather than take heed and reform her scandalous ways, Mrs. Cornish took to her heels. She and her husband "removed to Acomenticus" by 1644, Winthrop noting that the couple sought "outward accommodation" in their new neighborhood.[6]

In the shadow of Mount Agamenticus, amid the hardscrabble farms and the bustling waterfront of the settlement that Sir Ferdinando Gorges, the absentee Father of Maine, had grandiloquently dubbed a city in 1641, Mrs. Cornish found her "outward accommodation," far from prying Puritan eyes. Winthrop and his Boston brethren considered her new locale a fitting one for her licentious lifestyle, one shared by the region's "generally reckless adventurers."[7] "Some [in Maine]," wrote a visiting seventeenth-century ship's master, "were runaway seamen, some fugitives from justice, and some those vagrants from civilization who, by a strange instinct, seek seclusion from all civil and religious restraints. The state of society was distinguished by its lawlessness."[8] Just the place for Mrs. Cornish, by the Puritans' reckoning.

The rough-and-tumble aspects of life in Agamenticus notwithstanding, the jewel in Gorges's provincial crown also attracted such industrious and upright souls as carpenter Abraham Preble, scion of a Down East dynasty, who would dominate public life in York—in an honorable manner—into the eighteenth century. But to the Puritans in Massachusetts, "the planters and servers who had come over [to Maine] in the 1630s and the 1640s to fulfill the plans of Gorges . . . were soon left to their own devices"—in Mrs. Cornish's case, according to Winthrop, her own vices.[9]

Those alleged vices had brought Puritan authorities to Cornish's doorstep in Massachusetts. And although adultery took two, even in Winthrop's Boston and environs, the male participants of Cornish's Massachusetts trysts had somehow escaped mention in Winthrop's journal and in colonial court records.

Despite Maine's greatly inflated reputation for lawlessness and licentiousness of the sort embraced by Mrs. Cornish, one could go too far even there. Locals who savored clay pipes crammed with tobacco and a taste of liquor did not hold with murder. And, sometime in 1644, when the men of Agamenticus fished out the battered, waterlogged corpse of Mr. Cornish—the murder weapon still piercing his side—neighbors suspected his wife and "one Footman," a local with whom she enjoyed "fellowship," of having committed "murder most foul" and having crossed a colonial line from which there was no turning back even in a spot noted as the turf of colonial ruffians.[10]

Local authorities, headed by Mayor Roger Garde, noted that the corpse "bled abundantly" at the approach of Mrs. Cornish and that "so he [the victim] did also when Footman was brought to him."[11] (In some colonial minds, the age-old belief that a murder victim bled in the presence of his or her killer still held credence, the aggrieved reaching from the afterworld to provide blood evidence of the murderer's guilt. Mrs. Cornish and her lover Footman had flunked their "trial by corpse.") Despite the corpse's abundant bleeding, the authorities decided that "no evidence could be found against him [Footman]."[12] Mrs. Cornish's fate was a different matter.

"Something . . . discovered against the son of Mr. Hull," the town's minister, furthered suspicion in the case against Mrs. Cornish.[13] But no records—only Winthrop's mention of "something"—survived to indicate that some evidence had fueled speculation that the cleric's son had firsthand experience with the accused widow. Thus, courtesy of Minister Hull's son, Mrs. Cornish was hauled in and "arraigned before the mayor, Mr. Roger Garde, and others of the province of Maine."[14] She "persisted in the denial of the murder to the death," fighting back and refusing to submit meekly to a trip to the gallows, as her accusers piled "strong presumption upon her."[15] She not only asserted her innocence, but also scandalized her Agamenticus neighbors by "confessing to have lived in adultery with divers [many]" local men.[16] Cornish "charged two specially,"[17] one a man named Edward Johnson. She also revealed her second alleged paramour, "the said Garde"[18]—the mayor in whose deliberations her life rested.

Against Cornish's allegations of small-town scandal and her denials of the murder lay evidence of her wayward past—and present—and the body that had "bled abundantly" in her presence. Her accusers did not elaborate on why the blood evidence loomed so heavily against her but less against Footman. The "something" about Mrs. Cornish and the minister's son and the "presumptions" that followed led her accusers to a verdict of guilty.

In colonial New England, a chilling pronouncement by a magistrate generally preceded the jerk of the hangman's rope: "You [the condemned] are to return hence to the place from whence you came and from thence to the place of execution, there to be hang'd til thou beest dead—the Lord be merciful to thy soul!"[19] Thus, on an unknown date in 1644, death came in or around Agamenticus to the Maine Murderess.

Her name, her alleged misdeed, and her misfortunate demise known only by intriguing entries from a Puritan's journal, Mrs. Cornish merits a place of dishonor among colonial miscreants. For in her refusal "to take heed" of her "incontinent" ways—for shattering the First Commandment—she earned infamy as the first woman executed Down East.

Yet, a question lingers amid this murky tale of murder and mayhem. Did Mrs. Cornish act alone? After all, she possessed no shortage of male companions who, conceivably, could have helped her get rid of her clueless or long-suffering spouse. But the Maine magistrates who so quickly condemned Mrs. Cornish oddly found no evidence against her paramours. And a last look at one of Cornish's judges and alleged lovers bears mention because, even though Winthrop praised Mayor Garde's zealousness in unraveling the murder, the governor added a disclaimer about Garde's alleged adultery with the notorious woman: "But there might be skill [deception] in that," Winthrop wrote. "And he [Mayor Roger Garde] was but a carnal man, and had no wife in the country, and some witnesses came in against him of his acknowledgment to the woman. . . .But the mayor denied it."[20]

No hint that any man except Footman might have aided and abetted Mrs. Cornish appeared, and Garde emerged unscathed except for any damage his choice of company shed on his reputation. No one, however, could blame the mayor for scrambling to disavow any link to the Maine Murderess.

In many accounts of early Maine, a woman named Patience Boston, born in 1713, is cited as the first woman hanged in Maine. Like Cornish, Boston had racked up an unsavory record—curses, drunkenness, and theft among her criminal credits.

Benjamin Trot, an eight year old from Falmouth, Maine, accidentally stepped on Boston's toe. She picked him up, carried him over to a well, and tossed him into it. Before rescuers could reach him, the boy drowned.

Given the crowd of witnesses to the murder, and Boston's reputation, her ensuing murder trial in York did not last long. Neither jury nor judge found any mitigating circumstances; she was sentenced to hang. On May 24, 1735, Boston was "swung off" from York's gallows—the *second* Maine murderess to suffer the ultimate punishment. To Mrs. Cornish, hanged nine decades before Patience Boston, falls the infamous first.

The Harvard Hoodlums

H ere's a sorry saga that could turn Harvard grads crimson. It is a classic case of two of the best and brightest failing not only as students but as citizens.

An integral part of the Puritans' desire to found a bastion of "goodliness" in New England lay in their determination to forge a colonial equivalent of Cambridge University to train a steady stream of young ministers for New England's Congregational meetinghouses. The Puritans wanted their future college to produce only the highest caliber of young clerics.

In 1636 a handful of Puritan youths began theological training in a scattering of buildings along the Charles River. To prove how much they valued the new college, the colonists built the dormitory and the academic hall of costly red brick, in a settlement where even the wealthiest Puritans lived in wooden homes.

For the first three years of its existence, the school along the wooded banks of the Charles bore no official name, just the appellation "the college." But in March 1639, Governor John Winthrop and the colony's other founding fathers bestowed the name Harvard on the small, graceful brick buildings. The school's new title honored not a

Puritan luminary, but a Presbyterian minister named John Harvard. Harvard, who had set foot in Boston in 1638 but had died before making much of a mark in his new home, had willed the princely sum of 780 pounds sterling to the college. He had also left his four-hundred-volume library, one of the largest collections of books in the English-speaking colonies, to the school.

With his money and his precious tomes, John Harvard had propelled the college to the forefront of colonial academia. His grateful neighbors fervently believed that the deceased Presbyterian's largesse would turn out polished Harvard preachers who would carry the tenets of Puritanism to every corner of New England. One pair of notorious students would shake that notion.

In the early 1640s, two young men stowed their clothes and books in Harvard's dormitory and began their studies of Puritan philosophy, Greek, Latin, mathematics, history, and rhetoric. No one questioned the suitability of James Ward and Thomas Weld to assume their places among the newest crop of Harvard men. Ward, a promising young scholar, hailed from the family of Nathaniel Ward, one of the New World's preeminent intellectuals, a man who had codified his fellow colonists' rights into the landmark Body of Liberties.

Weld also carried a prime Puritan pedigree. He was the son and namesake of the Reverend Thomas Weld, a Massachusetts Bay mover and shaker who ruled the pulpit of the meetinghouse in Roxbury and served as overseer of Harvard's regents. With such connections and the confidence that his family name afforded him amid students and teachers alike, young Weld soon carved out a reputation as Harvard's leading hellion.

Weld struck up a fast friendship with Ward. Few at Harvard, however, guessed at the real glue binding the Puritan duo. None from Harvard Yard or on either side of the Charles River knew that the friends were partners in crime.

In the early spring of 1644, stunning news spread from the muddy paths of Boston, across the river, and to the college: someone had broken into two Boston homes in the dead of night, and while the unsuspecting occupants slept, the burglar or burglars had quietly rifled through chests, trunks, and drawers and had escaped with several rings and fifteen pounds sterling, a large chunk of colonial change. The suspicions of outraged Puritans naturally focused at first on the Town Dock, where rough-and-tumble sailors, or "tars," and outsiders held sway. But constables' waterfront investigations came up empty.

The search for the thieves then wound its way to the town's taverns. But the authorities' interrogations of assorted patrons gulping hard cider, port wine, or warm, frothy beer unearthed no bona fide suspects. Baffled, Winthrop and other notable Puritans, including the Reverend Weld, had little inkling about where to search next. Thoughts of the hoods still prowling the town led many Puritans to load their pistols or muskets before retiring.

No local envisioned that a break in the case would come from Harvard Yard. Such reasoning seemed as skewed as suggesting that clues lay in the settlement's meetinghouses. Yet a strange rumor wafted through Harvard's dormitory and swirled to the school's president, the Reverend Henry Dunster. Troubled by what he had heard, he contacted Winthrop.

Winthrop was equally taken aback by the rumor: two Harvard students suddenly seemed to have money to burn. To the anguish of Winthrop, the two students were none other than James Ward and Thomas Weld, sons of Puritan privilege. Refusing to settle the dismaying matter privately with the boys' prestigious fathers—his peers—Winthrop ordered a search of the students' quarters. The constables hit pay dirt—several pounds sterling and the missing rings.

Shock gripped the Puritans at the news that two Harvard men, not some nefarious types from the docks, had been caught red-handed with loot from the break-ins. At Cole's Inn, sailors and other outsiders who had come under suspicion for the burglaries drank in relative peace again and could chuckle at the authorities who had assumed that any Puritan was above suspicion.

How would the General Court's magistrates, not to mention a Puritan jury, mete out punishment to two privileged sons? The poorer sorts in Boston and environs would be enraged if the "poor little rich boys" were spared the sting of the lash or a humiliating stint in the stocks. Winthrop and the court turned over the burglars to their parents for the moment.

In June 1644, constables led the criminals into Harvard Yard, and the pair (about twenty years old) were "there whipped, which was performed by the president [of Harvard] himself," the Reverend Henry Dunster.[1] Then the constables dragged the bleeding "boys" to court. The magistrate ordered them to pay double restitution—"two fold satisfaction"— to the robbery victims or face a stint in jail.[2] Luckily for the youths, their fathers paid the damages.

America's first collegiate criminals had not escaped with a slap on the wrist. The colonial court had hammered home the reality that youths from influential families could not wriggle free from the same punishment that tradesmen's sons would have suffered. Weld and Ward learned their lesson and avoided another date with the court. The Reverend Nathaniel Ward, showing he had no hard feelings toward the Reverend Dunster or Harvard, later left the college six hundred acres of land in Andover, Massachusetts.

The Witch of Windsor

&

When one thinks of seventeenth-century witch-hunts and trials, the Salem, Massachusetts, debacle leaps to mind. But it was not in Massachusetts that the colonies' witchcraft scare began. In 1647, forty-five years before the Salem tragedy, a woman was tried for sorcery, convicted, and hanged in Hartford, Connecticut. Her name was Alse, or Alice, Young, and she was the first colonist ever executed for witchcraft.

Young's fatal foray onto history's stage lives in a scrap from John Winthrop's journal and a brief mention by Boston historian Justin Winsor. All that is known is that on May 26, Alice Young, of Windsor, Connecticut, was hanged for witchcraft.

After the noose "turned her off"—the colonial vernacular—her name faded, eclipsed by the unfortunate women and men dragged before magistrates in Hartford from 1662 to 1663 and in Salem in 1692.

BREAKING

THE

CHAINS

"Just to Stand
One Minute . . . A Free
Woman"

No one had ever made such a request to Sheffield, Massachusetts,
attorney Theodore Sedgwick. On a day in 1780, a careworn
middle-aged woman had emerged from the Berkshire hamlet's main
road, where farmers' carts heaped with produce clattered past the windows of Sedgwick's office, and had offered the thirty-four-year-old
lawyer a landmark case—one that posed both a legal and personal
dilemma to him. The woman, a local known only as Bett, was a runaway slave, the property of Sedgwick's close friend Judge John Ashley. She wanted the attorney to sue her master for her freedom, an
outlandish notion for the era.

A handsome man whose once-boyish visage had matured on Revolutionary War battlefields and in the snakepit of colonial politics,
Sedgwick did not blanch at controversy. But, as he pondered the request of the self-described "Nigrah" woman, he asked her what "doctrine and facts"[1] had prodded her into his office. According to writer
Harriet Martineau, an erstwhile friend of the
Sedgwick family, Bett replied, "By keepin' still
and mindin' things."[2]

"But what did [she] mean by keeping still
and minding things?" the lawyer queried.[3]

Bett answered that "fer instance when she
was waiting at a table, she heard gentlemen
talking over the Bill of Rights and the new
Constitution of Massachusetts; and in all
they said she never heard but that all the
people were born free and equal, and she

thought long about it, and resolved she would try whether she did not come in among them."[4]

Sedgwick had sat at that table on a frigid January evening in 1773. He and other local luminaries had trooped from various corners of the Berkshires to the home of John Ashley, in Sheffield. Within the pine-paneled walls of Ashley's study, the men "took into consideration the grievances which Americans in general and Inhabitants of this Province in particular labor under" at the whim of the British Crown.[5]

Twenty-six-year-old Theodore Sedgwick kept the minutes of that meeting, which produced a milestone tract dubbed the Sheffield Declaration. Although the proviso fell short of overt rebellion, its Berkshire creators wrote: "Mankind in a State of Nature are equal, free, and independent of each other, and have a right to the undisturbed Enjoyment of their lives, their Liberty and Property."[6]

According to Martineau, Bett carried platters of food and tankards of drink to the men as they crafted this lofty rhetoric.

Later, when the slave asked Sedgwick if the Sheffield Declaration's tenets of liberty truly applied to all "Mankind," she bore a vivid emblem of freedom denied: the seared flesh of her arm. Her mistress, Hannah Ashley, the wife of John, had recently inflicted the wound with a red-hot shovel "in a fit of passion."[7]

Although Sedgwick knew Bett's master as "the gentlest, most benign of men," Hannah Ashley's character was entirely different.[8] Bett's tormentor, in the words of Sedgwick's daughter Catherine, deserved her reputation as "a shrew untamable" and "the most despotic of mistresses."[9] Bett, chattel in the eyes of local slave owners, informed the lawyer that under no circumstances would she step into the Ashleys' home again. Despite four decades as a slave, she resented the "ill usage" and "the insult and outrage [of Hannah Ashley's abuse] as a white person would have done."[10]

When Bett fled the Ashleys' house, "neither demands nor entreaties could induce her to return."[11] Sedgwick, however, realized that if the Ashleys summoned a constable to seize Bett and drag her back, the law stood on their side. Hannah Ashley intended to do just that.

The attorney agreed to help the injured slave fight the Ashleys in court for her freedom. For the first time in New England's, as well as the fledgling nation's, history, the legality of slavery would face a courtroom test, from a forty-year-old Black woman demanding to "come in among" free Whites not as property, but as an equal.

Bett began her odyssey on a farm in Claverack, New York, near the border of Western Massachusetts. Born into bondage to Dutchman Pieter Hogeboom around 1744, she believed both of her parents had been seized by slavers in Africa, crammed and chained inside the fetid hold of a slave ship, and sold off to Hogeboom. Throughout her long life, Bett would treasure two mementos of her parents: an African "black silk gown" that had belonged to her father and a "short gown" her mother had worn.[12]

On the Hogebooms' farm, Bett and her younger sister, Lizzie, a "weak and timid girl," learned the household tasks they were expected to perform for the rest of their lives.[13] Tending the kitchen hearth and the simmering pots and kettles that hung on hooks above the flames, preparing meals for the Hogebooms, lugging those meals on platters and trenchers to the dining table, filling and refilling the family's mugs or cups with water, buttermilk, or other colonial beverages, Bett and Lizzie knew their subservient station in life by their teens.

The girls' routine did not encompass mere servitude, according to Theodore Sedgwick's son Dwight. "Slavery in . . . New England was so masked," he wrote, "that but a slight difference could be perceived in the condition of slaves and hired servants. . . . The younger slaves not only ate and drank, but played with the [masters'] children. They thus became familiar companions with each other."[14] The familiarity between slave children and their masters' broods, however, eventually evolved into the traditional, sharply defined chattel-owner relationship. When Bett and Lizzie entered their teens, their role shifted from playmates, as well as servants, for the white children to that of "cooks and nurses, and as such assisted by their mistresses."[15]

In 1758 Pieter Hogeboom died, and Bett, then about fourteen, and her sister were brought across the border to Sheffield, Massachusetts, and led to a classic clapboard New England home framed by trees and a lean-to at the house's rear. The sisters now belonged to Hannah Ashley, the youngest daughter of Pieter Hogeboom and the wife of John Ashley, a rising star in the Berkshires' legal and political circles. Bett's "patriarchal" new master and his wife had four children whom the two sisters would tend in addition to performing their myriad household chores.[16]

Betts's new home lay in the then unofficial capital of the Berkshires; Sheffield was the largest of the region's towns. And much of the area's legal business unfolded in the study of John Ashley, who, from 1761 to 1781, served as judge of Berkshire County's Court of Common Pleas.

By 1773, the tremors of revolt against the Crown were spreading from Boston to the Berkshires, and the house in which Bett and Lizzie fulfilled their drudgery and watched over the Ashley children furnished a meeting place for local men to discuss and debate the rising tensions between the colonists and their king, George III. As Ashley and his peers argued the rights of Man and other lofty concepts, the aproned, bonneted Bett not only served them food and drink but also, according to several later sources, "minded" the dialogues of Ashley and his guests. In their words, the slave did not hear references to the hue of a person's skin; she heard only that all men possessed a God-given right to liberty.

Bett's master proved a lukewarm rebel, a man who, in 1768, had signed Boston firebrand Samuel Adams's petition haranguing Britain's Parliament for its taxation of the colonies, but then buckled under pressure from stalwart Tories and publicly rescinded his support of Adams. Many of Ashley's neighbors condemned his lack of backbone. Still, his kindness and the respect he had garnered behind the bench of the local courts enabled him to weather rebels' ire.

Ashley's neighbors thought so well of him that in January 1773 they elected him chairman of a local committee formed to codify the rights that colonists believed were inherent—no matter what Parliament decreed. In that same month, men from Sheffield, Great Barrington, and other corners of the Berkshires dragged themselves from the warmth of their fireplaces and trudged through the snow to gather at the home of John Ashley.

Among the men who assembled in the judge's study was the young attorney, Sedgwick, who had been thrown out of Yale a few years earlier for unspecified "boyish gaieties."[17] The rakish youth settled down to study law at his cousin Mark Hopkins's office in Great Barrington, fall in love, marry, and meet his newfound obligations by opening a legal practice in Sheffield in 1766. Caught up in the revolutionary tide that swept through the region, the young member of the Berkshire Bar poured his energy and ardor into the evolving struggle for colonial rights. Not until 1776, however, a year after the bloody melees at Lexington and Concord, did Sedgwick espouse independence from the Crown.

Inside Ashley's crowded study that January evening in 1773, Sedgwick paid little attention to Bett or the other servants. He had weightier concerns at the moment: the other men had appointed him clerk. His quill would record the Sheffield Declaration, a document destined for fame.

No one knows how much of those lengthy discussions the illiterate Bett "minded" that night. Although Harriet Martineau's prose would conjure images of Bett's ears attuned to every word as she slid quietly through the crowded study with platters and pitchers, Bett hinted that her notion of freedom materialized not only that night but also in the following weeks as word of the Sheffield Declaration spread throughout the Berkshires to general approval.

The clerk, so busy recording the landmark rhetoric, never imagined it would fuel the personal rebellion of a slave in the Ashley household, or any other. Sedgwick's chief concern in January 1773 was that the declaration would articulate colonists' gripes against George III but would not advocate actual revolt.

In 1774, some of the Ashleys' Berkshire neighbors carried the milestone declaration a step farther. The men of Great Barrington shut down the region's courts until the creation of a state constitution asserting the inherent rights of Massachusetts citizens. Not until 1780 would the Berkshire Constitutionalists win their struggle, and by then the thirteen colonies had been embroiled in an all-out rebellion against the Redcoats for five years.

When the state's constitution finally took shape in 1780, the document's Declaration of Rights asserted: "All men are born free and equal, and have certain natural, essential, and inalienable rights."[18] Ideas articulated in John Ashley's study had materialized in the fledgling laws of the rebellious state.

In the very home where highly charged discussions had fueled so many of those guarantees of liberty, a burst of domestic violence prodded Bett to test those affirmations of freedom in a manner her master and his colleagues had never anticipated. Angered by Bett's sister, Lizzie, Hannah Ashley "resorted to a degree of violence very uncommon in this country [New England]."[19] She seized a smoking kitchen shovel from the hearth and swung it at Lizzie. Bett leaped in front of her sister and fended off the blow—but not before the metal seared her flesh with "a savage wound."[20]

When Bett stepped from the clapboard house and turned her back on her mistress, she headed where an outraged white in her predicament would have gone—to a lawyer.[21]

Once inside Sedgwick's office, the wounded slave, showing no compunction to flee from town but vowing never to return to Hannah Ashley, the most despotic of mistresses, convinced or challenged the attorney to win her freedom from that shrew untamable.

Sedgwick had changed greatly in the eight years since the Sheffield Declaration. Having literally risked his life and limb in the colonies' ongoing struggle for independence, he did not regard such terms as freedom and liberty lightly. But Sedgwick's decision to help Bett was puzzling to many. Under his ties of friendship and respect to the "gentle and benign" John Ashley, the attorney harbored conservative views that belied a penchant to roil the murky issue of slavery in New England. Some suspected that either his ego or the case's publicity lured Sedgwick to Bett's cause. Another theory, advanced by respected his-

torian Arthur Zilversmit, is that Sedgwick joined with evolving Berkshire Abolitionists to challenge the constitutionality of slavery in a
union of legal theory and zealotry. Sedgwick himself never fully revealed his reasons for taking up Bett's case. He simply went to work on
his new client's behalf, risking his long friendship with Ashley and
the wrath of local slave owners.

On August 21, 1781, the collective eyes of Berkshire citizens
turned toward an old white-framed building flanking the common of
Great Barrington. There, some of the region's top legal minds had
gathered to argue the landmark case of *Brom and Bett v. John Ashley,
Esq.*

A series of legal strokes and parries had preceded the moment
when Theodore Sedgwick entered the courtroom to confront John
Ashley. Shortly after Sedgwick first glimpsed the burn on Bett's arm,
the lawyer had filed a *writ of replevin*—a means of recovering property—at Berkshire County's Court of Common Pleas. He contended
that Bett had been illegally enslaved and held the right to recover,
in effect, herself. Sedgwick had also entered to the case another
plaintiff, a man named Brom, whom history knows only as the case
records described him—"a Negro Man . . . of Sheffield . . . a
Labourer."[22]

In describing the case's chief plaintiff, Bett, the court record referred to her as a "spinster" although she was widowed and had given
birth to at least one child. Sedgwick's contention that Bett's husband
had died "in the Continental service in the Revolutionary War"[23] never
mentioned whether he had been a free Black or a servant taken off to
war by his master.

Court officers served Bett and Brom's writs to Ashley and his son
John Ashley, Jr., the latter gambit suggesting that the enigmatic Brom
belonged to the younger Ashley. John Ashley, Sr., refused to back down
in his determination to recover his wife's property and drag Bett back
to his Sheffield home. Bett's proverbial day in court, one unlike any
New England had ever seen, would arrive on August 21, 1781.

In the weeks preceding the trial, Sedgwick charted his way through a legal morass, for there were no precedents to this emancipation case. He decided he needed help and, laying aside his ego, turned to one of the era's top legal minds, Tapping Reeve.

A thirty-seven-year-old resident of Litchfield, Connecticut, Reeve had cut a wide swath in New England legal circles. Would-be lawyers flocked to his office "for regular instruction in law in a methodical way"[24] and prompted him in 1784 to found the Litchfield Law School, the nation's first bona fide training ground for attorneys. But it was as a courtroom presence that Reeve had earned admiration throughout the region. Lauded by the renowned Reverend Lyman Beecher as "an eminently pious man," the portly, long-haired lawyer strode into the courtroom with the self-assured demeanor of a zealot intolerant of vice, especially liquor.[25] And, as with many confident of their inherent morality, he spoke with a bluntness that irritated his foes and often his friends. A prolific writer, he published conservative political polemics "characterized by a straightforwardness of expression which at times savors of lack of restraint."[26]

Reeve had ties to a family whose name would, to many Americans, prove synonymous with lack of restraint—the Burrs. As a teacher in the 1760s, he had wed Sally Burr, sister of Aaron Burr, whose brilliant and stormy career included a stint as one of Reeve's law students long before Burr killed Alexander Hamilton in America's most infamous duel.

At Sedgwick's request, Reeve, a man who loved a legal challenge, climbed aboard a horse and rode across the Connecticut border to Great Barrington. The chance to lend his legal expertise and his voice to the new nation's first emancipation case proved too tempting to pass up.

When August 21, 1781, arrived, another visitor to Great Barrington found the trial too tempting to miss. Shouldering his way into the courthouse amid the throng of local farmers, merchants, and assorted Berkshire notables was a tall, middle-aged Frenchman clad in the silk finery of his nation's nobility. The Duc de la Rochefoucauld, a wartime acquaintance of Sedgwick and his houseguest for a spell during a junket across the former thirteen colonies, would record his impressions of *Brom and Bett v. John Ashley, Esq.*

Even though the windows of the courthouse had been thrown open to catch any puff of a breeze in the summer heat, onlookers fanned themselves as they stared at the slave who had pitted two long-standing friends against each other. With his "prepossessing face and dignified, almost showy manner," which many locals found grating given his modest origins as a shopkeeper's son, Theodore Sedgwick commanded the jury's attention from the moment his broad-shouldered frame took center stage.[27] His colleague, Tapping Reeve, noted for his "soft dark eyes of rare beauty" and his "beaming expression of intelligence and benevolence," stood ready to lend his blunt brilliance to the case.[28]

Determined that not even the prowess of Bett's attorneys would prevent the court-sanctioned return of Hannah Ashley's runaway slave, John Ashley and his son had assembled their own duo of legal hired guns. David Noble, a local on the fast track to a judgeship, and John Canfield, like Reeve a Connecticut resident, possessed formidable trial records. Also in their favor was New England's tacit—if uneasy—acceptance of slavery. The thirteen colonies' first slave fleet had sailed from Boston in 1645, and many New Englanders had profited from the brutal institution. And in a region where property was a cultural cornerstone, the Ashleys did not stand alone in believing that Bett remained their possession, part of Hannah Ashley's legal inheritance.

The jury who would decide whether Bett and Brom were chattel or human beings with intrinsic rights filed into the courtroom and took their seats. As in all American courtrooms, only men served as jurors. Bett never stated whether any of the jurors in their tailed coats or homespun shirts were familiar to her. But many local men had entered her master's home on matters of law, business, or friendship during her nearly twenty-five years of bondage to the Ashleys.

The Ashleys' lawyers soon emphasized that Bett was the rightful property of Hannah Ashley, a legacy from her father, and had served the family for many years. Invoking many New Englanders' acceptance of slavery, but masking it in softer terms of "servitude," Noble and Canfield contended: "The Said Brom and Bett were at the time of Issuing the original Writ, the legal Negro Servants of the said John Ashley during their Lives." [29] Sedgwick, the Ashleys' lawyers asserted, held no legal right to issue a writ against Bett's lot as her master's property.

Sedgwick and Reeve unleashed a counterattack against long-accepted tenets of slavery's legality on several fronts. Bett and Brom, their lawyers argued, had not been the Ashleys' servants "during their lives" because they had been "illegally enslaved."[30] Although slavery existed in Massachusetts, Sedgwick and Reeve went on, "no antecedent law had established slavery and . . . the laws which seemed to suppose it were the offspring of error in the legislators."[31]

Then, the slaves' attorneys threw down their legal trump, one that the illiterate Bett had touched upon after fleeing from Hannah Ashley's kitchen shovel and turning up in Sedgwick's office.

Slavery, Sedgwick asserted, could not exist legally in Massachusetts. "Such laws [tacitly upholding slavery], even if they existed, were annulled by the new Constitution."[32] He concluded that Bett and Brom held the legal and God-given right "to come in among them" who were entitled to freedom.[33]

The lawyers' cases rendered, Bett and Brom could only wait and hope as Foreman Jonathan Holcomb and his fellow jurors weighed the Ashleys' case for slavery's status quo against the runaway slaves' claim of equality.

After their deliberations, "Jonathan Holcomb Foreman & His Fellows" returned to the courtroom.[34] Bett and Brom, the jury had adjudged, "are not and were not at the time of the purchase of the original writ the legal Negro Servants of him the said John Ashley."[35] Holcomb and his fellows not only delivered a landmark verdict, but also slapped Ashley with damages of thirty shillings for the burn his wife had inflicted upon her ex-slave, plus the trial's cost, five pounds, fourteen shillings, and four pence.

How heavily Hannah Ashley's "fit of passion" and "the honorable scar it left to the day of her [Bett's] death" influenced the jurors is open to speculation.[36] But if the jurors agreed with Dwight Sedgwick's later assertion that Hannah Ashley's assault upon Bett was an egregious break with typical New England master-slave relations, then the "degree and mode of violence" Bett suffered had indeed played a role in the verdict, as evidenced by the award of damages to the emancipated slave.

Ashley, who as a judge routinely presided over cases in which juries levied damages, did not appreciate being on the paying end. He filed an appeal, fomenting the possibility that a higher court could overturn the verdict of the Great Barrington jury and force Bett's return to Hannah Ashley.

Bett had to worry not only about the appeal, but also, for the first time in her life, about finding a job. Once again, Theodore Sedgwick stepped forward and offered her a post as a paid domestic in his home. With ten children and his wife Pamela beleaguered by emotional problems, the attorney needed the help of an experienced maid and cook.

From the moment that Bett stepped into the Sedgwicks' Sheffield home in 1781, she proved why the Ashleys were battling so hard for her return. To the attorney's children, she became "Mum Bett," "the main pillar of the household."[37] Theodore Sedgwick, Jr., would write: "Having known this woman as familiarly as I knew either of my parents, I *cannot* believe in the moral or physical inferiority of the race to which she belonged."[38]

The Ashleys still believed that Bett belonged in one place only: with them. John Ashley's appeal process in *Brom and Bett* continued. Then, a few months after the verdict, news of another slave case spread across the hills and farmlands of the Berkshires. In the new trial, *Caldwell v. Jennison*, the Massachusetts Supreme Court upheld Sedgwick's precept that slavery was unconstitutional in Massachusetts. Although the decision's wording proved murky and open to question, John Ashley, savvy to the vagaries of life behind the jurist's bench, realized that the high court's ruling had hamstrung his appeal. One historian would speculate that the good-natured judge had pressed for Bett's return merely to humor his wife's wish to recover her property. Bowing to the inevitable, Judge Ashley "confessed judgement,"[39] acknowledging the validity of the jury's verdict in *Brom and Bett*. Bett was literally free and clear under the law, the first slave to win liberation in a courtroom. She did so more than eight decades before Abraham Lincoln signed the Emancipation Proclamation.

The specter of a return to bondage dissolved, Bett legally adopted a new name: Elizabeth Freeman. She turned her full attention to the troubled Sedgwick household, first in Sheffield and then, from 1785 on, in a large Stockbridge home befitting Theodore Sedgwick's status as a lawyer and eventually a judge, a congressman, and a senator. Away on legal and political matters much of the time and with his wife Pamela so prone to "madness," Sedgwick relied on Bett to manage his children and Pamela's erratic behavior. Fortunately for her ambitious employer, Bett possessed not only every conceivable domestic and matriarchal skill, but also keen nursing abilities. Catherine Sedgwick, the brood's youngest, would write that Mum Bett was "the only person who could tranquilize my mother when her mind was disordered. She [Bett] treated her with the same respect she did when she was sane . . . her superior instincts hit upon the mode of treatment that has since been accepted."[40]

In 1811, another of Sedgwick's daughters, Susan, did not use words, but watercolors, to pay homage to Mum Bett. The only extant image of the slave who had bested her master in court, the painting depicts a plump, elderly woman with white curls peeking from a demure bonnet and wearing plain garb. Her eyes and demeanor reflect a woman who calmly handled the myriad crises of her life.

In 1785, not long after the Sedgwicks moved to Stockbridge, Bett faced one of those crises with characteristic aplomb. When the Shays Rebellion, fueled by farmers enraged at a whiskey tax imposed by the federal government, spread throughout the Berkshires, Theodore Sedgwick denounced the rebels and fought to suppress them. A band of farmers looking to settle scores with him burst from the snow-shrouded paths of Stockbridge in late 1785 and into the Sedgwicks' home. Theodore Sedgwick was away on business. With the troubled Pamela little help in a crisis, only Bett stood between the family and the musket-wielding men eager to ransack the house and put it to the torch.

According to Theodore Sedgwick, Jr., Bett "did not attempt to resist, by direct force . . . she, however, assumed a degree of authority."[41] Grabbing "a large kitchen shovel," she told them they "dare not strike a woman."[42] Whether she shamed them or surprised them, the insurgents left her and the family alone. But they were bent upon looting the house of their prosperous foe.

The men stomped through the rooms with Bett dogging their steps "to prevent wanton destruction."[43] At one point during the raid, a rebel found a bottle of porter and "shattered its neck."[44] Bett snapped that "if he or his companions desired to drink porter, she would fetch a corkscrew and draw a cork, as they might drink like gentlemen."[45] She also threatened to "lay flat with her shovel" any other intruder who broke open another bottle.[46] The rebels swigged at the porter, but "upon testing the liquor, the party decided that if gentlemen loved such cursed, bitter stuff, they might keep it."[47]

Theodore Sedgwick could easily abide the theft of his porter, but the possible robbery of his family's silver could ruin them. Bett, however, had hidden the Sedgwicks' valuables in her bedroom chest before the invaders had burst into the house. They rummaged through dressers, bureaus, and drawers, turning up nothing, neither coins nor gems. Finally, the brigands stomped into Bett's room. She pointed at the rude wooden chest.

"Oh," she said, "you had better search that—an old nigger's, as you call me."[48] The men never called Bett's bluff. They left the house, ransacked but still standing, and the Sedgwicks' valuables remained undetected.

In the following years, the Sedgwicks found other less dramatic reasons to laud Bett as the main pillar of their household. Pamela Sedgwick died in 1807, tormented to the end by her psychological demons, yet fortunate in having found a servant who had proven her nurse, her friend, and her helpmate in raising the eight Sedgwick children who would reach adulthood.

When Bett finally retired at an unknown date, she purchased a cottage in Stockbridge with money she had put aside over her years of service to the Sedgwicks. Her new home sat near the one in which she had tended the illness of Pamela Sedgwick and the bumps, scrapes, and ailments of her children and had defended them from the marauders of the Shays Rebellion.

The Sedgwicks revered Mum Bett, and when she fell ill in 1829, Catherine, on her way to fame as a novelist, visited the ex-slave's bedside daily in her cottage. "Even protracted suffering and mortal sickness . . . could not break down her spirit," Sedgwick wrote."[49]

Bett's illness slowly drained the strength that had, in her words, let her live "to be about a hundred years old."[50] On October 18, 1829, she signed her will with an X, the document confirming that she was a widow, a mother, a grandmother, and a great-grandmother. To her daughter, Bett left her pair of African gowns, the sole relics of her parents.

Mum Bett Freeman died on December 28, 1829. The Sedgwicks buried her in the family plot in Stockbridge Cemetery, her grave part of the "Sedgwick Pie," whose stones were arranged in a circular layout to ensure that on Judgment Day, writes Jon Swan, the first faces the family saw would be Sedgwicks'—and Bett's. She was the only Black buried there.

Today, an epitaph written by Charles Sedgwick adorns Mum Bett's headstone:

Elizabeth Freeman, known by the name of MUM-BET, died Dec. 28, 1829. Her supposed age was 85 years. She was born a slave and remained a slave for nearly thirty years. She could neither read nor write, yet in her own sphere she had no superior nor equal. She neither wasted time nor property. She never violated a trust, nor failed to perform a duty. In every situation of domestic trial, she was the most efficient helper, and the tenderest friend. Good mother, fare well.

Catherine Sedgwick, who would be buried next to Mum Bett, may have best eulogized the spirit of the slave who had dragged her master into court and won the nation's first emancipation suit. Elizabeth Freeman, Catherine Sedgwick recalled, once said: "Anytime, anytime while I was a slave, if one minute's freedom had been offered to me, and I had been told I must die at the end of that minute, I would have taken it—just to stand one minute on God's earth a free woman—I would."[51]

A Connecticut Yankee and Old Man Eloquent

～

On the night of July 1, 1839, a series of dull thumps awakened Don Jose Ruiz. The Spanish plantation owner threw off the covers of his cabin bunk and warily climbed the ladder to the main deck of the *Amistad,* a trim schooner bound from Havana, Cuba, to Puerto Principe.

Peering through the gloom that stormy night, he recoiled at the sight of the machete-wielding Black men who surrounded the ship's captain. Ruiz's mind screamed the two words guaranteed to chill the soul of any plantation owner—*slave revolt!*

A shout rose to the tall masts of the *Amistad,* "Murder!"

More than a thousand miles away, in New Haven, Connecticut, forty-six-year-old attorney Roger Sherman Baldwin did not yet know that the uprising surging across the decks of the *Amistad* would thrust him into America's first international slave trial and change his life forever. A nation's respect and rage awaited the New Englander—along with a landmark appearance before the U.S. Supreme Court.

Born on January 4, 1793, into a long line of Yankee luminaries, Roger Sherman Baldwin was the son of Simeon Baldwin, a justice of the state supreme court, and Rebecca (Sherman) Baldwin, whose father had signed the Declaration of Independence after working on its language with Thomas Jefferson. A slender child, Roger Baldwin read voraciously, studying the classics, especially Virgil, before his tenth birthday. His parents, realizing that behind their son's quietness lay a keen intellect, hired a tutor from New Canaan, Connecticut, and also enrolled the boy at the Hopkins Grammar School, where his brilliant cousin Henry Sherman taught.

Roger Baldwin's world consisted mainly of the schoolroom and his father's study, whose burnished wooden shelves held hundreds of books on history, philosophy, science, and the law. When his instructors at the Hopkins Grammar School informed Roger's parents that their fourteen-year-old son could learn nothing more among children his own age, the family pulled some strings at his father's alma mater, nearby Yale; in 1807, Roger Baldwin stepped onto the tree-lined, grassy little campus and walked into the red-brick colonial buildings with fellow students at least two years older than he. He left four years later, in 1811, an eighteen year old with a degree from one of the young nation's most prestigious universities.

The graduate had no doubts about his career path. He had chosen the family business—law and eventually politics. In his father's office, Baldwin clerked before his acceptance to the Litchfield Law School, the nation's first true classroom for aspiring attorneys.

At Litchfield, in a small frame house jammed with fellow students, Baldwin studied under Tapping Reeve, the brilliant lawyer who had joined fellow attorney Theodore Sedgwick to win Mum Bett's freedom in 1781 (see page 34). An instructor who spared little time for students who could not keep up with his rapid-fire lessons and whose questions could trip up even veteran attorneys, Reeve soon learned that young Baldwin possessed one of the sharpest minds he had encountered among law students.

At the end of the school's three-year course, grueling oral and written examinations loomed. The students had only one chance to pass them. In a letter to Baldwin's father, one of the teachers, Judge Gould, wrote about Roger Baldwin's test results: "I restore your son somewhat improved, as I hope and believe. At any rate, no student from our office ever passed a better examination."[1]

Judge Baldwin's restored son returned to the family's comfortable home, in New Haven, and won admittance in 1814 to the Connecticut bar, a minor feat, in his opinion, compared to Litchfield Law School's final examinations. On entering the starch-collared, frock-coated world of the Yankee attorney, Baldwin broke with tradition by opening his own practice rather than joining his father as a partner.

As with most attorneys of the day, Baldwin did not specialize in one form of law, but handled civil, criminal, and property cases alike. In an office always cluttered with briefs and correspondence and offering a fine view of the whaling boats, merchantmen, and warships carving the waters of New Haven's harbor, Baldwin soon built a thriving practice as word of his clear, legally airtight documents and reasonable rates spread. As the son of a man of means, Baldwin did not need to chase fees to pay his bills. Many poor clients sought his help, and he rarely turned them away, even though he knew that payment for his services would come slowly—if at all.

The tall, thin lawyer, who, whether in his office or in court, appeared in expensive, tailored black suits, with the occasional substitution of blue frock coats sporting gilt buttons and tan waistcoats, inspired confidence in his poor and rich clients alike with his measured, trenchant speech. The twenty-seven-year-old attorney inspired confidence of another kind in a lovely young member of Hartford, Connecticut, society in 1820. Blue-eyed, blond-haired Elizabeth Perkins was convinced that Baldwin, who had spent long hours riding on weekends from New Haven to Hartford to court her, would prove a fine husband. Spurning a small army of other suitors, she accepted Baldwin's proposal and married him in 1820. She would bear him nine children, six sons and three daughters, and accompany him on his climb to the highest rungs of America's legal and political system.

Settling with relish into his new role as husband and father in a New Haven mansion he bought for his bride, and never lacking clients, Baldwin could have coasted through life. But he plunged into Whig politics with successful runs for the New Haven Council and the Connecticut Senate.

As a staunch Whig and the grandson of a man who had fought in vain to free the slaves through the Declaration of Independence, Baldwin espoused the Abolitionist cause and began to take on cases that tested the boundaries of slavery. In one of his first Abolitionist actions, he represented a slave who had run away from Senator Henry Clay, of Kentucky, one of America's most powerful Democrats and a harsh enemy for any man, Whig or Democrat. When Baldwin won the case on a technicality, America's most zealous Abolitionist leaders took notice. So, too, did Clay and fellow Southern slaveholders.

In 1833, Baldwin served notice again to Southern slaveholders and Northern bigots with his defense of a White schoolmistress's campaign to teach young Black women in New Haven. Prudence Crandall brought her plan to open an academy for Blacks to a New Haven town meeting. From the largely male gathering, a chorus of boos and epithets greeted the slight, middle-aged teacher, clad in a plain gray dress and a bonnet. The members of the town meeting considered a motion to ban her school.

Roger Baldwin, risking votes on his future senatorial and gubernatorial runs, took the floor and asserted Crandall's right to teach children of any color and to do so anywhere she pleased. His neighbors listened to the lawyer, clad in one of his familiar dark suits, but voted nevertheless to ban Crandall's academy. She soon headed to Canterbury, Connecticut, opened her school, and ignited a statewide furor whose aftereffects would play a key role in the most important case of Baldwin's legal career.

The events drawing Baldwin into the landmark slave case commenced on that stormy night aboard the *Amistad* nearly six years following his defense of Crandall before his irate New Haven neighbors.

The strange voyage of the *Amistad* began no differently than that of any other slaver setting sail from Havana. Although Great Britain and Spain had signed a treaty in 1817 outlawing the African slave trade, Havana still flourished as the clearinghouse of that peculiar institution. Spanish colonial officials, their pockets bulging with bribes of $15 per slave, allowed slavers to cram the squalid barracoons, or slave quarters, with kidnapped African men, women, and children. The corrupt officials issued "Ladino papers" to verify that all slaves sold in Havana were Spanish-speaking natives of the New World and exempt from the provisions of the 1817 treaty.

Wearing chains around their hands, necks, and feet, fifty-three Blacks were dragged from the Havana barracoons in late June 1839 and packed like kindling into the four-foot-high hold of the *Amistad*. The two-masted vessel's long, graceful lines and elegant sails belied the manacled and moaning human cargo concealed below decks.

Two additional passengers, men of means, boarded the ship. The urbane arrogance of countless plantation owners also glinted in the dark eyes of Don Jose Ruiz, who owned forty-nine men in the hold, and Don Pedro Montez, a former sea captain who had purchased three young girls and a boy. As the *Amistad* slipped through the waters of Havana's bustling harbor, the two planters and the crew anticipated an uneventful three-hundred-mile jaunt to Puerto Principe. Montez later recalled, "For three days the wind was ahead and all went well."[2]

The slaves, Mende from Sierra Leone, their muscles knotted in agony, their chains clanking, were led on deck a day or two after the ship reached open waters. One of the Blacks, crazed by thirst, grabbed a dipper of water. Captain Ramon Ferrer ordered a sailor to whip the offender, and after the tips of the lash had torn the slave's back, the sailor cruelly rubbed salt and gunpowder into the victim's bloody stripes.

As they were herded back to the hold, the Africans passed the ship's cook, Celestino. Leering at the slaves, Celestino dragged his finger across his throat and pointed toward a simmering cooking pot. The terrified slaves immediately understood his gestures: their throats would be cut and their bodies eaten by the crew. This cruel joke would be the cook's last.

If the crew and the planters had taken more than a cursory look at their cargo, they would have noticed the regal bearing and intense eyes of a slave named Singbe-Pieh, known to history as Joseph Cinque. Among his fellow slaves, Cinque was the acknowledged leader. The son of a Mende chief, he possessed the decisive intelligence of a warrior-king and the muscular frame of an athlete; he had no intention of submitting to the fate Celestino had described.

Once in the hold, Cinque exhorted his people to make a choice—death or revolt. His fiery words stoked a rage that filled the Africans' aching limbs. Pulling their chains in unison, the slaves eventually broke the giant padlock that bound them to each other. Having shed their irons, they stole into the main cargo hold and armed themselves with two-foot-long, razor-sharp machetes normally used to cut sugar cane. Cinque then led his people onto the main deck of the *Amistad* around 4 A.M.

The first crewman the slaves saw was Celestino, sound asleep in his galley. Cinque raised his machete and sliced into the cook's body. The blade rising and falling again and again, the cook died without a whimper. The strokes of the machete awoke Ruiz.

Near the ship's helm, Captain Ferrer suddenly noticed the horde of armed slaves swarming the galley and ordered his cabin boy, a mulatto named Antonio Gonzales, to throw them some bread. Gonzales had no time to move. One of the Mende rushed Ferrer, who dodged the Black's hissing machete and plunged his sword into the man. An instant later Cinque was upon Ferrer. The slave leader's blade split the captain's head in two.

Two crewmen dove overboard, and Ruiz, who had seen Ferrer fall, swung an oar at several approaching slaves and fled to the ship's after-cabin. Montez suddenly appeared, grabbed a club and a knife, and lunged at Cinque. But the elderly slaveholder proved no match for the powerful Mende, whose remorseless blade gashed Montez's arm and face. The Spaniard lurched down the hatchway to the main hold.

While Montez hid beneath a spare sail, Ruiz surrendered after the slaves gestured they would spare both of the planters. The Mende barely reached Montez in time to save him from Cinque's machete.

Cinque, his fury finally ebbing, decided to sail the *Amistad* to Africa. He knew enough to steer by day toward the eastern track of the sun; however, none of the Africans could navigate by night. Montez was forced to pilot the ship back to Africa. The Mende sang jubilantly, believing they were headed home—an ocean away from the barracoons of Havana.

But as the weeks passed, Africa loomed no closer on the horizon. Every night and on overcast days, the Spaniard guided the *Amistad* northward, ever closer to the shores of the United States. As the ship's stores dwindled, seven of the Mende died.

When a number of coastal ships reported sightings of a filthy schooner flying no flag, the U.S. Navy dispatched the steam frigate *Fulton* to find the suspected pirate ship. The *Amistad*, meanwhile, drifted off Montauk Point, the eastern edge of Long Island, on August 25, 1839. Cinque ordered Montez to drop anchor in the sheltered waters off Culloden Point. Then the Mende leader sent a search party, led by a slave named Banna, or Burnah, who spoke fragments of English, ashore to find food and water.

The success of the search party, who used gold doubloons taken from Ruiz and Montez to purchase some potatoes, two large dogs, and a bottle of gin from a startled White, prompted Cinque to lead a second longboat ashore. As the Blacks filled water casks in a nearby stream, five White men in wagons approached Cinque and his men. Henry Green and Peletiah Fordham, both sea captains, gaped at the necklaces and bracelets of gold doubloons jangling from the Blacks' necks and wrists. The captains' amazement quickly gave way to fear when they noticed that several of the Blacks were carrying guns. Through sign language, the slaves assured Green and Fordham that no harm was intended. The Whites' gestures that Cinque and the others were no longer in slave country sparked dancing and cheering by the Mende.

From the top of a dune, Green and the other Whites stared at the weather-beaten schooner in the cove and gawked as the slaves offered the captains a fortune in gold doubloons in exchange for sailing the *Amistad* to Africa. But the gold gave the seamen another thought: the capture of the *Amistad* and salvage fees for its treasure.

On the following day, August 26, a warship suddenly rounded Culloden Point and moved swiftly toward the *Amistad*. Cinque and several other Blacks, who had returned to the shore, scampered to their longboat and rowed frantically toward the schooner. When Green spotted the Stars and Stripes fluttering above the deck of the onrushing ship, he knew any chance of collecting salvage money for the *Amistad* had vanished.

The American ship was the naval brig *Washington;* its captain, Lieutenant Commander Thomas R. Gedney. Aware of the rumors of a pirate ship in the area, Gedney sent a heavily armed boarding party to the battered schooner.

When Lieutenant Richard W. Meade and the boarding party clambered over the gunwales of the *Amistad,* they found scores of hollow-eyed, emaciated Blacks and two weeping White men. Meade, fluent in Spanish, listened in amazement to Ruiz and Montez's account of the slave revolt, and placed the Blacks under guard.

Cinque suddenly leaped on deck, saw the armed sailors, plunged overboard, and began swimming for shore. An American longboat rowed him down and then rounded up the terrified slaves on the beach. The slaves' pleas for Green and Fordham to save them echoed pitifully across the sand.

Returned to the *Amistad,* Cinque delivered a speech that "raised the blacks' excitement to such a pitch"[3] that Meade had him led away by force to the *Washington*. After Cinque promised to reveal a hidden cache of gold doubloons aboard the *Amistad,* Gedney allowed him to return to the slaver the next day. Cinque stepped on board the *Amistad* and addressed the other Blacks. Antonio Gonzalez, knowing a little Mende, gave a flowery translation of Cinque's speech: "Friends and brothers, I would not see you serve the white man. . . . You had better be killed than live many years in misery. . . .I could die happy if by dying I could save so many of my brothers from the bondage of the white man."[4]

When the slaves "yelled, leapt about, and seemed to be animated with the same spirit and determination of their leader," the Americans hustled Cinque back to the *Washington.*[5] With the *Amistad* in tow, Gedney laid a course for New London, Connecticut.

When the brig and the slaver docked amid merchantmen and whalers in New London's harbor, a mob of curious sailors, dock workers, and passersby lined the waterfront. John J. Hyde, editor of the *New London Gazette,* boarded the *Amistad* on Tuesday, August 27, 1839, and later wrote that the ragged sails, barnacle-covered hull, and filthy decks of the slaver made it look like *The Flying Dutchman.* He described "the Ethiop crew,"[6] some dressed in stolen silks, others nearly naked, and all of them wasted from hunger. On board the *Washington,* Hyde visited Cinque and wrote, "We also saw Cingue [*sic*] . . . in irons, unusually intelligent . . . with a composure characteristic of true courage and nothing to mark him as a malicious man."[7]

Hyde's vivid impressions, which ran in New York's newspapers, enflamed Abolitionists throughout the Northeast; many magazines and other newspapers depicted the *Amistad* captives as bloodthirsty cannibals, adding to public hysteria and playing into the hands of proslavery Americans. Lewis Tappan, a well-known merchant and staunch Abolitionist, joined forces with other foes of slavery to found the Committee of Friends of the *Amistad* Africans. Donations poured in from Abolitionist groups and countless Americans who uneasily tolerated slavery but were moved by the plight of the *Amistad* prisoners.

The *Amistad* affair rapidly escalated into an international uproar.

The Spanish minister to Washington, Angel Calderon de la Barca, demanded the return of the ship and the slaves to their owners. The Spaniards' intentions were clear: they wanted the United States to hand over the *Amistad* captives.

The Africans were moved from New London, to Hartford, to New Haven, where their jailer charged throngs of curious spectators one New York shilling apiece to view the Mende in their cells. On sunny days, guards took the captives to the town green for exercise, drawing huge crowds who tossed coins to the puzzled Blacks.

President Martin Van Buren, besieged by Spanish demands for the return of the slaves, by British protests that Spain had violated the 1817 treaty, and by the outcry of Abolitionists and Southern slaveholders, was caught between the proverbial rock and a hard place. With no chance of reelection without Southern votes, "Matty Van" was strongly inclined to return the *Amistad* and the slaves to the Spanish. His attorney general, Felix Grundy, of Tennessee, stated, "A delivery [of the slaves] to the Spanish minister is the only safe course for this government to pursue."[8]

Van Buren ordered the U.S. attorney for Connecticut to prepare a case on behalf of Montez and Ruiz. After a series of proceedings in Hartford, the trial was set for early January 1840 in the district court of New Haven. Tappan and his fellow Abolitionists were horrified that Judge Andrew T. Judson would hear the case. Judson had spearheaded the successful campaign to shut down Prudence Crandall's academy for young Black women in Canterbury, Connecticut, in 1833. Confident that Judson would deliver the correct ruling, Van Buren ordered the naval brig *Grampus* to anchor at New Haven and to await the judge's order to sail the slaves back to Cuba.

Van Buren was concerned about the attorney to whom the slaves' desperate friends turned. Roger Sherman Baldwin stood at the apex of his legal career; the attorney knew not only how New Haven's courts operated, but also how to argue a case in Judson's court without alienating the bombastic judge. Even Baldwin, however, wondered if any lawyer could successfully argue the *Amistad* case before Judson. Would

Judson limit the defense attorney's use of evidence and instruct the jury to disregard key points made by the slaves' advocate?

Also worried about Judson's bias, Tappan and his allies hatched a plot to snatch the slaves from the courtroom and to sail them aboard a swift schooner to Canada. Within clear sight of each other in the waters off New Haven, the navy brig and the Abolitionist schooner swayed from their anchor chains. The vessels' crews eyed each other.

On a snowy January morning in 1840, Roger Sherman Baldwin walked into the old New Haven courthouse and entered the crowded courtroom with a clear-cut legal strategy—to prove that his clients were illegally kidnapped Africans. The normally unflappable attorney later revealed that he also entered the courthouse with a bona fide case of nerves.

Perhaps the most important person to Baldwin's defense strategy was James Covey, the interpreter for Cinque and the other captives. Professor Josiah Willard Gibbs, of the Yale Divinity School and one of the captives' most ardent supporters, had found Covey aboard the British warship *Buzzard*. Having completed a mission against slavers off Sierra Leone, the *Buzzard* was docked in New York. An eighteen-year-old Black seaman, Covey spoke fluent Mende.

Using Covey as a mouthpiece, Baldwin put Cinque on the stand. His dark eyes flashing with emotion, his face and bearing regal, Cinque revealed, beneath Baldwin's careful, concise questions, how he [Cinque] had been kidnapped by Portuguese slave peddlers, clapped in irons, and then whipped, beaten, and hauled across the Atlantic to the Havana barracoons. At Baldwin's signal, Cinque squatted on the courtroom floor to show astonished onlookers how he and the other slaves had been packed into the *Amistad*'s hold, his heart-rending testimony fueling the emotions of the Africans' many supporters in the court gallery.

In a clever legal stroke, Baldwin questioned the three little girls owned by Montez and proved that they could not speak Spanish, as their Ladino papers asserted. The only tongue the girls knew was Mende.

Baldwin also summoned Dr. Robert Madden, a world-famous English opponent of slavery and a member of the commission formed to oversee Spanish compliance with the 1817 treaty. Madden, who had helped freed Africans in Havana for three years, testified that Cinque and the other Mende had arrived at Havana from Africa in a Portuguese slaver, the *Tecora,* and had been herded into the barracoons.

Baldwin had proven that the *Amistad* slaves were kidnap victims in the eyes of Spain's own treaty. But he and the slaves' supporters knew that hard evidence probably would not sway the prejudices of the judge who had closed Prudence Crandall's academy for young Black women.

The tension hung tangibly in the drafty courtroom as Judson prepared to deliver his verdict on January 13, 1840. The judge decided in favor of the slaves—but no cheers filled the room. Everyone waited to see if Judson would restrict his decision. To no one's surprise, he declared that the crew and officers of the *Washington* were entitled to salvage money for the *Amistad.* The slaves' lawyer and friends then braced themselves for the ruling that would doom Cinque and his people.

"These Negroes were imported in violation of that law [the 1817 treaty]," Judson began, "and by the same law of Spain, such Negroes are declared free, and, of course, are not the property of Spanish subjects. . . .Cinque . . . shall not sigh for Africa in vain. Bloody as may be their hands, they [the slaves] shall yet embrace their kindred."⁹

A wild volley of cheers erupted inside the courtroom as Abolitionists, stunned by the unexpected ruling of Van Buren's judge, hugged each other and swarmed the grinning Baldwin. But the celebration was short-lived; the adroit Van Buren had considered the remote chance of the judge's surprising action. The United States attorney William Holabird, acting upon the express orders of Van Buren, immediately filed an appeal. Judson had no choice but to order that the Africans be returned to the New Haven jail.

The president had every confidence that the U.S. Supreme Court, almost entirely composed of slaveholders, would overturn Judson's verdict. The shadow of a Spanish gallows fell once again over the *Amistad* captives.

As Cinque and his bewildered people chafed in their New Haven cell, where Abolitionists taught them English and Christian doctrine, a new and formidable ally added his voice to the Africans' cause. Ex-president John Quincy Adams, seventy-three years old and still a powerful presence in Congress, pushed through a resolution that opened all government documents on the *Amistad* case to the public. A letter from Van Buren to Secretary of State John Forsyth, a Georgia slave owner, underscored the president's attempt to rig the verdict of the New Haven court, fueling bitter controversy between North and South.

When donations to the slaves' cause ebbed in the fall of 1840 and the slaves' lawyers—with the exception of Baldwin—deserted the case as payments stopped, Tappan and fellow Abolitionist Ellis Gray Loring, of Massachusetts, traveled to the mansion of John Quincy Adams in Quincy, Massachusetts, and pleaded with Old Man Eloquent to act as co-counsel for the Africans before the Supreme Court.

His bald pate framed by tufts of white hair and long side-whiskers, his eyes rheumy with age, Adams said that he was too old and too long away from any courtroom to accept the case. But his visitors' arguments that Adams could reignite interest in the Africans' plight and help Baldwin to save the captives from Spanish nooses finally swayed the ex-president's conscience. Over the objections of his son, Charles Francis Adams, who worried about his father's health, Old Man Eloquent accepted the formidable task, realizing that Baldwin would bear the brunt of the actual pleading.

In November 1840, Adams met Baldwin at his office, and Baldwin escorted him to the slaves, now jailed in nearby Westville. The *Amistad* captives huddled inside a drafty, thirty-foot-long, twenty-foot-wide cell. Adams later wrote that he was impressed by Cinque's appearance and intelligence.

The trial began on February 22, 1841—George Washington's birthday. Baldwin and Adams entered the round courtroom in the east wing of the Capitol, the light that streamed through a bank of windows bothering Adams's eyes. As Baldwin squinted at the black-robed jurists holding the power of life and death over the Africans, he spied only two judges, Joseph Story, of Massachusetts, and Smith Thompson, of New York, who could be expected to vote in the slaves' favor.

To the crowded gallery of spectators the government's attorney, Henry D. Gilpin, spoke first. He asserted that no American court had the right to question the validity of the *Amistad*'s Ladino papers, issued legally by a foreign power on its own soil. Citing numerous precedents in international law, he argued that America's laws regarding fugitive slaves applied to other nations' runaway slaves when they reached American territory.

Baldwin, wary of angering the Southern justices, carefully and unemotionally assailed the government's case. Many of the New Haven lawyer's arguments were buttressed by the input of another attorney sitting in the packed gallery: Theodore Sedgwick, Jr., the son of the man who had won Mum Bett's freedom (see page 34).

"Can the government become a party to the proceedings for the enslavement of human beings cast upon our shores and found in the condition of free men within the territorial limits of a free sovereign state?" Baldwin asked.[10] Adams later described his partner's argument as "sound and eloquent."[11] Although the ex-president would opt for a far different approach when his turn to speak came the following day, both sides knew that no matter how brilliant Adams's discourse, the judges' view of the case hinged squarely on the arguments Baldwin had rendered.

A large crowd jammed the courtroom on February 23, 1841, anxious to hear the words of Old Man Eloquent. Tormented by doubts that he would be equal to his momentous task, Adams faced the Supreme Court judges. "I shall show how another department of the government of the United States [the Presidency] has taken with reference to this case the ground of utter injustice."[12]

His voice tinged with anger and indignation, Adams harangued

Grundy, Forsyth, and Van Buren: "Was ever such a scene of Lilliputian trickery enacted by the rulers of a great, magnanimous, and Christian nation?"[13]

The judges and the audience sat spellbound as Adams branded Van Buren "a Spanish puppet, a man-robber, a jailer, and a catchpole who would appease the public vengeance of the African slave-traders of the barracoons."[14] In a stunning four-and-a-half-hour diatribe that would have taxed the energy of even the youngest lawyer, the aged statesman assaulted the government's case not on legal grounds, but on moral grounds, and castigated the evils of slavery in front of slave-holding judges.

Washington D.C. buzzed with excitement after the Court adjourned for the day, but Adams was not yet finished. The sudden death of Supreme Court Justice Philip Barbour on the evening of February 23 postponed the proceedings until March 1, 1841. When the Court reconvened, Adams once again mesmerized the crowd and the judges with the force of his demands for morality and justice. He argued that a decision to return the captives to the Spanish and to certain death would threaten "the blessing of freedom" for every American and would promote "the . . . tenure of executive discretion, caprice, or tyranny . . . at the dictate of a foreign minister."[15]

Adams closed his three-and-a-half-hour argument with a moving appeal to the consciences of the justices, imploring them to honor the impartial legacy of John Marshall and other former Supreme Court judges, "all of them gone to receive the rewards of blessedness on high."[16]

As Old Man Eloquent, exhausted by his impassioned argument, returned to his seat, everyone in the chamber sensed that the venerable old statesman had delivered a verbal tour de force virtually unrivaled in American history, a speech worthy of Cicero, of ancient Rome. Justice Story later wrote that Adams's argument was "extraordinary for its power, for its bitter sarcasm, and its dealing with topics far beyond the record and points of discussion."[17]

Adams's harangue of Van Buren had eclipsed Baldwin's eloquent but understated assault upon the government's case, yet every lawyer present, including Adams himself, understood that there was no chance of Adams having shamed the slaveholding justices on moral grounds. Only if Baldwin's canny, step-by-step dismemberment of "the record and points" of the government's case compelled the Court to lay aside their prejudices and deliberate as Supreme Court judges were sworn to do—with utter impartiality—did the slaves have a chance.

On March 9, 1841, the Court's decision was rendered. To the hushed chamber, Story said, "They [the *Amistad* captives] were kidnapped Africans, who by the laws of Spain itself were entitled to their freedom."[18] Cinque and his people were free. Only one justice on the pro-South Supreme Court had dissented.

The Africans, accompanied by missionaries, were eventually sailed back to Sierra Leone. Cinque soon learned that his wife, his three children, and his father had been sold into slavery. He later became a tribal chief, counting many of the ex-*Amistad* captives among his followers.

Abolitionists distributed the full text of Adams's Supreme Court speech throughout America, infuriating Southerners who believed that his words would foment slave rebellions. A Virginian wrote: "May the lightning of heaven blast you [Adams and Baldwin] and direct you to depart from His [God's] presence to the lowest regions of Hell!"[19]

Old Man Eloquent's words, barbed with the forces of conscience, morality, and justice, had seared the collective psyche of the nation. In their defense of the *Amistad* captives, John Quincy Adams and Roger Baldwin had issued a challenge that foreshadowed the bitter and bloody conflict that would finally free America's slaves.

After the trial, Roger Sherman Baldwin was elected governor of Connecticut and then United States senator. He staunchly backed Abraham Lincoln for the presidency in 1860 and lived long enough to witness the Emancipation Proclamation.

On February 19, 1863, with the Civil War's outcome still in doubt, Baldwin died of a probable heart attack. Lauded as "the ablest lawyer that Connecticut ever produced" and as a man who, in his later years, "still walked with a firm step,"[20] he rarely received in life, or after death, the credit he deserved in the Amistad case. The verbal pyrotechnics of Old Man Eloquent aside, the Connecticut Yankee had shouldered "the main responsibility" for the successful outcome of the landmark slavery trial.[21]

The Gentle Crusader: Sarah Hale

With each scratch of her quill upon paper, history unfolded: the pretty, dark-haired author was composing America's first anti-slavery novel. The writer, however, was not Harriet Beecher Stowe, and the book was not *Uncle Tom's Cabin*. The year was 1827—twenty-five years before Stowe's classic enraged slaveholding Americans.

The thirty-nine-year-old widow was crafting *Northwood* out of conviction and necessity, although she had already launched a career that would carry her to the heights of the nineteenth-century publishing world. But Sarah Josepha Hale's chief renown would come not from *Northwood*, from her future status as America's first successful woman editor, nor from her modest crusade for women in the workplace. Her immortality would reside in the opening lines of a bit of doggerel she would write for children: "Mary had a little lamb . . ."

Sarah Josepha Buell was born in the Merrimack Valley hamlet of Newport, New Hampshire, on October 24, 1788, the third of Gordon and Martha Buell's four children. Hale, her younger sister, and her two older brothers grew up on the family farm. Their father, a fiercely patriotic former militia captain in the Revolution, also kept a tavern and owned real estate throughout the area.

Although many girls in the region received little formal education, Sarah's mother, a woman with "a mind clear as rock-water," was
determined that her children would learn the Bible and classics of
Western literature, all of which they read in front of the farmhouse's
hearth, the fire's glow flickering across the pages of Milton, Bunyan,
and Shakespeare.[1] Martha Buell imbued her children with her belief
that women were not mere appendages of their husbands and that
the gentler sex could study the weightiest topics without overtaxing
itself. But she grounded her forward-thinking approach in conservative New England tenets and in the Protestant faith, both of which
would remain integral elements of Sarah's life.

Death was another element of life for which Martha Buell prepared Sarah. When Sarah was a child, her mother brought her to the
bedside of a dead relative and forced the girl to touch the corpse's
cold forehead. Harsh as the lesson seemed, it introduced Sarah to
life's harshest reality.

Years later, Sarah preferred to recall the lessons her mother taught
from the family's many books, and the latitude she had allowed in her
children's reading. At the age of seven, Sarah read a British romance
novel titled *The Mysteries of Udolpho,* the sort of fare that many right-
thinking New England parents would have banned from their book-
shelves. For young Sarah, however, it marked a turning point because
its author was a woman writing in an era when proper women simply
did not publish their work. "How happy it made me!" Hale would remember. "The wish to promote the reputation of my own sex and my
own country were among the earliest mental emotions I can recall."[2]

In her teens, Sarah expanded her education when her brother Horatius matriculated at Dartmouth College and instructed his sister in
a homegrown course of study based on his classes, her voracious intellect absorbing his every lesson.

Sarah Hale gleaned such a knowledge of reading, writing, and
basic mathematics, seasoned with the classics, that by her eighteenth
birthday she had opened a school for local children. Although their education was Spartan, the students left her classroom with rudimen-

tary reading skills and enough "ciphering" to manage household account ledgers and handle money.

Money became a problem for the Hales in 1812, when her father's tavern failed less than a year after the death of Sarah's mother and sister from a fever. As grim as 1811–1812 proved for Sarah, she took solace in the company of a new neighbor, David Hale. A young attorney who had opened a practice in Newport, Hale was captivated by the local schoolteacher, whose sculpted cheekbones, glossy ringlets, wide eyes, and wit more than compensated for her family's lack of means. On October 23, 1813, the lawyer and the twenty-five-year-old schoolmistress married and settled in their own Newport home.

The next nine years, as Hale would often recall, were the happiest of her life. She reveled in the traditional roles of wife and mother, and with five children—three boys and two girls—born between 1815 and 1822, the latter role consumed most of Sarah's days and nights.

The demands of family life notwithstanding, Hale did not neglect the scholarly pursuits that had so intrigued her husband from the couple's earliest days of courtship. Although she no longer taught, she read and discussed the classics with her husband from 8 to 10 every night, and he introduced her to important contemporary works. The couple's home brimmed with books.

Unlike arranged marriages of the era, the Hales's was forged in genuine love and deepened with the years. In 1818, when Sarah developed a respiratory problem, David Hale took her on a fresh-air junket throughout New England, and she regained her health. In those days, many husbands would have sent their spouses on such a trip, but would not have accompanied them.

Sarah Hale professed no desire to seek anything beyond marriage and motherhood, but began writing poems, articles, and stories that David Hale encouraged her to submit to local newspapers. He edited her efforts, steering her away from the ornate prose of the era and toward a leaner style (still flowery by later standards). By 1822, her work had appeared in several publications.

In that same year, Sarah Hale's world imploded with the sudden death, "as with a stroke," of her husband, two weeks before the birth of their fifth child, William. "And to my throbbing heart," she wrote, "thy babe I press which thou wilt never see, and never bless."[3]

Hale faced not only personal tragedy, but also bleak financial prospects: her husband had left a meager estate, and her relatives could offer little aid to the widow and her children. And in the 1820s, an era utterly dominated by men, few career paths lay open to women.

She took an immediate step toward self-sufficiency by opening a small millinery shop with her sister-in-law. Hale also continued to write, thoughts of a literary career tugging at her even though she realized that publishing was one of society's most formidable male bastions.

Her fingers numb from hours of sewing at the millinery shop, the demands of her children incessant, Hale somehow picked up her quill each night. She enjoyed her first noteworthy whiff of literary success in 1823 with the publication of her book *The Genius of Oblivion*, a slim volume of poems that touched on traditional women's concerns—home and family—and resonated with heartache over her husband's death and a longing for her past life, one in which her husband had been "creation's lord."[4] Her husband's Masonic Lodge brothers had assumed the printing costs.

Hale's verse did not win her financial freedom from the millinery shop. Her writing appetite whetted, however, she began to work on a novel whose theme focused on an incendiary topic—slavery.

Hale had little knowledge of slavery beyond her reading. Her motive for writing *Northwood* was more to extoll small-town New England's virtues than to condemn the South. Still, while believing that Whites were the superior race—a common view in her region—and even that the Bible sanctioned slavery, she decried its effect on America.

Night after night she labored over *Northwood*, "literally with my baby in my arms."[5] Striving to depict "Life North and South, Showing the True Character of Both," although she had never ventured beyond New England, Hale juxtaposed the values of a Yankee town

(Northwood) to the troubles of a Southern plantation.[6] And embodying the noblest traits of all her novel's characters was a young tutor named Stuart. A man of modest means, a wide-ranging intellect, staunch Masonic ties, and morality, the handsome teacher read and studied with his wife, whom he cherished most in his life. No one in Newport had to read between the lines to grasp that Stuart was David Hale.

The protagonist of Sarah Hale's novel is not the estimable Stuart, but Sidney Romilly, a young Northwood man of "expansive forehead, large, luminous eyes," and the "promise of uncommon genius."[7] In his New England hometown, he mirrors the Yankee values of industry and Protestantism taught to him and his siblings by their father, James Romilly.

Everything changes for Sidney with the arrival of Horace Brainard, Hale's Southerner, husband of Sidney's Aunt Lydia (Romilly). Childless, longing for an heir to his plantation fortune, Brainard convinces James Romilly to let him and his wife adopt Sidney. Realizing that the offer presents a financial windfall for the boy, James Romilly agrees. Sidney leaves for South Carolina with his stepfather, and, as Hale would later reveal, also takes leave of Yankee values.

A scion of inherited wealth; charming; sophisticated; a lover of billiards, the race track, and the theater; and a Roman Catholic—a factor always worthy of mistrust among Puritanical New Englanders—Brainard appears, on the surface, a lazy, frivolous man. However, he is also a doting husband, solicitous of young Sidney, and kind to a fault with his slaves, whom he treats less as property than as human beings.

Over seventeen years, Sidney's New England values erode. The Brainards buy him the finest clothes, send his despairing tutor packing, and introduce their stepson to Charleston society. One of the foremost reasons for Sidney's moral descent, writes Hale, is his reliance on slaves to answer his every wish. Only the fact that "Sidney had never forgotten he was Yankee born, although half raised on a Southern plantation" curtailed a total immersion in hedonism.[8]

Following nearly two decades in the South, Sidney returns to

Northwood for a visit. Then, the sudden deaths of James Romilly and Horace Brainard not only devastate Sidney emotionally, but also financially; the Romilly farm is failing, and Brainard has frittered away his fortune in bad business deals.

These tragedies jolt Sidney back to his Yankee roots. He faces his problems with stoicism and hard work, rescuing the family's farm by working it with his genteel hands. "Till within a few months," he says, "pleasure has been the idol of my pursuit; and I have, I believe, sought it in every place except where alone it is to be found—in a virtuous home."[9]

Sidney also finds virtue in a local girl and woos her. Once reformed from his Southern ways, fortune again follows him: his fiancée is an heiress and, through mysterious circumstances Hale never completely clarifies, he regains Brainard's fortune.

Northwood having saved Sidney, he returns to the Brainard plantation to run it, not with Southern indolence, as characterized by Hale, but with Yankee morality. High among the Southern weaknesses that had almost ruined Sidney Romilly was his reliance on slaves. Hale's major condemnation of the "peculiar institution"[10] emerged "not in its effect on the slave but its effect on the master."[11] Unlike hardworking Yankees seeking wealth, Southern plantation owners, she asserted, became indolent because slaves labored on their behalf. She wrote that scions of plantations "often give promise of great talent, [only] to smoke cigars in a verandah, or lie in the shade reading cheap novels."[12] In Hale's view, this laziness whittled away their morality. "Thus the system of slavery increases the temptations of sin," she wrote, "and only the most resolute courage in duty and humble reliance on Divine aid can struggle on successfully against the snares of evil around the slaveholder."[13] Buttressed by traditional Yankee values, Sidney Romilly remained "a gentleman."[14] His wife, Annie, "supplied the moral force while the man was kept busy with material concerns and with politics."[15] According to her scheme of America, women such as Annie Romilly must serve as the moral buffer against Yankee greed and Southern self-indulgence and idle pleasure.

In the second edition of *Northwood*, published in 1852, Sarah Hale rendered her solution to slavery in a stance advocated by the American Colonization Society and repudiated by slave owners. The society, founded in 1817, endorsed freeing the slaves and shipping them to African colonies; one of the organization's members was New Hampshire Senator Daniel Webster. Like her state's fiery politician, Hale espoused that the slaves be converted to Christianity, set free, and ferried to Africa "to plant Free States and organize Christian civilization."[16] She feared that if the slaves remained in America, "the black man would still be, in our land, a servant."[17] Hale abhorred the idea of a war of liberation sought by Abolitionists "who would sever the Union rather than see a slave within its borders . . . [and] forget the *master* is their brother, as well as the *servant.*"[18]

Throughout *Northwood*, Hale urged that "constitutions" and "compromises" between North and South offered the solution to slavery. Southerners would rightfully charge that her near-idyllic portrait of her barely disguised hometown of Newport celebrated Yankee superiority. She also spoke out against Northerners' preoccupation with wealth and materialism, however.

The original publication of *Northwood*, in 1827, vaulted the New Hampshire writer to national attention; her book was the first successful novel by an American woman. With its examination of the deepening cultural chasm between North and South, *Northwood* sold so well that it was printed in England under the title *A New England Tale.*

Anathema to outraged Southern readers, a celebration of Yankee virtues to Northerners, *Northwood* also gained the struggling Yankee widow a name in literary circles. When Boston minister John Laurie Blake, impressed by the antislavery novel, offered Hale the chief editor's slot for a monthly women's magazine he planned to publish, she accepted, forever turning her back on the millinery shop.

In April 1828, Hale said her good-byes to friends and relatives and climbed aboard the Boston stagecoach, sad to leave the village where she had spent virtually all of her forty years and the house where every book and every stick of furniture conjured wistful memories of the union of body, soul, and intellect she had known with David Hale. Hoping that the job in Boston would support their children far better than the hat shop she hated so much, she had no choice but to leave.

Hardest of all for Hale as the coach clattered from Newport was leaving her children with relatives. She would be living in a boarding-house and working too many hours to care for them properly. Future scholars' attempts to brand her a neglectful mother would carry little weight; there was no hypocrisy in the cash-strapped widow's desire to provide for her family the best way she knew how—by capitalizing on her skill with the written word.

In the first issue of *Ladies' Magazine,* Hale promised her readers that she would "mark the progress of female improvement and cherish the effusions of female intellect."[19] She broke with traditional editorial practice by refusing to pirate stories and articles from other magazines, running only original material. Her formula worked—the publication's circulation inched upward to 10,000.

Male writers and poets expecting to bully the editor of *Ladies' Magazine* into leaving their copy alone while doling out any payment they demanded learned otherwise. "Beneath the soft exterior of motherhood and femininity, Sarah Hale was a shrewd and businesslike woman whose later dealings with male contributors . . . proved her more than a match for the Yankee entrepreneurs who were making their way in literature."[20]

Hale's tough-minded stance toward male writers lay unrevealed in the pages she edited. Concentrating on what she termed the "women's sphere," she harangued outspoken feminists such as Frances Wright.[21] Of the cries of Wright and company for the vote, Hale huffed: "I consider every attempt to induce women to think they have a just right to participate in the public duties of government as injurious to their best interests and derogatory to their character. Our empire is purer, more excellent and spiritual"—such as that of *Northwood's* Annie Romilly.[22]

Hale's success with *Ladies' Magazine* so impressed a rival publication's owner that in the mid-1830s he launched a relentless campaign to lure her to the editor's slot of his magazine, *Godey's Lady's Book.* Louis Antoine Godey was a thirtyish entrepreneur determined to make his women's magazine America's foremost, a man whose pleasant, whiskered features and paunchy physique belied his iron-willed ambition. He believed that Hale understood the minds and the concerns of his target readership—middle- and upper-class women—better than any American editor and that her abilities could translate into unprecedented circulation of his magazine. Hale, unwilling to move to Godey's Philadelphia offices from Boston, where she was becoming a celebrity in tony Brahman drawing rooms and a nationally acclaimed fund-raiser for the completion of the Bunker Hill monument, rebuffed Godey's commercial advances. With her son Horatius at Harvard and her family in Newport, she intended to stay put.

Godey persisted, and Hale, realizing that his magazine was poised to become the nation's favorite publication for women, finally accepted his offer after he purchased the *Ladies' Magazine* and melded it into one publication, *Godey's Lady's Book,* in 1837. Hale edited the magazine from Boston for her first four years with Godey and ultimately moved to Philadelphia in 1841, once again setting her valises down in a succession of rooming houses. Her children grown and well educated, courtesy of her earnings as editor of *Ladies' Magazine,* Hale focused on her private ambition—to better the lives of American women.

As editor of *Godey's Lady's Book,* Sarah Hale garnered wealth and nationwide fame. Still, she was not a strident advocate of women's rights, despite her lofty perch in the publishing world. She continued to extol the virtues of home and family. She aimed the magazine at "an untapped and as yet inarticulate group of Mrs. Hales—middle-class women; women of the sewing circle rather than of the salon. . . . women coping with life on serious terms, earnest about philanthropies and progress, proud of their new country, busily endowing the old-fashioned religion with a new outlook—not the pampered and over-leisured dolls of Boston and provincial parlors, but leaners upon domestic broomsticks and supporters of books."[23] Hale, evincing a dual mission that made her hard to typecast for future historians of her century's women's movement, "consecrated [her magazines] to duty and domesticity, and the preparation of women for a larger and more serious sphere."[24] Her editorial approach sent Godey's circulation rate soaring to more than a million annually by the Civil War.

Hale's pages, however subtly, did steer women from viewing themselves as mere appendages of their husbands. In the 1850s, despite the reluctance of her boss, Louis Godey, Hale tackled controversial topics, but excluded any disturbing accounts of the Civil War. She wrote: "Every young woman in our land should be qualified by some accomplishment which she may teach, or some art or profession she can follow, to support herself creditably, should the necessity occur."[25] Hale, who knew that necessity all too well, encouraged her readers to seek work as teachers and nurses.

To the dismay of many men, Hale asserted that women should train not only as nurses, but also as doctors. She used *Godey's* to publicize America's first woman doctor, Elizabeth Blackwell (see "Calling Dr. Lee," page 76), and the nation's first women's medical school, the Female Medical College of Pennsylvania. Some scholars have argued, however, that Hale's support of women physicians lay less in the battle cries of the era's feminist movement than in traditional views of feminine modesty, such as her assertion that male doctors treating women's more intimate ailments bordered on "unscriptural and unnatural."[26] She noted that countless women chose "to suffer the extremity of danger and pain, rather than waive those scruples of delicacy which prevent their maladies from being fully explored."[27] Female physicians, she believed, would mean better care for the nation's women.

Although Hale used the *Lady's Book* to advance her opinions, fashion articles, short stories, poems, recipes, household advice, and health pieces turned the magazine into the most successful women's publication of the nineteenth century. A shrewd judge of talent, Hale introduced her readers to the stunning, macabre work of a former West Point classmate of her son David. Edgar Allan Poe thrilled—and chilled—the *Lady's Book*'s readers with "The Cask of Amontillado" and other stories. Along with Poe's work, Hale ran verse and fiction from the likes of Hawthorne, Emerson, Longfellow, and Holmes, paying high rates—up to $30 per poem.

While advancing the careers of great writers, Hale did not neglect her own literary work. She wrote more than twenty books, including the nine-hundred-page tome *Women's Record, or Sketches of All Distinguished Women from 'The Beginning' till A.D. 1850*, not to mention her articles in *Lady's Book*.

Of all Hale's convictions, her belief that wife and mother were her most important titles never wavered. Her children were all well-adjusted overachievers; her youngest, William, graduated second in his class at Harvard and became one of America's most prominent lawyers. Hale's namesake, Sarah Josepha, founded and operated the Boarding and Day School for Young Ladies, in Philadelphia.

Sadly, no amount of pride could temper the loss of four of her children. Her first, David, the youngest graduate of his West Point class, died of a fever shortly after his mother took the job at *Godey's*. Some scholars have suggested that Sarah Hale published the work of her son's West Point classmate Poe not only because of his talent, but also because of his link to her deceased son. Her moral and financial support of the troubled writer and his wife and child buttresses that theory.

Hale endured these losses by immersing herself in her work and refusing to wallow in self-pity. The stoicism her mother had instilled in her so many years earlier, when she forced Sarah to touch the forehead of her dead relative, had steeled Hale for the inevitability of personal tragedy.

In the final years of her life, Hale lived and worked in the Philadelphia mansion of her daughter, Frances, and her daughter's husband, a physician named Hunter. "Godey's Lady" sat for unbroken hours behind a massive desk in the center of her bedroom, sifting through neat rows of manuscripts awash in the light of a green-shaded banker's lamp, incessantly dipping her gold pen into an inkpot resting atop a nearby tray, and reaching again and again for the bowl of grapes she always kept on hand.[28] Her lifelong regimen of sensible diet and exercise paid off, furnishing the octogenarian the stamina of someone decades younger. "I never saw her when she was not working," one of her grandchildren would later recall, "except at meals and Sunday nights."[29] But her grandchildren knew, as had her own children in years past, that they were always welcome in her office. Seated on a huge chintz sofa amid the bookshelf-lined walls of Hale's bedroom, her grandchildren loved to read and to talk with her as she worked.

Hale continued to relish her status as the arbiter of women's fashions throughout the 1800s. Stylish women waited to buy new hats, outfits, and shoes until they had read Hale's assessment of the latest trends. She took her role as fashion plate seriously, dressing conservatively but elegantly in tailored, lace-trimmed black dresses, her hair neatly coiffed and her bearing erect. One of her grandchildren said that "when dressed for church, she was an imposing spectacle, rather like a duchess of fiction."[30] In a classic case of "do as I say, not as I do," she advised women on changes in hairstyles for nearly five decades, but never changed the ringlet curls her husband had known so well.

In her daughter's house in December 1877, Hale wrote her final missive for *Godey's*: "Having reached my ninetieth year, I bid farewell to my countrywomen, with the hope that this work of half a century may be blessed to the furtherance of their happiness and usefulness in their Divinely appointed sphere."[31]

On April 30, 1879, Sarah Hale died of natural causes. *Godey's Lady's Book* began a slow decline, brought on in large part by readers who no longer agreed with such conventional views as Hale's advice regarding the vote; in 1898, the final issue of *Godey's* appeared, a nineteenth-century relic as the twentieth century loomed.

Hale's ascent from her rural New England origins to her status as the nation's first successful woman editor and as the author of the first antislavery novel make her a most remarkable woman. Oddly enough, however, the doggerel "Mary had a little lamb," published as "Mary's Lamb" in a volume of verse titled *Poems for Our Children* in

1830—three years after *Northwood*—eclipsed all of Hale's earlier literary feats.

Of the special status that *Northwood* brought to the creator of "Mary's Lamb," no doubt exists. The foreword of the second edition professed Hale's hope that reason, not warfare, would end slavery. "And from the glorious old Granite State, where the scenes of this novel begin," she wrote, "have come forth those great men, 'Defenders of the Constitution'—who 'know no North and no South'—but wherever the sacred Charter of Union stretches its cordon of brotherhood, and the Eagle and the Stars keep guard, is their country. In the same spirit our book goes forth."[32]

In her capacity as editor of *Lady's Book*, the author of *Northwood* bowed to pressure from Southern readers and banned the work of Abolitionist Sarah Jane Clarke from going forth in the magazine's pages.

Despite the hopes Hale expressed in her revision of *Northwood,* the novel's time had passed. Stowe's work mirrored the polarization that had gripped North and South in the quarter century since *Northwood*'s original publication. In 1827, Hale's call for compromise had seemed reasonable and possible. In 1852, America's first antislavery novel appeared naive and dated. Sarah Hale's little lamb, however, proved timeless.

Calling Dr. Lee

On March 1, 1864, a cultural trailblazer stood among the graduating class of the New England Female Medical College. Rebecca Lee had overcome far more than male opposition to the idea of female physicians: she was the first Black woman to hold a medical degree, and she attained it during the height of the Civil War and less than two years after President Abraham Lincoln signed the Emancipation Proclamation. All of the new physicians clutching their Doctress of Medicine degrees from the Boston school that day were, in a sense, medical pioneers. Elizabeth Blackwell, America's first woman doctor, had earned her sheepskin only fifteen years previously.

Having overcome staggering social obstacles in her thirty-odd years to win the prized degree, Rebecca Lee left the familiar Commonwealth Avenue campus to embark on a milestone career; she would prove her medical mettle despite the misgivings of several white faculty members.

Although Lee's career path and her diagnostic and healing abilities are readily observed in her 1883 book, *A Book of Medical Discourses in Two Parts,* much of her early life remains enigmatic, her treatise offering only tantalizing bits of her background. Various scholars write that she was born in Pennsylvania or Richmond, Virginia, in 1833; however, recent research by historian Ann Rollins reveals that Lee was born a free Black in Delaware in 1831 and, in Lee's words, raised by a "kind aunt . . . whose usefulness with the sick was continually sought."[1]

Under her aunt's tutelage, Lee decided at an early age that she, too, wanted "to relieve the suffering of others."[2] In 1852, having trained as a practical nurse and midwife by tending ailing children and pregnant women, the twentyish Lee headed north to Boston, a hotbed of Abolitionism and the site of a growing community of free Blacks. She settled in Charlestown and soon found work as a nurse with several White physicians.

Her employers were so impressed with Lee's intuitive feel for medicine and her way with patients that they recommended her to the New England Female Medical College, the precursor of Boston University's medical school. In 1859, her application was accepted.

Although Lee's formal education prior to 1859 is obscure, it is not only possible but probable that her White classmates, most of upper- and middle-class backgrounds, possessed an advantage over the Black nurse. But Lee's years of ministering to the sick gave her a hands-on knowledge that served her well in the classrooms and laboratories of the stately granite and brick Boston medical school.

Lee plunged into her studies. Although her tuition, up to $2,000, was paid by a state scholarship, unlike the wealthier students, she had to work to support herself. Financial duress forced her to interrupt her studies for two years, but not to abandon her dream of a medical degree.

Whatever insults or ostracism she may have encountered at the Commonwealth Avenue campus, she did not let the bigotry deter her. Nor did she bow to the male disapproval facing all female medical students of the day.

A more ominous threat to Lee's hopes arose on February 25, 1864, on the eve of her triumph. The following passage appeared in the notes of the college's faculty: "Some of us have hesitated very seriously in recommending her."[3]

The dissenters never indicated their specific qualms about Lee in print, but stated that they would award her a degree "out of deference to what we understand to be the wishes of the Trustees and the present state of public feeling."[4] The "public feeling" mentioned by the faculty alluded to Boston's strong Abolitionist roots; without documented elaboration, however, the reluctance of some teachers to endorse Lee remains a riddle.

In the limited world of medicine open to female doctors then, obstetric practices offered the most logical and lucrative route for Lee and her fellow graduates. Mrs. Hassenfuss, a graduate of Lee's alma mater, specialized in the delivery of babies, offering formal training traditional midwives did not possess, and she did quite well. "Although she [Hassenfuss] was never sought by the well-paying portion of the Boston community," wrote one observer, "she held a very reputable position among her patients and among such of the profession as had business with her."[5]

Dr. Lee, too, focused her skills on women and children, but did so far south of Boston once the Civil War ended. She hung her shingle in Richmond, Virginia, home to large numbers of newly freed slaves in dire need of basic medical attention, and married a man named Arthur Crumpler.

The exact length of Dr. Rebecca Lee Crumpler's practice in Virginia is sketchy, but by 1872 she had returned to Boston and moved into a Beacon Hill brownstone at 67 Joy Street. That same year, the *Boston Almanac & Directory* listed the nation's first Black woman doctor and her office's address: "Female Physicians, Crumpler, Rebecca, Mrs., 20 Garden [Street]."[6]

Targeting her practice toward women and children and living in a city with an entrenched Black community, Crumpler upheld the highest tenets of her profession with her self-avowed credo to treat all patients "regardless of remuneration."[7] Although she did not comment overtly about racism in medicine in *Medical Discourses,* she did address class prejudice in Brahman Boston: "It is just as important that a doctor be in attendance before the birth of a poor woman's child as that he should be present before the birth of a child of wealth."[8]

In the decade after her return to Boston, Dr. Crumpler labored "to mitigate the afflictions of the human race."[9] As her expertise in the examination room grew, so did her desire to eradicate traditional but unsound home remedies practiced in laborers' hovels and Brahmans' mansions alike. In the early 1880s, she labored to put her medical observations and treatments to paper at a desk in her new home, in Hyde Park.

Dr. Crumpler, depicted in a commemorative medallion a century later as an attractive, strong-featured physician wearing a high, stiff collar, her hair pulled back in a neat, businesslike bun, brought her compendium of treatments and advice to Boston publisher Cashman, Keating & Company, and in 1883 the firm's release of *A Book of Medical Discourses in Two Parts* marked the first medical handbook written by a Black woman in America.

Crumpler's 144-page tract, "Containing Miscellaneous Information Concerning the Life and Growth of Beings; the Beginning of

Womanhood; also the Cause, Prevention, and Cure of Many . . . Complaints of Women, and Youth of Both Sexes," offered much advice that would prove as sound a century later as in 1883.[10] To pregnant women, she issued a warning: "Over-indulgence in intoxicating liquors and tobacco will cause sickly, diminutive offspring, to say nothing of premature births."[11]

Crumpler also cautioned mothers to avoid another form of alcohol abuse, condemning the age-old practice of lulling infants to sleep with liquor, as well as such drugs like laudanum (opium) and such herbal remedies as catnip tea. "Babes should move about if they have life enough in them," she wrote. "They should, by no means, be stupefied."[12] Lee also advised mothers that when infants who should be sleeping began to squall, "the first milk from the breast is [often] the only medicine needed."[13]

Along with her faith in breast-feeding and her harangues against alcohol abuse, Dr. Crumpler advocated other medical measures steeped in common sense, but new to many Americans of the 1880s. She shunned the use of strong soap for infants because its alkalinity severely irritated their skin. And for readers who did not grasp how soft a baby's bones were, Crumpler warned that under no circumstances should a parent press a baby's skull.

Crumpler's medical specialty, women and children, resounds in virtually every segment of her book. She wrote of her desire that *Medical Discourses* become a "primary reader in the hands of every woman," and dedicated it to "mothers, nurses."[14] Crumpler exhorted those mothers to pay attention to every sign of marked change in their children's health. "There is no doubt that thousands of little ones annually die at our very doors from diseases which could have been prevented or cut short by timely aid. . . .My chief desire in presenting this book is to impress upon somebody's mind the possibilities of prevention."[15]

Crumpler's advocacy of preventive medicine complemented her ability to address common health problems through "perscriptions" that parents could prepare at home. She offered such home-brewed formulas as her "Vegetable Alternative," a mix of water, "fresh Indian posey, and red water pepper herbs . . . white pine bark . . . horehound herbs . . . pulverized mandrake root," and sugar.[16] The result was a syrup for the treatment of everything from "bloating, worms, [and] cough" in children to "old colds . . . morbid craving for tobacco, alcoholic beverages or other blood-poisoning idols" in adults.[17]

Dr. Crumpler's book and the tidbits of her life depict a physician whose practice was "ahead of her time."[18] Under the very noses of teachers who had doubts about her abilities, she practiced medicine with the utmost competence and professionalism while shouldering the dual burdens of sexism and racism.

Dr. Rebecca Lee Crumpler died in 1895. Her accomplishments have slipped into obscurity. At this writing, however, her reputation is slowly resurfacing as aspects of her life emerge from such sources as old records of the New England Female Medical College.

At 67 Joy Street, on Beacon Hill, a plaque dedicated in 1995 emblazons a brick wall flanking the entrance to Dr. Crumpler's former home. The memorial proclaims:

Rebecca Lee Crumpler
1831–1895
First African American
Woman to Earn a Medical Degree

FUN, FOOD, AND THE FINER THINGS IN LIFE

First Class
All the Way

〜

E verything looked different. From the moment that the Tremont House, in Boston, opened its doors on October 16, 1829, a new world of comfort and service greeted the patrons fortunate to sample the amenities of America's first modern, world-class hotel.

Standing outside the main entrance, a well-dressed, twenty-nine-year-old architect peered proudly at the stately granite walls of the five-story edifice. Isaiah Rogers had reason for satisfaction: the Tremont House would justly earn him the sobriquet "the father of the modern hotel."

His own father had doubted his son's ability to accomplish the feat. Isaac Rogers, Isaiah's father, was a Marshfield, Massachusetts, ship-builder and wanted his son, born on August 17, 1800, to run one of the family's chief assets, a farm. A boy who loved to draw and carve wood, and who proved a standout pupil in South Shore schools, Isaiah Rogers recoiled against his father's wishes, the pair often at odds at the dinner table.

In 1816, the youth stunned his parents with his announcement that he had signed an apprentice agreement with a Boston carpenter named Shaw and would move immediately to the big city. Years passed before he and his father would reconcile over the decision.

The apprentice worked for Shaw until turning twenty-one, learning the trade well. But as Rogers drove carts of sawed wood and also crafted stairs, moldings, and other fittings at Boston construction sites, he began to study every detail of how structures—from private homes to office buildings—took shape. Whenever he spied architects unrolling blueprints across tables on site, he begged them to explain every penciled or inked detail, from drawing board to finished edifice. Many architects chased him away, but one in particular, Solomon Willard, was amused by the earnest youth and took time to explain the basics of architecture.

With no financial help forthcoming from his estranged family and with little money of his own, Rogers could not afford formal architectural instruction. But Willard and several other designers noticed that Rogers retained every design tidbit they threw his way. He proved himself as adept with a pencil as with a saw.

In 1821, the end of his apprenticeship, Rogers took a carpentry job in Mobile, Alabama. His true reason for heading south, however, soon became apparent. Several Mobile entrepreneurs wanted to build a theater and announced an open competition for the structure's design. They were not looking for anything elegant, just functional and inexpensive. The winning design came from the drawing board of twenty-two-year-old Isaiah Rogers.

The jubilant carpenter gave his first patrons their money's worth— the cavernous, plain, and inexpensive building they required. Despite the modest configurations of his design for the Mobile Theatre, Rogers's commission placed him at least on the same level as formally trained young architects just leaving college.

In 1822, Rogers returned to Boston, with a visit to the downtown offices of his mentor, Solomon Willard. As the stout, dapper Willard— one of America's foremost architects as well as a master mason and gifted sculptor—studied the young man pleading for a position, it became obvious that Rogers had come a long way from the sawdust-covered carpenter's apprentice of a few years earlier. That he had won a design competition without benefit of formal training convinced Willard that Rogers possessed a measure of unhoned architectural genius. Rogers left Willard's office with an entry-level job.

Pitted against young men holding diplomas from the nation's finest architectural programs and traveling in the highest social circles, the carpenter labored over his drawings long after his associates had departed for dinners at Boston's toniest restaurants with high-society belles and a night at the theater. He also eclipsed his peers' efforts through his combination of natural talent and innovation, qualities no professor could instill in a student. Willard's clients praised Rogers's design skills and his ability to incorporate customers' whims without cost overruns, and his boss assigned him to important jobs, from lucrative restorations of Beacon Hill brownstones to multi-story warehouses.

In 1826, grateful to Willard but chafing to control designs from foundation to roof, Rogers decided to branch out on his own. To his relief, Willard approved and, realizing the special nature of the twenty-six-year-old man's abilities, forged a loose partnership that would allow the pair to pool their talents on future projects. For Rogers, the union was wise and profitable, as the elder architect was a far better businessman than his departing employee.

Rogers exited Willard's firm with far more than his boss's blessing and support. In 1823, while overseeing a construction site for Willard in Portland, Maine, Rogers had met Emily Tobey, a pretty, well-connected young woman, and married her after a short courtship. They settled in Boston.

Rogers's reputation for innovation and for accommodation of his clients' own "designs" soon filled his drawing board with commissions. At first, most of his work was profitable but small in scope. Then, in 1827, like architects all over America, he learned that a consortium of Boston businessmen had purchased a lot on Tremont Street and were entertaining open bids for the design of an unprecedented hotel—a "palace of the people"[1] to rival Europe's grand hostelries. For the winning architectural firm, a hefty payday and the potential for worldwide fame beckoned. The lot's owners informed contestants that money was no object; innovation, elegance, and, above all, comfort were the key design features the hoteliers were seeking.

Rogers scrutinized the Tremont Street site and went to work on his bid. Pouring every bit of imagination he could muster into his sketches, studying the designs of classic hotels of London, Paris, Milan, and Rome, he devised a plan for a five-story brick and granite edifice with a grand main entrance that would feature four giant columns in classical style surmounted by a stunning archway. But the true splendor of his vision lay with the regal interior, whose touches won Rogers the prized commission.

On July 4, 1828, as holiday crowds stopped to watch, a band of Boston politicians, Brahmans, and Rogers stood along the large Tremont Street lot. As applause echoed from the crowd, the cornerstone of the Tremont House Hotel was placed.

The glow of the ceremony soon dissolving, Rogers had little more than a year to raise the hotel. His bosses did not want any stoppages in the construction short of a blizzard. Warming themselves as best they could around small fires and in ramshackle lean-tos, the project's masons and carpenters worked in round-the-clock shifts. Countless wagons groaning beneath loads of granite and timber clattered up and down Tremont Street; the rasp of saws, the clang of hammers, and workmen's shouts filled the street incessantly, irritating some passersby, but fascinating most, as evidenced by the crowds who stopped to marvel at the building taking shape. They usually saw the well-dressed Rogers, blueprints in hand, striding in and out of the structure. Often, he removed his coat, rolled up his sleeves, picked up a saw or hammer, and worked a full carpenter's shift. His crews, accustomed to highbrow architects treating tradesmen with aloofness or barely disguised disdain, gave Rogers the same respect he showed them. Few work stoppages of any sort plagued the Tremont House, an almost unheard-of development on Boston construction sites.

On October 29, 1829, with a brass band booming popular tunes, a stream of ornate carriages pulled up in front of the Tremont House and deposited assorted Brahmans and other socialites on the steps of the hotel's pillared portico. Rogers watched the crowd from the lobby.

From the instant the visitors—by invitation only at the grand opening—finished gaping at the classical exterior and strolled into the main lobby, they grasped why the Tremont would soon eclipse the Exchange Coffee House, on Congress Street, as New England's premiere hotel. For that matter, they realized why the Tremont House humbled all other American hotels.

Although the soaring, dignified exterior and spacious entryway proclaimed that this establishment offered something special, the true beauty of Rogers's design became evident as the first genteel guests ambled into the high-ceilinged, columned lobby and signed their John Hancocks in a bound-leather ledger resting atop a burnished mahogany reception desk. Patrons began to sense the unprecedented accommodations that awaited. And Isaiah Rogers had designed all of the amenities.

Unlike any other American inn or hotel of the era, the Tremont provided single rooms. Guests venturing into other hostelries were accustomed to proprietors' rooming complete strangers spoon fashion in a single bed, wondering if the snoring stranger alongside them was some sort of miscreant. As a European traveler recalled, he would lay half-awake all evening in America's inns worrying about who might slide into bed with him. Even worse, owners of such hospitality suites often attempted in a pinch to pile strangers of both sexes under the same bedcover. A raffish young man wrote of "a late night" in a New York inn "when five young ladies came into [his] room" and began to disrobe for bed.[2] "I raised my head," he later wrote, "and desired to be informed which of them intended me the honor of her company."[3] The women smiled at him—and arranged a bedroll for themselves on the floor.

Some guests at America's hotels reveled in situations like the one in which the young blade found himself. A popular travel anecdote of the late eighteenth century told of a staunchly religious Connecticut woman who harangued her nephew for his womanizing on the road. The nephew explained: "But we're not so very different. Suppose that in traveling, you came to an inn where all the beds were full except two, and in one of those was a man and in the other was a woman. Which would you take? The woman's to be sure. Well, madam, so would I."[4] Such was the hotel scene of the 1800s until the Tremont House opened its 170 rooms to the public, or at least the well-heeled public able to afford the new hotel's pricey $2-per-night rate.

When patrons wriggled their keys into their singles' locks, another "hospitality first" emerged, for the Tremont was the first American hotel to provide individual locks and keys. Upon entering their rooms, which were tastefully decorated and featured clean, comfortable beds, guests encountered other unprecedented amenities: a washbowl, a pitcher, and a cake of soap for each visitor. In other hotels, roommates shared all of the above. And Tremont guests didn't have to worry about knocking over bowls or pitchers in the dark—rooms came equipped with innovative gas lamps with which even the clumsiest fingers could cope.

If the hotel's patrons did have trouble figuring out how to use the lamps or any of the Tremont's other conveniences, yet another new marvel of technology provided help. Each room boasted an electric-magnetic annunciator featuring two buttons. All a guest had to do was press them, and the device set off a small, ringing disk in the main office to dispatch employees to the customer's room.

Although high society seldom praised the Tremont's attentive staff—they believed that too many compliments to servants made them forget their station—some of the highborn patrons' loftiest praise went to two working-class heroes, the hotel's plumbers, Thomas Philpott and Thomas Pollard. The "princes of pipes" had installed private bathrooms, yet another hotel first, replete with flush toilets that earned plaudits as a modern miracle from guests and tradesmen alike. The idea had been Rogers's.

The society sorts soon ventured from their private bathrooms and plush digs and headed down the hotel's sweeping staircases to its elegant dining room. There, repasts turned out by world-class chefs and served on fine china atop costly white linen tablecloths conquered the privileged palates of people for whom only the best fare would do.

One frequent Tremont House guest discovered, in the glittering dining room, what he believed to be the landmark hotel's true secret of success; and that secret was not the sumptuous food. "You eat in a crowd," wrote the Reverend George Lewis, "sitting down with fifty, a hundred, sometimes two hundred at a table, to which you are summoned by a sonorous Chinese gong. The only place of retirement is your room, to which you have the key."[5] Later chroniclers of American

89

life would agree with Lewis's assessment that the Tremont's revolutionary balance between public and private amenities, "this congenial mix," was the "cunning sum of its achievement."⁶

The stellar reputation of the Tremont House bloomed from the first day its magnificent doors opened. Many of the era's elite embarked on pilgrimages to Boston for no other reason than to settle into one of the grand hotel's luxurious rooms, to sample its cuisine, and to peruse the massive library. Among the notable guests who signed the ledger in the hotel's first decade were President Andrew Jackson and famed writers Charles Dickens, William Thackeray, and Alexis de Tocqueville.

Throughout the rest of the nineteenth century, anyone determined to build a first-class hotel in America looked to the bible, a book entitled *A Description of the Tremont House with Architectural Illustrations.*

Unfortunately, many Tremont House imitations outlasted the original. In 1895, developers purchased the still-popular establishment with the intention of building a bigger and better hotel. The "palace of the people" fell victim to the wrecker's ball. An era had ended, but in the gleaming lobbies and plush environs of today's finest hotels, the traditions of the Tremont House flourish. America's first modern hotel had proven worth every penny of its steep $2-per-night rate.

The creator of that hotel had quickly capitalized upon its success. The Father of the Modern Hotel lived up to his billing, designing many of America's legendary hostelries: the Astor House, in New York; the stunning second St. Charles Hotel, in New Orleans; Louisville's immortal Maxwell House; and the superbly rendered Corinthian-style Charleston Hotel, in South Carolina. In 1841, he brought the world-class hotel to Maine with his lovely Bangor House.

The largely self-taught architect, acclaimed in 1850 by the *Illustrated London News* as the finest hotel designer in the world, never lost his sense of the practical amid his favored Greek revivalist themes. In 1863, he patented a burglar-proof safe for his hotels' patrons.

In his sixties, his workaholic career caught up with Rogers and he suffered a series of heart attacks. He succumbed on April 13, 1869, having designed the nation's first first-class hotel and having provided his family a first-class lifestyle.

Each time an American walks into a hotel with all the amenities, Isaiah Rogers's fingerprints appear from lobby to suite. J. M. Fenster, a historian of famous hotels, observes: "Even in 1994, the Tremont House would seem new; ambition that powerful can't change."[7]

"The Mansion of Happiness"—America's First Board Game

All eyes peered at the eight-sided wooden top spinning dizzily across the gaming board, for the printed number that would face upward as soon as the whirling teetotum stopped would decide the fate of the players. If the wrong digit appeared, a stint in the pillory, the stocks, or a cell loomed for the misfortunate gamester.

In 1843, this scene played out not in the waterfront gambling dens, but in the parlors of the middle and upper classes throughout New England. The game of chance featured neither wagered wads of cash nor demon dice. From Rhode Island to Maine and everywhere between, parents and children alike were gathering around parlor tables, and, in the glow of oil lamps or candles, spinning the teetotum and moving wooden pegs across the brilliantly colored spaces and artwork of America's first successful board game—The Mansion of Happiness. No mere fad, the pastime would launch a worldwide industry and earn Salem, Massachusetts, status as "The Cradle of the American Board Game."

In the early 1840s, Ann W. Abbott, the thirtyish daughter of a

Beverly, Massachusetts, minister, strolled into a gabled, wood-frame building in the neighboring town of Salem with a business proposal. Standing at 230-232 Essex Street, in the seaport's commercial hub, the structure housed the clattering printing presses of W. & S. B. Ives Company.

The bespectacled fifty-year-old proprietor, William Ives, had proven himself the quintessential Yankee businessman—shrewd, hard-working, and able to recognize a golden opportunity when he heard one. And in 1840, the prim and proper minister's daughter had presented just that: she had invented a children's card game called Dr. Busby and had convinced Ives to print and market it. The vividly hued cards depicting Dr. Busby and a cast of his patients and acquaintances offered children and their parents a fast-paced, free-wheeling parlor pastime that netted both creator and inventor a tidy profit.

Now, three years later, Abbott showed Ives her new creation, The Mansion of Happiness, which she pitched as an "instructive, moral, and entertaining amusement."[1] Ives was looking at America's first bona fide board game, and the notion intrigued him.

Ann Abbott had devised the idea, but Ives—if he decided to cut a deal with her—would bear all the financial burdens to bankroll, print, and market the game. The risks notwithstanding, the Yankee merchant gambled on Ann Abbott, the woman who had introduced him to Dr. Busby.

At first glance, the serious visage of William Ives, a man who literally spent his working life elbow-deep in printer's ink, hardly cast him as the fun-and-games sort. Abbott, however, had chosen her backer sagely. Born in Salem on February 15, 1794, to sea captain William Ives and Mary Bradshaw Ives, the mariner's namesake, his three younger brothers, and one sister had grown up in a proper New England household in which the virtues of hard work and devotion to family governed the children's lives.

In the opening decades of the nineteenth century, Ives's Salem teemed with merchant ships laden with the wealth of the Orient,

Africa, and Europe—spices, gems, silks, pepper, opium. And tars prowled the city's waterfront for liquor and women after months at sea. For the right-thinking parents of William Ives, keeping children on the straight and narrow posed a formidable task.

Captain Ives and his wife did not need to worry about their eldest child, however. The sea held little allure for him; William Ives fell in love with books and newspapers. He got his first whiff of newsprint when he served as an apprentice to Thomas C. Cushing at the *Salem Gazette*. After learning everything from setting type to writing good leads, Ives left to print his own newspaper, the *Observer* (later the *Salem Observer*), on January 2, 1823.

In partnership with his twenty-two-year-old brother Stephen, Ives formed the W. & S. B. Ives Company, which lasted until Stephen quit in 1838. Realizing that a newspaper's costs could ruin a family man, Ives not only printed the *Observer*, but also turned W. & S. B. Ives into a bookseller, printer, binder, and publisher.

With business booming, Ives took a bride on May 12, 1824. She was Lucy Gardner, of Hingham, Massachusetts, and by the time Ann Abbott carried The Mansion of Happiness to W. & S. B. Ives headquarters in 1843, Ives and his wife had seven children.

A family man, a successful businessman, and a pillar of the community—William Ives seemed a solid, but unremarkable, sort. He fit the profile of the industrious, God-fearing Yankee who believed a man generally got exactly what he deserved in life. Befitting a family man who happened to be a publisher, Ives churned out religious and educational tracts for children, including a weekly magazine called *The Hive* from 1828 to 1830.

When Ann Abbott brought Dr. Busby to Ives in 1840, he had begun selling toys and other children's items and realized the potential in her idea. Her reappearance in 1843 with The Mansion of Happiness would push Ives from the realm of the successful businessman to that of a cutting-edge gamesman.

Ives soon crafted Abbott's idea into a sleek wooden game board embossed with sixty-seven squares that led to the players' ultimate destination—The Mansion of Happiness. Reflecting traditional Puritan tenets of moral rectitude, Abbott and Ives disdained the use of dice in favor of an eight-sided teetotum.

Across those sixty-seven squares, players advanced wooden pegs according to the whims of the teetotum and prayed that their pegs would find such spaces as Justice, Humility, and Piety and avoid such pitfalls as Poverty, Cruelty, and Passion. A journey to The Mansion yielded fascinating glimpses not only of Yankee religious values, but also of the world according to a Massachusetts minister's daughter. Her virtuous squares featured images of healthy, beatific men, women, and children. Piety depicted a kneeling maiden, hands clasped in prayer beneath a stately tree. Honesty showed a dignified man in a modest brimmed hat and a sober but well-cut frock coat, his features dour but filled with propriety.

To the minister's daughter, a demure young woman standing in front of a church symbolized Humility. The young woman rendered on square 31, Chastity, appeared in plain garb and wore a similarly sweet expression, but without a church in the background.

As the players raced their pegs from the first square, Justice—a long-haired young woman balancing the scales of justice but not wearing a blindfold—to the sixty-seventh, the Mansion of Happiness—a domed, pillared edifice framed by gracefully spreading trees and a lush lawn—more than two centuries of New England history, culture, and tradition unfolded. Puritan punishments beckoned the Drunkard, a man lurching against a lamppost with his stylish top hat askew on square 47, or the Perjurer, a rogue lying to a magistrate on square 43. A misfortunate turn of the teetotum that dispatched players' pegs to such nefarious characters' squares decreed a loss of turn and a humiliating stint in the stocks or on the pillory.

For players who had navigated their pegs into the home stretch—within ten squares of the cherished Mansion—the number 57 posed one of the game board's more ominous pitfalls: the Robber. A sinister figure in his slouched hat, the thief assailed yet another of Abbott and Ives's virtuous young women as she pleaded on her knees to no avail while the highwayman seized her cash and valuables. A visit to the Robber's realm resulted in the removal of a player's peg to prison for two precious turns.

Along with the sinners and saints, players encountered familiar and welcome New England sights. The Water, square 6, presented two young couples in a rowboat on the ocean, one of the women clad in a stylish bonnet, one of the beaus manning the oars. Just nine squares into the journey, the Inn awaited—a familiar, slope-roofed, clapboard structure that welcomed travelers to all corners of New England.

Square 50 guaranteed players a different sort of welcome. There, an edifice of grim granite blocks and barred windows and doors beneath a squat roof hinted of unspeakable dangers and evil. That stop—The Prison—often ruined players' chances in the race for The Mansion.

In parlors across New England and beyond, the trip across Abbott and Ives's sixty-seven colorful squares delivered on Abbott's promise that young and old alike would find the game "instructive, moral, and entertaining amusement." Americans visited The Mansion of Happiness repeatedly, those sojourns not only confirming Abbott and Ives's creation as the grandfather of all board games, but also ringing up profits for several decades.

Ives capitalized upon the game's success by releasing other board games in the 1840s. In 1844, he offered customers Pope and Pagan, a forerunner of historically themed games that would swell into a lucrative niche of the toy industry. And mindful of the first successful games issued by his firm, Ives reissued Dr. Busby and unveiled other card games such as Characteristics.

Ives's success soon proved the axiom: "imitation is the sincerest form of flattery." His first major imitator and competitor materialized in Springfield, Massachusetts. The interloper, Milton Bradley, introduced The Checkered Game of Life in 1863, which was published by Brooks & Brothers, a Salem rival of Ives. The new game shared more than its Salem origins with Ives's parlor pastimes. As with The Mansion of Happiness, morality and virtue were the compass for

The Checkered Game of Life's players as they strove for Happy Old Age, while hoping to avoid such vices as sloth, crime, disgrace, and ruin. One of the virtual vices of Bradley's conception was poverty, which he, like many Yankee businessmen, linked to laziness.

No one could accuse Bradley of either laziness or lack of vision. During the Civil War, he designed Games for Soldiers, a neat, light-weight package of board games that troops could easily stuff into their packs or satchels. In every theater of the conflict, Union troops whiled away the tedium of camp life by reaching into their packs and selecting from nine pasteboard-mounted games including checkers, chess, backgammon, five forms of dominoes, and, of course, The Checkered Game of Life, whose goal of Happy Old Age took on a special meaning to men facing death on any given day. For a few hours, the sounds of gamepieces and laughter diverted thousands of soldiers' thoughts from the specter of Confederate cannons and muskets and disease-wracked companions lying in infirmary tents.

Patriot and canny entrepreneur, Milton Bradley parlayed his games into a genuine American success story. But another New Englander took the parlor-game revolution of Ives and Bradley to an even higher level.

George Swinerton Parker, born in Salem in 1866, a year after Union soldiers carried home their worn packages of Bradley's board games, had grown up playing Dr. Busby, The Mansion of Happiness, and any other board game on which he could get his hands. Following the death of his father when Parker was ten, money woes beleaguered the family; at sixteen Parker was hatching an idea to lift his family to security. In 1883 he designed, in his opinion, a better board game than those he had played.

Fed up with parlor games heavy with pious virtues, the teenager created a game he dubbed Banking. Unlike Ives and Bradley's, Parker's theme prized riches over religion; Banking's goal was to amass the most wealth. On the youth's game board, opportunity awaited those who borrowed money from the bank at 10 percent interest and funneled it into a range of deals either profitable or ruinous. Smarts, and a little luck, governed the squares of Banking.

Practicing what his game preached, the teenaged Parker spent his savings of fifty dollars, accrued by selling produce from his garden in Medford, Massachusetts, on five hundred copies of Banking. With ten dollars he became a "drummer" (New England jargon for traveling salesman), pitching his board game to department stores and toy distributors in Boston and Providence.

Those hard-nosed Yankee retailers who spared some time for the precocious youth found his game promising, and George Parker sold almost all of his stock, netting nearly a hundred dollars. By the time he was twenty, the tall, thin, and pale Parker had become a fixture in the board-game arena and was on his way to amassing kingpin status in the field of fun and games. The titles of his most popular game and his company would aptly highlight his career: Monopoly and Parker Brothers. The headquarters of Parker's operation was Salem.

William Ives, the board-game trailblazer whose success had inspired George Parker and Milton Bradley and had launched the business with a distinctly New England sensibility, died on December 12, 1875, in his Salem home, at 390 Essex Street. He had lived long enough to glimpse the board-game mania he had ignited with The Mansion of Happiness, and, unlike so many innovators who never reap the profits of their notions, he had garnered financial reward.

A decade after Ives's death, Parker, paying the ultimate commercial compliment to his fellow Salem native, purchased all rights to five of Ives's games, including Dr. Busby and The Mansion of Happiness, despite Parker's pronouncement years earlier that The Mansion of Happiness was "preachy"[2] and not enough fun. He promptly reissued the grandfather of all board games, America's first.

The creator of that preachy game remains enigmatic. But among the collections of the Peabody-Essex Museum, Ann W. Abbott's game buttresses Salem's claim as the birthplace of board games.

97

The Lunch King: Walter Scott

As traffic flows along the Cranberry Highway in Wareham, Massachusetts, drivers spot a sign and, beneath it, a metallic railway-style car with horizontal stripes. Directly below the sign hovers a clock. Drivers check the clock and their watches, decide they have time, and pull into the parking lot of the Millpond Diner.

As hungry customers of the 1990s pass through the front door and by the gray steel walls and opaque glass windows, the aromas of strong, hot coffee and a sizzling grill set mouths watering—as they have for decades. And when customers pay their checks at the antique cash register, they know they have spent time in a genuine American joint—a real diner. Most patrons might not know, however, that the diner is a New England tradition founded more than a century ago by a Rhode Island character dubbed "The Lunch King."[1] But King of the Diner is an equally fitting name for Walter Scott.

On an evening in 1872, savory scents filled the air and wafted into the offices of the *Providence Journal*. Curious late-shift workers spilled onto Westminster Street and converged on the source of the delightful smells: a small, one-horse freight wagon parked along the sidewalk. The hungry night owls quickly lined up to buy hot coffee, ham sandwiches, boiled eggs, sliced chicken pie, and a range of other edibles. To the editors, reporters, and leather-aproned pressmen, the price—a nickel for most orders—was right. The patrons did not know, nor would they have cared, that cultural and culinary history was materializing curbside; the lunch wagon was destined to evolve into that most American of eateries, the diner.

Walter Scott, a twentyish, mustachioed entrepreneur, sat on a wooden box jammed inside the wagon and between its two open windows. One window facing the sidewalk, the other the street, Scott worked both windows at once, serving up coffee and meals from dusk to dawn that night. By the time he had shuttered his windows and nudged his horse and wagon home, he knew he had hit upon a winning idea: to cater to night-workers and nocturnal revelers with homemade foods after Providence's restaurants closed their doors at 8 P.M.

From his earliest years, Walter Scott had sold food on Providence's streets. Born in Cumberland, Rhode Island, in 1840 to poor but industrious parents, he was forced to leave school early on and help feed his brothers and sisters. The boy lugged crates of food and baskets of candy from street corner to street corner and hawked his goods to passersby, one of an army of young street vendors sweating in summer and shivering in winter. He rose before dawn to peddle the morning editions of the *Journal,* the *Herald,* and the *Star,* then ran home for a quick nap. By late morning he hit the streets again, selling fruit and candy.

In his teens, Scott landed a job as a compositor and pressman on the *Journal*'s late shift. Having noticed that his fellow workers carried lunches to work every night, Scott began to show up at work with ham and chicken sandwiches made by his mother, now a widow, and with an urn of steaming coffee. Each morning, he headed home with his sandwich box and coffee urn empty, his pockets crammed with copper.

Scotty, as his friends and fellow workers called him, continued his side job at the *Journal* with his bosses' blessing, as well as their orders for sandwiches and coffee. By the mid-1860s, business was so profitable that he built a rude handcart and piled ever-increasing loads of food and strong coffee into it every night. But to the increasing disappointment of the *Journal*'s night shift, the sandwich selection became skimpier. Every night, as Scotty rolled his handcart to work, other Providence night owls would swarm him with big appetites and cash in hand. The trade from passersby and from his stops at the *Star* and the *Herald,* not to mention the *Journal,* not only filled his change box, but also forced him to rethink his side business.

Scott had much to ponder. Married, the father of a son, he wanted to provide for his family far better than his ailing father had. Scott earned more money from his food cart than he did during his grueling night shifts. Thirty-two years old in 1872, he decided a career change was in order: he would quit his job at the *Journal* and devote all his considerable energies to his night-lunch concern.

Scott was convinced that Providence's night owls and late-shift workers offered a bottomless and steady market for food on the fly and that the heavy loads of pennies and nickels his cart raked in every night proved that the profits outweighed the risks. He not only persuaded his wife that the business would point the way to a more comfortable life, but also enlisted her help. If they were going to take the plunge, she would have to pitch in with the preparation of the menu, one that Scotty planned to expand far beyond simple sandwiches.

When Scott quit his job, the *Journal* lost a skilled pressman but gained a sorely needed food service. He quickly got that service into motion with his purchase of a squat, spoke-wheeled freight wagon, and a workhorse named Patient Dick. With his first full-time supply of food stored inside the wagon, Scott harnessed Patient Dick and nudged horse and livelihood toward the Westminster Street curb outside the *Journal*.

Within minutes, Scotty's former coworkers spilled out of the building and lined up at the wagon's windows. Working with the same speed and dexterity he had shown on the line of the morning edition, he dispensed his new and improved cuisine—and piled up the nickels.

The nickels purchased a range of homemade items from Scott's kitchen. Customers gobbled not only the sandwiches of thickly sliced ham or chicken, already something of a trademark for the vendor, but also boiled eggs, butter-smeared slices of bread baked by the Scotts, and, for big appetites and big wallets, a plate of sliced chicken priced at thirty cents. For dessert, customers chose from fragrant, freshly baked apple, squash, mince, huckleberry, or cranberry pies, each slice costing a nickel. The term "slice" does not do justice to the portions hungry workers wrapped their hands around, for Scotty cut half a pie for each sweet-toothed patron.

From dusk to dawn every morning, newspaper workers and other late-night sorts watched and listened for Patient Dick and Scotty's creaking wagon as the two made their rounds through the city's streets. Only a man with a strong constitution could handle the long hours and every extreme of New England weather, from scorching summer heat to winter storms. But Scotty, with stamina to match that of Patient Dick and the ability to ward off colds and other ailments with ease, kept his night-lunch wagon rolling even in blizzards. If the pressmen and reporters could make it to work, so could he.

Scott's hardiness, an image reinforced by his stocky build and square-jawed, mustachioed and goateed visage, served him well in an unsavory aspect of his innovative business. The men lining up at his wagon did not number just honest workmen such as those he had labored with on the *Journal*. From every corner came drunken vagrants and dandies alike, with little inclination to pay for their meal. Scott soon had to contend with rowdies who grabbed their food at the window and fled before Scott could spring from his perch. Through bitter—and costly—experience, he honed a talent for sizing up potential runners at a glance and devised a clever way of holding them hostage until they paid their bill: as he handed a suspicious fellow a meal, Scott snatched the man's hat and held it until cash crossed the counter.

In a wooden crate inside the wagon, workers' caps and nobs' tophats piled up. Many owners of the headgear sheepishly returned to the wagon a day or two later, paid up, and retrieved their hats. All was forgiven—unless they ran again. If the hats remained unclaimed, Scott sold them to local haberdashers.

Raised in the rough streets himself, Scott knew that some potential runners would not give up their hats without a fight. A small, burnished hickory club offered a solution. "If a man got too gay, I had a spring billy that took some of the gayness out of him," Scott would later say. "Nobody ever wanted more than one taste of billy."[2]

A "Fox Point rough"[3] learned that hard lesson outside Scott's night-lunch wagon when he refused to pay for his ten-cent meal. Scott grabbed the man's hat, ducked as the rough's fist whistled at him, and sprang at him across the window's counter. Across the sidewalk the two men grappled. "I fell on top," Scott recalled, "and pounded his head on the pavement until he cried enough."[4]

Scott rolled off the man, and both lurched warily to their feet. The welcher asked for his hat.

"He didn't get it," Scott would later say. "My son, who watched the fight, was holding the hat, and he became so nervous that he tore it to pieces without knowing what he was doing."[5]

Scott took the shreds from his son and handed them to the Fox Pointer. "I told him that he was lucky to escape so lightly."[6]

The night-lunch vendor learned that *he* might have been the one to escape lightly: his foe was an ex-convict noted for "biting off a man's nose in a fight." "I was thankful that he didn't get hold of mine while we were wrestling," Scott admitted.[7]

Luckily for Scott, most of the wrestling around his wagon took place between paying customers who jostled each other for Scott's specialties, such as his time-tested chicken sandwich. "For my chicken sandwiches," Scott boasted, "rooster fowl was always good enough. I bought the best of native birds and cooked them under the best condition. Nobody ever kicked at a chicken sandwich that I passed out."[8]

In a classic example of waste not, want not, Scott found a use for bits of chicken and other remnants dotting his cutting board: the "chewed sandwich."[9] Despite its unappetizing moniker, the item—meat scraps between bread slices drenched in butter or mustard—was a cheap and popular entree.

With chewed sandwiches and Scott's other fare attracting crowds whenever Patient Dick and the wagon stopped, one customer decided to load up a lunch wagon himself. Ruel B. Jones, a Providence police officer, resigned from the force in 1883, copied Scott's wagon and menu, and carved out a route outside curbside saloons and gentlemen's clubs. His business took off, and he was dispatching a fleet of seven wagons each night by 1887. Another interloper upon Scott's night-turf was Mike Stapleton. He cruised Westminster Street, filching Scott's customers with a brand-new item—the hot dog.

Despite the escalating food fray on Providence's streets, Scott continued to thrive, the pies and the bread from his own kitchen and his fresh chicken and ham continuing to attract hungry crowds around his wagon.

The original Lunch King kept up with his competitors by expanding his menus, adding hot dogs and other items to his larder. But he did so grudgingly, particularly peeved by the cost of condiments customers demanded. He longed for the evenings when even "tough customers" had not "wanted the earth for every nickel they spent."[10] In the good old days before Jones, Stapleton, and others spoiled night-lunch customers, according to Scott, whenever someone ordered "an egg sandwich, they didn't demand a slice of onion to go with it."[11] He wished that people would not "swamp their beans in catsup or slather mustard on a 'dog' until you couldn't see the 'dog'."[12]

Lamenting that he "lost several dollars a week in free onions, wasted mustard and excess catsup," Scott harangued whoever among his rivals had "invented the slice of onion with the fried egg."[13] He huffed: "I know *I* didn't. With eggs and everything else high, there wasn't much profit in a sandwich at five cents, especially if you added the piece of onion."[14]

Despite his complaints, Scott, his only son at his side, would head out with a full wagon every day and sell most of his stock. Then, one evening in 1917, his night-lunch wagon did not rattle up Westminster Street and creak to a halt in front of the *Journal* building. Walter Scott had decided to retire at the age of seventy-six. Tired of the competition and long nights, his son did not want to take over the business.

A *Journal* regular soon showed up at Scott's door to find out why the still robust lunchman had finally shuttered up his wagon. To the reporter's query, Scott replied: "I guess I've done my share in putting the night lunch on the map, and I'm perfectly willing to step back and let others do the scratching for the dollars that came pretty easy in the old days."[15] But in a feisty aside, Scott claimed, "I'd probably be in business still if things weren't so high."[16]

By the time he retired, those pricey "things" on mobile menus included corned beef hash, ham and beans, beef stew, lamb tongues, coffee, rolls, corned beef and beans, pork and beans, cold ham sandwiches, boiled frankfurters, boiled eggs, and donuts.

Scott died of natural causes in 1924, less than seven years after his last night-lunch shift, but he lived long enough to see his idea turn into the stationary roadside diner, a New England notion destined to become an American icon. No one can say who took the wheels off first, but by the late 1920s, night-lunch stands had multiplied all across America and had become part and parcel of the nation's life.

The inspiration of the night-lunch wagon comprised, in the words of Richard J. S. Gutman, author of the definitive *American Diner,* "the diner's humble beginnings."[17] The credit for that idea belongs to Walter Scott, the Lunch King.

In recent years, Americans fed up with fast food that tastes the same from New England to the Pacific coast have rediscovered the concept of diners, where menus might be similar, but no two eateries' burgers taste the same. The public's resurgent interest in classic diners—from modest wood-frame lunchcars to glitzy steel, chrome, and neon motifs—has brought the diner back to the American landscape.

Because of the 1990s' renaissance of classic diners, the legacy of Walter Scott and his Providence night-lunch wagon thrives—although at a steeper price than the nickel's worth of 1870s New England.

Lillian Nordica:
The Down East Diva

On a summer evening in 1894, thousands of onlookers peered at a stout, square-jawed woman. Clad in a simple maiden's gown, she stood on the stage of the world-famous Festspielhaus, in Bayreuth,

Germany, bathed in the stage-lights' glow, and began to sing one of opera's most challenging roles,
Wagner's Isolde.

From the first soaring soprano note that
floated out over the hilltop amphitheater, the
prima donna Lillian Nordica enthralled the
crowd. "Her voice rang out with thrilling
clearness, power, and brilliancy."[1] The so-
called Lily of the North, the toast of European
nobility and American high society, was accustomed to the opera world's adoration. But she
never let the plaudits swell her ego, because
she never forgot that she was Lillian *Norton,*
of Farmington, Maine.

The youngest of six daughters, Lillian was born on December 12,
1857, to Edwin Norton and his wife, Amanda Elizabeth (Allen) Norton. The family's bloodlines were distinctly old Yanke. Lillian's father was a direct descendant of Thomas Mayhew, the first colonial
governor of Martha's Vineyard; her mother was the daughter of one
of New England's most famous revivalist preachers, "Camp-Meeting"
John Allen.

Lillian Norton's father farmed a tract not far from the Sandy River
but struggled to provide for his family. He and Amanda also opened
the Blue Mountain House for boarders, but the venture fell apart.
While he considered music his true vocation, he had failed to earn a
living as a fiddler. Amanda Allen shared her hard-pressed husband's
love of music and had met him when both added their voices to the
choir at Farmington's tidy little Methodist church. Although she and
her husband did not possess the talent for a career in music, they were
determined that their fourth child would make a name in America's
music halls, both popular and classical. The grandly named Wilhemina Kossuth Norton had been blessed with a gifted singing voice from
her earliest years.

Shortly before Lillian's seventh birthday, the Nortons sold the Blue

Mountain for $2,000; left behind the familiar church, the old court-house, the Sandy River, and other landmarks of Farmington; and moved to Boston. Besides Edwin Norton's failures as a farmer and rooming-house owner, the parents had another, more important reason to abandon their fields for the city: they were realizing that Wilhemina's raw talent required the ministrations of a skilled voice teacher. In 1867, Amanda Norton arranged an audition with Professor John O'Neill, of the vaunted New England Conservatory of Music. A glowering Irishman with swept-back hair and a bristling mustache, O'Neill bore a resemblance to later Boston musical great Arthur Fiedler. He agreed that "Willie" showed promise and offered to train her.

Voice lessons from a teacher of O'Neill's stature did not come cheaply. In Boston, Edwin Norton worked in a Harrison Avenue photography studio, and Amanda took a sales clerk's job at Jordan Marsh. With the older Norton girls pitching in with their salaries from clerical posts, the family garnered just enough to support themselves and pay for Willie's studies.

Then, in November 1868, during a visit to Farmington, Willie was stricken with typhoid fever. At 5 A.M. on November 24, the girl on whom her family had pinned their financial future died; the tragedy shattered the Nortons and Willie's teacher, John O'Neill, who lamented the loss of his star pupil.

For nearly two years, the Nortons struggled with their loss. Amanda, who had nurtured Willie's voice and had monitored her music lessons, was disconsolate, going through the motions at work and home. Then, gradually she became aware of Lillian's voice as the girl sang around the house. For the first time, Amanda recognized the natural vocal talent of her fourteen-year-old daughter.

With characteristic decisiveness, Amanda brought the girl to the office of Professor O'Neill. "The spotlight on her for the first time,"[2] Lillian realized that she was about to audition before this imposing figure in frock coat and starched collar.

Out of deference to Amanda, the music professor agreed to hear

Lillian sing. He ordered her to sing the scale, and when she easily hit a high C in a clear but unpolished soprano, he "burst into a laugh . . . of sheer delight."[3]

O'Neill then offered her a place at the conservatory as one of his voice culture students, warning her that he would drop her if she did not progress as he wished or if she did not work diligently. Her mother immediately accepted O'Neill's offer.

Lillian spent the next four years inside the windowless acoustic rooms of the conservatory, the clicks of metronomes atop pianos and the chords of student accompanists at the keys marking her time and her progress. Lillian Norton stood in front of Professor O'Neill and sang until her throat and chest ached. O'Neill criticized her for every missed note, every minor slip on the nuances of classical music's greatest soprano parts. Many of his students quit after a few sessions, but O'Neill's caustic, relentless commentary never cowed Norton; she simply worked harder, often spending hours on one note until she had perfected it. Later, she described this period as "stained with tears and sodden with discouragement."[4]

Norton graduated from the conservatory with high honors, her once unrefined soprano now strong, clear, and technically polished. She had appeared in various choirs and concerts with Boston's famed Handel and Haydn Society, singing the lead in Handel's *Messiah* as well as other challenging oratorios. Now, however, as she accepted her diploma, her plain black dress a sharp contrast to the pricey clothing of her classmates, the true test of her talent loomed.

Taking over from O'Neill as the guiding hand of Lillian's career was her mother, who would chaperon her eighteen-year-old daughter through the glamorous but backstabbing music world of the era. In the summer of 1876, mother and daughter boarded a train for New York City and began a journey that would carry them farther than either imagined, farther than Amanda's former dreams for Wilhemina.

The pair's first stop in New York was at the Broadway brownstone of noted opera teacher Madame Marie Maretzek, who had heard Norton sing in Boston and offered to hone O'Neill's disciple further.

The ex-diva strengthened Norton's soprano until it could fill a cavernous music hall.

Amanda Norton, sensing the moment was right for her daughter to turn professional, brought her to an audition for Patrick Gilmore's band. One of America's favorite touring ensembles, they played classical pieces and popular tunes for New York City blue bloods, Boston Brahmans, and wild and woolly Westerners alike. Some of America's finest divas had fronted Gilmore's band, and as he studied the stout teenager from Boston, she did not fit his preference for lead singers. Most were gorgeous, or possessed at the least genuine stage presence.

As Norton began to sing, her hand gestures and facial expressions struck him as awkward. But on hearing her voice, Gilmore decided he could work on her appearance and her acting. He signed her on and then informed her that on September 30, 1876, she would make her professional debut at one of America's most famous venues, Madison Square Garden.

When her big night arrived, Norton performed for a throng including New York socialites. Polite applause greeted the gowned young singer, her dense brown hair pinned up fashionably. Amanda Norton watched anxiously from the wings. Her daughter's debut went smoothly, but it was several weeks later, at a concert with Gilmore's band at Steinway Hall, that Lillian Nordica's first critical plaudits came. On November 29, 1876, a *New York Herald* review proclaimed: "She has a voice of great beauty of tone, considerable compass and richness of expression . . . Such material is susceptible of being developed into the proportions of a great singer."[5]

Professor O'Neill was angered by his former pupil's career decision. "After all my training, all my advice, that you should come to this . . . [singing] with a brass band." Norton was undeterred: "I pocketed the sarcasm in the best of humor. . . . I felt I was doing wisely in getting before the public."[6]

Backstage after her first concerts, Norton reveled in her first wave of admiration from dandies who kissed her hands, and jeweled matrons who showered her with compliments.

Gilmore took his latest discovery on the road for the next year and a half. As her popularity climbed, so did her poise. Gilmore eventually paid her a percentage of the gate receipts.

In 1878, Gilmore booked a European tour, and Norton, after a day or two of seasickness, rallied to packed evening concerts in the ship's ballroom. But as the vessel finally neared Liverpool, she agonized that in Europe, home to legendary opera stages, her talent would fall short of the true prima donna's.

Her worries evaporated in the din of standing ovations at London's Crystal Palace and Paris's Trocadero. With each sold-out performance by his soloist, Gilmore came closer to losing her. Several of the world's most prominent opera teachers were poised to turn the young woman from a skilled songstress into a true diva. Gilmore could not compete with them, especially since Amanda Norton was pushing Lillian to study with one of the European maestros.

When the moment he had dreaded came, Gilmore did not waste time pleading with or bullying his young star. She left him to study with one of opera's most famous names, Antonio Sangiovanni. Norton and her mother packed their valises, loaded their steamer trunks, and took a train from Paris to Milan, Italy.

Sangiovanni was a gifted teacher with a genuine eye and ear for talent. Having studied with respected voice and drama instructor Francois Delsarte during the Gilmore Band's Paris dates, Norton was prepared for another European voice coach.

From Norton's first lesson at the Milan Conservatory, Sangiovanni realized that O'Neill had hammered outstanding technical proficiency into Norton's voice, but Sangiovanni felt Norton's stage character was weak. His first measure to redress the deficiency proved cosmetic but critical to her success in European opera houses, where nobility and assorted highbrows snickered at American names. Sangiovanni transformed the guttural syllables of "Norton" to "Nordica."

Sangiovanni's next step to prepare his pupil for the world's harshest opera critics was to immerse her in a regimen that would enable her to master ten operas in six months. If Lillian had not had her mother to cook meals, to buoy her from her doubts, and literally to help her to bed each night, Professor Sangiovanni's program would have overwhelmed her.

On March 8, 1880, promoting the singer as "Lillian Nordica, the Lily of the North," Sangiovanni debuted his pupil in the role of *Don Giovanni*'s Elvira. Her American accent dismayed a few purists, but her clear soprano conquered even the sternest critics in attendance.

On one Italian tour, she played in thirty-five operas, including *La Traviata, Faust,* and *Rigoletto*, and garnered ebullient reviews whenever she performed. Admirers filled her dressing rooms with flowers and with notes brimming with praise for the Lily of the North. In the restaurants and shops of Milan and Brescia, opera fans mobbed not only the singer, but also her mother. Nordica's popularity led to an invitation from the Russian Imperial Opera, in St. Petersburg, and she accepted.

Even though they were accustomed to New England winters, Norton and her mother found the arctic winds and ceaseless snow of Czar Alexander II's magnificent capital hard to bear. The cold reception the American singer received from female headliners of the Imperial Opera and the theater's directors proved harder to handle. Relegated to secondary roles, Nordica at first complained to anyone who would listen. Then, her New England common sense, as she referred to it, compelled her to listen closely to her fellow prima donnas and to make comparisons. Eventually, Nordica concluded that her mezzo-soprano, although polished, required more range and power.

For two seasons, from 1880 to 1882, Nordica performed for the czar and Russia's nobility, but during the summers she and her mother rented a flat in Paris, and the singer studied with arguably the opera world's greatest voice coach, Jean Baptiste Sbriglia. The results were astonishing. One of Nordica's rivals lamented that, with Sbriglia's help, Nordica learned to "sing a high C that thrilled the soul."[7]

On July 22, 1882, having left the Russian opera for good, Nordica strode onto the stage of the Paris Opera as Marguerite in *Faust*. Her mesmerizing performance launched her into the ranks of the world's foremost divas at the age of twenty-four.

Although a handful of purists continued to complain about her American accent, most European opera buffs enjoyed the exotic nuances her speech lent to the arias of the masters. Nordica herself longed to hear others with that same accent, and when the Mapleson Company, a rival of New York's Metropolitan Opera, asked Nordica to come home and sing at the city's Academy of Music, she eagerly accepted.

Lillian Nordica returned to America not only as a sophisticated star of European opera, but also as a married woman. In Paris in 1882, she had been courted by Frederick Allen Gower, a handsome, urbane, and brilliant businessman-inventor who had worked with Alexander Graham Bell and who was Nordica's second cousin. He had attended all of her performances at the Paris Opera and overwhelmed her with flowers, love letters, dinners in the city's finest restaurants, and strolls along the Seine. Independently wealthy from his stake in the Gower-Bell Telephone Company and a noted ladies' man, Gower, a Maine native, fell in love with his cousin—with her celebrity, critics would charge—and they married in Paris in January 1883.

Meanwhile, Nordica's appearances with the Mapleson Company enthralled New York opera fans. An astute businesswoman, she embarked upon a lucrative nationwide tour but lavished much of the profits on her father, mother, and sisters, as she would throughout her life.

Although Nordica's career was secure, her marriage floundered. Her husband was a hot-tempered man unable to focus his scientific genius on any project for long; in one writer's opinion, Gower was "beyond a doubt psychopathic."[8] Nordica, hoping that a change of scenery would help the marriage, accepted a series of engagements in London in 1884. Her mother accompanied the troubled couple at Lillian's insistence.

London proved no help to the marriage. Nordica was welcomed as a star into the drawing rooms of royalty, but her husband was dismissed as a lout. In desperation, Nordica retired to a London townhouse, hoping that a more stable home life would mollify her erratic spouse. Nothing helped. Fearing for her sanity, Nordica left the house, rented another for herself and her mother, and filed for divorce on grounds of abuse. Before the divorce was finalized, she became a widow: in an attempt to cross the English Channel in a balloon, Frederick A. Gower, a skilled aerialist, vanished—presumably drowned.

In the decade following Gower's death, Nordica devoted herself completely to opera, singing throughout Europe. Having made her home in London, she became the toast of the British popular musical stage. Royals and commoners flocked to her public venues, including a memorable state concert at Buckingham Palace. Her performance so impressed the Prince and Princess of Wales that they thanked her for the privilege of listening to her voice. A short time later, by personal invitation of Queen Victoria, Nordica performed at Westminster Abbey. Nordica did not disappoint; her powerful, mellifluous version of the hymn "Let the Bright Seraphim" awed listeners in the packed church.

In the summer of 1894 Nordica embraced one of the greatest challenges in her career when she traveled to Bayreuth, Germany, to train for the role of Elsa in the first Bayreuth performance of Wagner's *Lohengrin*. For the first time, she faced a daunting operatic challenge without the one person whose love, support, constant companionship, and occasional criticism had helped her overcome despair: Amanda Norton had died of pneumonia in London in 1891. Her daughter wrote:

> I can never tell all that I owe to my mother, so just, so discerning, so thoughtful of my welfare, and of my every interest . . . My mother spurred me on by her criticism, for she was a severe critic . . . Her courage, energy, perseverance, and pride enabled her to meet the greatest discouragements bravely, and guided me to a way out of them . . . But it was her wisdom, her courage, and her sympathy that won me a way through it all.[9]

Nordica especially longed for her mother's comfort and counsel in Bayreuth, where Cosima Wagner, wife of the immortal composer and "the high priestess of the [Wagnerian] cult," forced Nordica to practice long, grueling hours each day, berating her "American voice," her stilted acting, and her plumpness—hardly a drawback in the opera world of the 1890s.[10]

Nordica fought the Teutonic terror with her time-tested weapon: unstinting devotion to her craft. The singer would later relate that she often went to bed with Madame Wagner's insults echoing in her ears. But Nordica worked diligently with Wagner's hand-picked voice coach, Julius Kniese, to master the role of Elsa.

On a pleasant summer evening in 1894 Nordica entered the hilltop theater, crowded with Wagnerian experts able to detect the slightest flaw in a singer's interpretation of the composer's heroines, Elsa, Isolde, and the three Brunhildes. Although Nordica was booked for the entire Bayreuth season, Cosima Wagner would have no qualms about sacking the diva if the critics tore apart her performance.

Later opera scholars would wonder at Cosima Wagner's choice of Nordica for the roles of the Teutonic maidens, for her voice "seems to have been clear and beautiful rather than heroic in the now accepted Wagnerian manner."[11] In rehearsals, her acting lacked the flair that Madame Wagner demanded.

Nordica, however, was prepared for the challenge.

From the moment she strode onto the stage at the Bayreuth Festspielhaus, the temple of the Wagnerians, her lovely soprano conquered even those opera experts who preferred a heavier, more dramatic approach to Wagner. Not only was Nordica a smash as Bayreuth's first Elsa, but also as Isolde, which became one of her trademark roles. According to critic H. E. Krehbiel, Nordica sang Wagner "with a distinctness of enunciation and a truthfulness of expression. . . . It was wonderful how Mme. Nordica rose to the opportunity which Wagner's drama opened to her. The greater the demand, the larger her capacity. . . .her voice rang out with thrilling clearness, power, and brilliancy."[12]

In the aftermath of Nordica's rave reviews at Bayreuth, the singer's career entered a new phase in which she experienced the trappings of celebrity that only the most acclaimed singers enjoyed. She traveled throughout Europe and America in a private railway car equipped with plush couches, large beds, and a first-class kitchen and wine rack. Nordica shipped the car back and forth across the Atlantic according to her schedule. In fine restaurants, at high-society fetes—anywhere she appeared in public off stage—Nordica wore a diamond tiara in her coiffured, upswept hair.

Despite her growing wealth and celebrity, Nordica rarely displayed the bombastic nature of her fellow prima donnas. She never lost sight of her modest, New England origins. She did her own sewing in the privacy of her railway car or in grand hotel suites, and boasted to friends that she "could put on a good New England patch as well as anybody."[13]

Nordica's humility was due not only to her upbringing, but also to her work ethic. Few opera stars strove harder to hone their craft, and few approached their careers with such an honest grasp of their strengths and weaknesses. Having realized early on that many other singers possessed stronger voices, Nordica never stopped studying with the era's best coaches, no matter how hard they pushed her. A noted opera critic of the 1890s commented that "[Nordica's] ability comes with willingness and desire."[14]

The ability that led Nordica from her success at Bayreuth to nearly fifteen years of acclaim at New York's Metropolitan Opera for her roles as Wagner's heroines was rivaled by her inability to find a good husband. After her ruinous first marriage to Frederick Gower, a decade passed before she fell in love again. Although her fame and wealth attracted many suitors over the years, the diva had spurned all offers. But when Zoltan Dome, a Hungarian tenor whose good looks and suavity far eclipsed his talents on stage, wooed her in 1896, she paid attention, despite his reputation as a rogue. He accompanied her on her 1896 American tour, and, on May 28, in Indianapolis, they married.

Dome abandoned his mediocre career, and for the next seven years he traveled with Nordica and squandered her money at gambling tables and gentlemen's clubs featuring dubious entertainment. The forty-five-year-old Nordica divorced Dome in 1903.

The singer wed her third husband, George Washington Young, in London on July 29, 1909. An affluent banker, Young did not crave Nordica's money but, handsome and urbane like Dome and Gower, he too disappointed Lillian. Although she did not elaborate on her marital problems, she wrote to her sisters, less than five years after the marriage, that she had been "duped, betrayed, deceived, and abused." "I am just a poor picker of husbands," she confided.[15]

In 1913, Nordica's troubled personal life and her grueling schedule began to wear her out; her voice began to slip, time's passage inevitably forcing her to strain for—and often miss—notes she had once sung with ease. Her last full performance, as Isolde, was on March 26, 1913, in Boston, where her career had begun so many years ago. But she would not slow down. Taking leave of her sisters, she headed west on a worldwide tour across the United States and on to Australia, Java, East Asia, Russia, and London.

Nordica took the stage in Melbourne, Australia, on November 25, 1913, and despite her waning voice, earned warm ovations from theatergoers. Within days of the performance, she collapsed from exhaustion and neuritis, missing her boat from Sydney to Batavia (present-day Djakarta). Rallying after a few days of complete rest, she booked passage on the *Tasman*, a Royal Dutch Mail ship.

On December 27, 1913, the *Tasman*, bound for Djakarta, grounded on a jagged coral reef in the Gulf of Papua. For several days, the trapped ship was lashed by storms. Finally, the vessel's engines coaxed the keel from the coral. The *Tasman* limped to Thursday Island; in her cabin below decks, Lillian Nordica had contracted pneumonia.

The diva's condition worsening, she was ferried to Batavia, in Java, in April 1914. For the next year, Nordica convalesced in a local clinic. Telegrams and letters from admirers flooded her room, urging her to get well and take the stage again. The letters heartened her, but her performance in Melbourne had been her last. On May 10, 1914, the fifty-six-year-old diva died.

As her will stipulated, Lillian Nordica's body was taken to London, where she and her mother had spent many of their happiest years. The diva's funeral was held there on July 6, 1914, at the King's Weigh House Church. Her remains were cremated and interred at the plot of her last husband's family, in the New York Bay Cemetery, in Jersey City.

The Lily of the North, New England's first world-famous prima donna, had reached the operatic heights her family had once dreamed of for her ill-fated older sister, Wilhemina. On the grandest stages of the globe and at the glittering fetes of royalty, the Down East Diva never forgot her Yankee roots.

At Portland, Maine, on March 17, 1943, "several thousand people including music lovers and hundreds of shipyard workers . . . stood for an hour in a drizzling rain" to cheer the launch of the U.S. Navy's latest World War II Liberty ship—the U.S.S. *Lillian Nordica*.[16] She went on to see heavy action in European waters, earning the nickname "the Lucky Lillian." Her captain, Robert Bloxom, said: "She has well served the country . . . and honored the great lady whose name she bears."[17]

'Tis
the Season
⟨⟩

Christmas cards and department store Santas—both are part and parcel of the Yuletide season. While most frantic holiday-shoppers are familiar with them, many Americans might not know the New England roots of these cherished traditions.

In 1874, a young art student named Mrs. O. E. Whitney presented Boston printer Louis Prang a watercolor sketch of a red bud about to bloom and sporting a graceful stem and a few leaves. Whitney was hoping that Prang might purchase her design for one of his postcards.

The printer was impressed with the simple, beautiful image rendered on a black card, but not even he grasped how popular the sketch would become. He purchased the design, printed it on small cards with a Christmas greeting, and sold more than a million of them. Whitney's little sketch had become America's first commercial Christmas card (Albany printer Richard H. Pease designed a Christmas card in the early 1850s, but was not successful with it).

Knowing a good thing when he saw it, Prang went on to become America's first Christmas card titan, foreshadowing the rise of Hallmark and other greeting card companies. Whitney joined his staff, and continued to design many other Christmas cards for Prang & Company.

Another Christmas tradition—bringing one's tots to the local mall and placing them on Santa's lap—is also a New England creation. Thanks to the film classic *Miracle on 34th Street,* legions of Christmas shoppers believe that Macy's Department Store holds bragging rights to the notion of store Santas, but that assumption is wrong. In the Yuletide season of 1888, James Edgar, owner of Edgar's Department Store, in Brockton, Massachusetts, donned whiskers and a red suit and entertained hordes of local tykes, not to mention their parents. Edgar wore his festive garb for many holiday seasons to come, and stores all over the country began to mimic his Yuletide brainstorm.

Department store Santas and Christmas cards are two customs that would have enraged New England's Puritan settlers. To them, Christmas smacked of pagan ritual and was a holiday that symbolized the hated Catholic church.

The Puritans reviled Christmas celebrations so much that in 1659, the Massachusetts Bay Colony passed a law stating that anyone caught celebrating the holiday would be fined five shillings. Although the edict was repealed in 1681, Boston's public schools remained open on Christmas Day until 1870, four years before Whitney and Prang's holiday card hit the region's stationery stores.

You Said a Mouthful

~~~

On March 4, 1634, a new business opened its doors in Boston. The establishment also opened many disapproving Puritan eyes; Cole's Inn was New England's first recorded tavern.

Run by Samuel Cole, the inn took off as thirsty locals ambled up to the bar for draughts of ale and hard cider. The General Court of Massachusetts sought to curtail drinking at Cole's and anywhere else in town by enacting a 1639 law that banned "the common custom of drinking to one another" as "a mere useless ceremony" that "draweth on the abominable practice of drinking healths."[1]

Although Cole's Inn was open less than a decade, Puritan party poopers failed miserably in their attempt to discourage settlers from raising their tankards. Taverns with such names as Noah's Ark and The Bunch of Grapes followed Cole's Inn and packed in the locals.

One business Puritan leaders did not quibble with was the "cook's shop," opened in 1643 by a Boston woman named Goody Armitage. Little information about the colonial chef and her menu survives, but various historians have hailed her establishment as the thirteen colonies' first restaurant.

More than two centuries after Goody Armitage placed platters of steaming victuals in front of her customers, a Maine man cooked up fare of a different sort on his Franklin stove. In 1850 John B. Curtis, of Bangor, scraped raw spruce from nearby trunks and heated it into a sticky concoction he dubbed "State of Maine Pure Spruce Gum"— America's first chewing gum. He parlayed his creation into a profitable business over the next thirty-plus years, stocking general stores' shelves with brands such as Trunk Spruce, Yankee Spruce, and 200 Lump Spruce. He also sold a variety of paraffin-based gums—Licorice Lulu, Four-in-Hand, Sugar Cream, Biggest and Best, and White Mountain.

From his brick factory in Portland, Curtis ruled the chewing-gum world until Thomas Adams, William K. Wrigley, and other entrepreneurs produced chicle gums that tasted far better than Curtis's chewy creations and turned spruce and paraffin products into quaint memories.

BUILDING

A

BETTER

MOUSETRAP

Captain Morey's
Horseless Carriage

A group of scientists stared at the sixty-five-year-old man and at the buckboard carriage with which he was tinkering. Stout, his arms muscular for a man of any age, his face creased and deeply sunburned from decades at the helm of a ship, he belied the image of a wan, bespectacled man of science. He held no pedigree from Harvard or Yale, but his experiments with steam power, chemicals, and machines had won him patents that rivaled the feats of his era's foremost engineers and innovators.

None of his competitors had yet attempted the experiment that unfolded in a fenced lot flanking his workshop that day. For Captain Samuel Morey, of Orford, New Hampshire, had attached his patented liquid-fuel engine to the buckboard as a means of propulsion. Although various inventors had affixed steam engines to carriages, an internal-combustion engine had never powered a horseless carriage. Until now.

Having completed "what he thought were satisfactory tests in the yard," Morey gripped the engine's crank, turned it, and continued to do so.[1] Its flywheel began spinning, and he cranked faster and faster. Suddenly, an electric spark crackled and, within the device's two iron cylinders, ignited a small tin dish of turpentine mixed with oxygen. The engine sputtered to life. The buckboard shook as the onlookers gaped. The road test of America's first internal-combustion horseless carriage was underway—in *1828*, nearly seventy years before Henry Ford strode across the world's automotive scene.

Samuel Morey was born on October 23, 1762, in Hebron, Connecticut, to Israel and Martha (Palmer) Morey. Israel Morey, like many ambitious men in the region, saw opportunity in the sparsely settled woodlands and arable soil of the Connecticut River's upper reaches. Shortly before Samuel's fourth birthday, the family moved to Orford,

New Hampshire, a scattering of log cabins along the river and on the future border of New Hampshire and Vermont.

Israel Morey, a gregarious man, opened a tavern where local lumbermen, farmers, peddlers, and rivermen slaked their thirst and talked with the innkeeper about everything from the price of regional timber bound for New England shipyards to the ongoing furor between New Hampshire and New York for the future Vermont. From his tavern, Morey dispensed hard cider and home-brewed ale, and served dishes that featured venison and other game from the adjoining forest, as well as perch, pickerel, bass, and other fish from local ponds and lakes. He not only provided well for his family, but also earned a reputation as an astute, forthright man with an ability to sway others to his side of issues. The tavern owner, whose cool head and quick fists persuaded unruly patrons to calm down or leave the smoke-filled, low-ceilinged inn with his help, soon emerged as one of the frontier's leading men. By 1775, he also stood as one of Orford's fieriest advocates of rebellion against the Crown, typifying the independent nature of rural New Englanders who viewed themselves as beholden to few in their own communities, let alone the monarch and Parliament an ocean away.

In his son, Samuel, the rebellious tavern owner instilled his streak of independence and self-sufficiency, as well as the virtues of discipline, hard work, and determination.

Boys like Samuel Morey grew up fast in frontier New England, especially when exposed to hard-working, hard-nosed patrons of a riverfront tavern; young Morey also received another type of education, in a one-room schoolhouse. In New England, compulsory education often began in the "dame school," where both boys and girls learned the alphabet and the rudiments of mathematics.

Grammar school for boys commenced when they were seven or eight years old. Shivering in the faint heat thrown by the school's central fireplace in winter, sweating in the close atmosphere of spring and summer, Morey and other youths sat for hours on hard wooden benches, poring over primers. To enforce discipline, the schoolmaster carried a rod and used it often.

Samuel Morey proved little problem to his teachers, absorbing his lessons diligently and displaying a natural aptitude for mathematics. His first natural-science lessons, combined with his love of tools and boats, ignited a passion that would govern the youth's life. When freed from his lessons or from his chores of sweeping and washing at the tavern, he would scurry to local blacksmiths' forges to study the combination of artistry and brute force that fashioned everything from farm implements, to axes, to fittings for river vessels. He would also spend hours by the river, studying the skiffs, barges, and other craft plying the Connecticut.

By the time he was fifteen, Morey had evidenced an intellect pointing toward study at Dartmouth or some other New England college. But in the 1770s, only sons of wealth or boys with affluent patrons continued their formal education. And, even if Israel Morey wanted to send his son off to college, larger events gutted that dream.

When the Revolution erupted in the spring of 1775 at Lexington and Concord, the men of Orford quickly chose sides, most throwing their support behind the Rebels. Israel Morey, practicing what he had preached in his tavern, rode off at the head of local militia, who would patrol the frontier. His neighbors had elected him their colonel, and he had elected Samuel to run the tavern and take care of his mother until the war's end.

Even when his father returned for good, a general by the conflict's end, any opportunity for Samuel Morey to attend college had passed. A young man now, he needed a trade, and he turned, as so many in the borderlands did, to the forests. He became a lumberman, but, imbued with his father's innate ability to lead, he wasted little time felling white pine, spruce, and fir for other men's profit; Samuel was running his own timber business in Orford by his twenties.

With a profitable company, his rugged good looks, and his status as the son of a local luminary, Morey presented an attractive marital prospect to the young women of Orford. It was vivacious, dark-haired Hannah Avery who conquered her competition. Their marriage would last more than sixty years.

His new bride and his thriving business lent Samuel Morey respect in the community, but he wanted far more. Beginning in 1780, he had been buying and studying every scientific and mechanical journal and tome he could find and had been conducting experiments with heat, light, and steam in a shed. By 1790, his financial success allowing him to fund more intricate experiments, he possessed a university-caliber knowledge of general chemistry and the mysteries of steam power.

The Yankee businessman-inventor was determined to harness steam power for his own profit and for other people's benefit. He had seen incessant manual labor grind down even the hardiest lumberman and believed that steam-powered machines could make laborers' tasks easier, and improve production. Better technology, such as the massive wooden chutes he built to transport logs from remote mountain forests, obsessed him. His fascination with technology won him regional fame in the 1790s, when he was elected to oversee the construction of river locks at Bellows Falls. By the time he completed that task, ships could travel to the farthest settlements along the Connecticut River, and Samuel Morey's engineering skills attracted attention even from academic quarters. He struck up a friendship with Professor Benjamin Silliman, a renowned Yale chemist who would create America's first carbonated water, ushering in the bottled-water and soft-drink industries. He also would serve as advisor, if not mentor, to the budding inventor.

Morey's fascination with steam and his love of the water inevitably thrust him into a race with other American inventors to build a practical steamboat that would free ships from the whims of the wind. The man who did so would win not only scientific laurels, but a potential fortune.

In 1787, John Fitch had displayed the first steam-powered vessel on the Delaware River, a six-paddle affair that could reach a speed of three miles an hour. Morey entered the steamboat fray in the early 1790s, with a steam engine mounted on a small paddle wheeler. His venture followed three years of experiments that included several burst boilers.

With the help of a few friends, Morey lugged the craft to the Connecticut River, slid it into the water, and eased his way to the bow, where the engine was perched. The machine started with a hiss, which, in the early days of steam power, often signified an impending explosion. The small boat quivered, then chugged down the river, the bow dipping dangerously close to the river's surface (if the cold water had come into contact with Morey's pressurized boilers, it could have blown up the inventor and his invention). But, the boat remained afloat. The ebullient Morey headed back to his workshop, brimming with improvements for his next steamboat.

Morey returned to the river in 1793 with a small paddle wheeler that held two men. Every hour he had been able to spare from his business concerns and his family was reflected in the many innovations of his newest steam engine, also mounted in the bow.

With a stronger hiss than his old engine emitted, the compressed steam of the new one propelled the top-heavy boat along the river at four miles an hour—a mile faster than Fitch's Delaware boat. In the following months, Morey increased the vessel's river runs until he had navigated it all the way to Hartford.

The year 1793 proved auspicious for Morey not only because of his successful steam trials on the Connecticut, but also because he was awarded his first U.S. Patent, for a steam "spit," a jib for ships. Patents for a rotary steam engine, a windmill, a waterwheel, and a steam pump followed.

His experiments with steam ever costlier, Morey took his boat and his ideas to New York City for three consecutive summers in the mid-1790s to search for financial backers. Morey had not thrown all of his assets into his inventions; he did want, however, to avoid that scenario.

New York entrepreneurs realized that commercially viable steamboats represented the future of river, lake, and ocean travel and that the first to come up with a suitable ship would steal a march on the business world. They scrutinized Morey's patents, the innovations that now powered his stern-wheeled craft at five miles an hour, and, most of all, the inventor himself. Robert R. Livingston, the fiftyish chancellor of New York and one of America's wealthiest men, had followed the experiments of Morey, Fitch, and others as they unraveled the commercial applications of steam. He was willing to bankroll the right inventor.

In 1796 or 1797, the courtly, silver-haired Livingston met with the jut-jawed Orford innovator. Confirming Morey's belief that a fortune lay in steam power, Livingston offered the New Englander $7,000 for exclusive use of his patents for steam travel on the Hudson River. Although $7,000 was a sizable figure in the 1790s, Morey nonetheless felt he was being shortchanged by Livingston, a man who traveled in the highest circles of power and influence and who, as President Thomas Jefferson's ambassador to France, would negotiate the Louisiana Purchase. Morey refused the deal.

Livingston responded with a second offer, one wrapped in a challenge to the inventor's ego. If Morey could build a steamboat capable of traveling eight miles an hour, Livingston promised to pay him an alleged $100,000. Morey took up the technological gauntlet. Some would later assert that *he* was taken.

Morey plunged into the task, driven by pride and gain alike. He wracked up another key steam patent, for an engine powered by a crank and suited to boats of any size. In 1797, he set up a workshop in a Bordentown, New Jersey, shipyard and poured his expertise into the biggest engine and ship he had yet built. His side-wheeler steamboat would, he believed, crack the eight-mile-per-hour barrier.

On the Delaware River near Philadelphia, Morey cranked his engine on a summer afternoon, and the boat's side paddles dipped into the water and pulled the ship forward. The jaunt proved the smoothest and quickest that one of Morey's boats had taken. But one major hitch developed: no matter how vigorously the steam drove the paddles, the vessel would not reach the magic eight miles per hour.

Morey went back to the workshop—without the cash from Livingston. In 1803 and 1815, he garnered patents for two more steam engines, but in 1807, another inventor captured the acclaim that

Morey had chased for so long, from New Hampshire to Philadelphia. Robert Fulton and his *Clermont* won the steamboat race with the aid of a deep-pocketed backer—Robert Livingston.

Sometime before Fulton successfully tested the *Clermont* on the Hudson River in 1807, Morey, according to his own accounts, visited the handsome, forty-two-year-old inventor in New York. The son of a Pennsylvania farmer and, like Morey, a self-made man, Fulton had built a 150-foot boat that eclipsed anything built by Morey. The Orford inventor, however, would later assert that he showed Fulton a scale model of a steamboat whose innovations Fulton stole. While no concrete proof of the charge exists, Morey certainly had a legitimate gripe with Fulton and Livingston's deal: the *Clermont*'s top speed was five miles an hour, three miles an hour slower than the speed the diplomat had required of Morey's boat.

Morey believed that Fulton had robbed him, purloining most of his designs from the model Morey had shown him. Though Fulton and his ship reaped worldwide fame, Morey would carry to his grave his certainty that improvements in the *Clermont*'s steam engine and paddle-wheel design had come from his patents—without acknowledgment. Morey never claimed he had invented the first steamboat, as others would on his behalf, especially his friends in Orford. But some scholars would assert that the boat he had built for Livingston in 1797 was the first practical steamboat.

Morey, rather than wallowing in his defeat and allowing his anger at Fulton and Livingston to fester, began spending less time with his business and more hours in the sturdy, beamed workshop he had built several hundred yards from his Orford home. His lab was far enough away from the house so that if something went awry amid the shelves of chemicals and the steam boilers that were scattered across several tables, his wife and daughter would be safe. And so Captain Morey, as his friends called him, continued his experiments in Orford.

His financial status comfortable, Morey eventually turned his scientific scrutiny to another labor-saving source of power: liquid fuel. The inventor's new scientific course stemmed in some part from his resentment of Fulton, but in larger part from his correspondence with Professor Silliman, who suggested that chemicals and natural vapors offered cheaper and even more viable sources of power than steam. Intrigued by the possibility of rendering steam-powered ships and other steam-powered machinery obsolete before their day had truly arrived, Morey concentrated on his new obsession, but did not abandon his steam experiments entirely.

Undaunted by working with chemicals equally as or more volatile than pressurized steam, Morey slept little and spent countless hours experimenting with various gases, vapors, and ignition methods, from flame to electric sparks. Hannah, long accustomed to her husband's nocturnal experiments, trusted in his proven ability, or luck, not to blow himself up. The inventor never mixed new combinations of gases and chemicals without first consulting with Silliman about the compounds' properties. Eventually, Morey developed a feel for how much or how little of ` substance he should use, breaking away from the chemical training wheels his mentor provided.

The longer Morey studied and tested flammable liquids as a potential power source, the more he shifted his emphasis from steam to gas and vapor. In 1820, the inventor built his last steamboat— and his first gas-powered vessel. After a decade of trial and error, Morey had at last invented a vapor-fueled engine. He had mounted it aboard a boat he dubbed *Aunt Sally*. Not much bigger than a dinghy, the craft was shaped from keel to bow to stern to conform to his new engine.

In 1820 the fifty-eight-year-old inventor eased the *Aunt Sally* onto Fairlee Pond, ignited the vapor engine, and waited for it either to explode or to launch the boat forward. The water began to churn beneath the sputtering, backfiring, stern-mounted engine. Suddenly, just as Morey's steamboat had chugged across the Connecticut River nearly three decades before, the *Aunt Sally* lurched along the surface.

Morey did not reveal all the secrets of the *Aunt Sally*'s engine until April 1, 1826, when he was awarded a patent for a "gas and vapor engine."[2] His invention came two years later than New Yorker

M. Isnard's internal-combustion engine, but the New Englander's creation, with features and technological expertise eclipsing Isnard's crude design, represented "the *first* successful application in America of internal combustion principles."[3]

On his patent application, Morey stated: "I, Samuel Morey, of Orford in the County of Grafton and State of New Hampshire, have discovered or invented . . . a machine or engine, for mechanically mixing or preparing gases or vapors with atmospheric air . . . by means of which a power is derived applicable to nearly every mechanical purpose."[4]

The features of this two-cylinder engine provided hints of internal-combustion power plants that would not appear until the late nineteenth century, when they would be hailed as revolutionary. Among these innovations were Morey's "poppet valves," his rough but workable carburetor, and his water-cooling system. Among the invention's most amazing features was its "two-cycle explosive engine," fired by an electric spark. The volatile fuel was "common proof spirits mixed with a small mixture of turpentine" in a small tin dish. Its heat source was a common table lamp. Drawing from his work with steam engines, Morey started the internal-combustion process by cranking two 180-degree levers that set a flywheel into motion, producing rotary movement.

Morey described his vision of his patent's future: "A working model has been set in motion . . . and should no unfortunate difficulties present themselves in its operation on a large scale, it will be the greatest improvement which has been made for many years, particularly in its application to locomotive engines."[5]

Before the Age of Steam—which Morey helped launch in America—had arrived in full force, he was heralding the era of internal combustion. Morey, never one to sit on his patents, in 1828 traveled again from Orford to Philadelphia with hopes of winning financial backers through two remarkable experiments.

In the first test of his patent, Morey installed his gas and vapor engine on a small boat on the Schuylkill River and propelled it across the water long enough to attract serious scrutiny from scientists and backers. Morey's previous patents and his articles for his friend Benjamin Silliman's *American Journal of Science and Arts*, the nation's first bona fide scientific journal, had earned the captain renown in scientific circles, but his reputation lay in steam power. In its infancy, internal combustion intrigued academics and businessmen, but lagged far behind steam in popularity. Now, the Orford inventor was pressing Americans to consider an even more volatile source of power. For his second major experiment in internal combustion, Morey would move his laboratory from water to land.

Many of Morey's competitors in steam power had attached boilers to horseless carriages. In the mid-1820s, Thomas Blanchard, of Springfield, Massachusetts, patented a horseless steam carriage that "could run forward and backwards, steer properly and climb hills, aided by a set of interchangeable gears which would transmit the driving force to the rear axle in two speeds."[6] Most inventors who truly believed in the future of the horseless carriage viewed steam as the inevitable means of propulsion. Morey had agreed—until he commenced his dangerous experimentation with liquid fuels.

In 1828, Morey invited a group of scientists and possible backers to his temporary workshop in Philadelphia to prove that the real future of transportation lay not in steam, but in internal combustion. As the guests, lured in part by Morey's reputation as a pioneer of steam, in part by curiosity about his latest patent, walked through the gate of a fenced lot fronting Morey's ramshackle laboratory, they encountered a buckboard carriage sporting a two-cylinder engine. Further inspection revealed that two hand cranks and a flywheel, standard sights on many steam engines, would set the engine in motion. But closer scrutiny showed that no cumbersome steam boiler would power the machine. A dish of turpentine, assorted spirits, and compressed air would bring the engine to life and usher in the age of liquid fuel.

Morey, still vital despite worsening rheumatism—the result of countless days and nights in lumber camps, on ship's decks, and in cramped workshops—reached for the engine's cranks and spun them several times, hard. Within the cylinders a spark flared and ignited the fuel with a series of loud pops. The carriage began to rock.

The now white-haired inventor climbed toward the driver's "tiller," ready for the test drive of America's first internal-combustion carriage. Suddenly, Morey "lost his hold, tripped, and fell flat onto the ground" in front of the gaping scientists and his assistants.[7]

"Stop her! Stop her!" he yelled.[8]

But the crowd scattered as the buckboard lurched across the yard and toward the gate.

Morey staggered to his feet and chugged toward the careening wagon. George Sellers, one of the witnesses, would later recall: "The thing ran across the street, through the gutter, over the sidewalk," bowling over terrified passersby.[9] Finally the buckboard "turned a somersault into a brickyard . . . a complete wreck."[10]

Samuel Morey had unwittingly orchestrated the first witnessed—even if involuntarily unmanned—run of a liquid-fuel car in American history. He had also fueled America's first auto accident. Fortunately, the runaway horseless carriage had not caused any injuries—except to Morey's ego.

Morey soon returned to Orford, his prototype a bust. He would never halt his experiments and studies completely, but in his latter years, he became more of a scientific dabbler than the vital force he had once been. Retiring late in life, he and Hannah moved to a large estate in Fairlee, Vermont, overlooking the pond where he had cruised the *Aunt Sally* to the chattering strains of his gas and vapor engine.

On April 17, 1843, Captain Samuel Morey died at the age of eighty, embittered to the end about the fame Fulton had won through, Morey believed, the theft of his ideas on steam power.

Morey's name and his patents slowly slid into obscurity. Nearly a century after his death, the people of Orford and Fairlee resurrected his name by dedicating the Samuel Morey Memorial Bridge, on the New Hampshire and Vermont Interstate. Various writers strove to anoint him as the true inventor of the steamboat, a faulty assertion although he was one of the pioneers of America's Age of Steam and built his first steamboat on the Connecticut River at least fourteen years before Fulton's *Clermont* embarked on her maiden voyage on the Hudson.

Lost in the furor of the steamboat wars was Morey's milestone work with internal combustion. The first American to invent a modern liquid-fuel engine, the first to invent a motorboat, the first to affix an internal-combustion engine to a horseless carriage—Samuel Morey merits a niche in the pantheon of American inventors. Each time a car of the 1990s purrs, roars, or clanks, the legacy of the Orford lumberman, riverboat captain, and self-taught engineer and inventor fills drivers' ears. For in 1826, nearly seven decades before gas-powered autos claimed America's roads, Morey's "gas and vapor" patent, the work of a true Yankee genius, heralded the future: "It [the internal-combustion engine] . . . will be the greatest improvement which has been made for many years, particularly in its application to locomotive engines."[11]

Today, in Vermont, a measure of immortality embraces the Orford inventor. The scenic lake on which he took the *Aunt Sally* for a liquid-fueled spin bears the name Lake Morey.

A Spark of Genius

In December 1833, a Vermont blacksmith gaped at a device inside the Penfield Iron Works, in Crown Point, New York. The contraption was an electromagnet "shaped like a horseshoe, the arms ten or twelve inches long, and spreading six inches, and with wire back and forth, perhaps an inch thick," wrote the dark-haired observer, Thomas Davenport.[1]

The blacksmith knew immediately that his life would change because of what he saw. The magnet, suspended in air, held aloft a 150-pound chunk of iron. "Here to me was one of the wonders of Nature and Providence," Davenport would write. "Like a flash of lightning the thought occurred to me that here was an available power which was within the reach of man. If three pounds of iron and copper wire would suspend in the air 150 pounds, what would three hundred pounds suspend?"[2]

Davenport turned to several other men, all gaping at the electromagnet. "In a few years," he later recalled saying to them, "steamboats will be propelled by this power . . . and ere long the mysterious power will supersede steam, for shall this mighty agent which suspends between heaven and earth this mass of iron serve no other purpose than to excite our wonder and admiration?"[3]

Davenport decided that he would be the one to unlock the secrets of "this mighty current"—electromagnetism.[4] He would earn acclaim, heartache, and eventually ruin in his quest to "harness the red lightning of heaven" for mankind's benefit.[5]

Thomas Davenport, born in poverty in Williamstown, Vermont, in 1802, the eighth of eleven children, received only three years or so of formal education in a "little red school house."[6] He showed a penchant for arithmetic, and pored over mathematical problems "alone and unaided far into the night if necessary, until he had mastered" them.[7] Tom always had great patience," his brother Oliver later said. "When he went to school, he would never go up to the master to help him do a hard sum, but would keep everlastingly at it and generally he didn't have to give it up."[8]

Following his father's death from a "spotted fever" that ravaged the region, the fourteen-year-old boy was apprenticed to local blacksmith, Captain Samuel Abbott.[9] Although Davenport, a frail youth, did not fit the brawny, rough-and-tumble image of the village smith, the youth mastered the arts of hammer and anvil inside Abbott's forge.

In 1823, when Davenport's apprenticeship expired, he set up his own forge in Brandon, Vermont. He prospered, and in 1827 he married Emily Goss, a beautiful, intelligent neighbor, and built her a spacious brick home. "Happily wed, intelligent, sober, upright, diligent," Davenport appeared to be a young man slated to make a mark in his community.[10]

In 1833, with $18 in his pocket to buy iron for his forge, Davenport strode into the Penfield Iron Works, not only to shop, but also to view that modern marvel—the electromagnet, dubbed the galvanic battery. According to his brother Oliver, Davenport's first sight of the horseshoe-shaped magnet, its wires, and its battery cups would become his financial undoing.

Between the $18 and his sale, without permission, of his peddler brother Oliver's horse, the blacksmith came up with $75 to purchase a broken galvanic battery in Albany. He immediately conducted an experiment that no trained scientist had tried: he snipped the device's wires to break the circuit and reattached them to restore the current, proving that this process could stop and start the surge at will. A jubilant Davenport wrote that the possibilities of his discovery hit him "like a flash." He envisioned electricity powering ships, trains, and industrial machinery and replacing "murderous steam."[11]

According to Oliver Davenport, his blacksmith brother began spending less time at his anvil and more hours "working and working" on his battery and studying any available tracts on electricity and magnetism.[12] "His idea was to make a wheel revolve by the force of magnetism, and he seemed possessed with the idea. . . . He worked at his wheel early and late."[13]

Many wives would have been horrified if their husbands had neglected their livelihood as Davenport did, but Emily Davenport not only encouraged her spouse, she also became his assistant. When he failed time after time to sever the current quickly enough to keep the wheel spinning, he lamented to Emily: "It's no use, there is no power short of the Almighty quick enough to do that."[14]

Emily, who had paid close attention to her husband's experiments and journals, asked, "I wonder if quicksilver isn't a conductor?"[15]

"We'll try it," her husband said.[16]

Oliver Davenport would later write: "They did, and after working all night one night 'til three o'clock in the morning, they made the wheel turn."[17]

The successful experiment was the turning point for Davenport. Despite his father-in-law's howls of protest and with his wife's ongoing support, the blacksmith neglected his forge almost completely and plunged into electrical experiments. As Emily Davenport jotted down her husband's observations, he took the electromagnet apart; unwrapped its wires; used his smithy's skills to fashion a larger, horseshoe-shaped magnet; coated it with glue; and, after his wife shredded her white silk wedding gown by her own choice, sheathed the device's coils in the silk.

In July 1834, the erstwhile blacksmith and Emily powered a seven-inch wheel at thirty revolutions per minute using four electromagnets supplied with current from battery cups. The world's first practical electric motor had materialized in Davenport's workshop.

But Davenport's machine did not impress the people of Brandon, Vermont. The inventor complained that his achievement was somewhat tainted by "the ridicule and derision of my neighbors and friends."[18]

Others thought differently. Buoyed by the support of Professor Turner, of Middlebury College, and electrical genius Joseph Henry, the Albany scientist whose galvanic battery had so inspired Davenport, he began a torturous and financially disastrous quest to patent his invention. A fire at the Patent Office, in Washington D.C., consumed his first application and model in 1836. Davenport begged and borrowed the funds to build another model, and on February 25, 1837, the world's first patent for a practical electric motor was issued to the Vermont blacksmith.

To prove his motor a safer alternative to steam power, Davenport labored day and night to refine his discovery, even creating a miniature circular railway powered by electricity. Several prominent scientists from Middlebury College, Rensselaer Polytechnic Institute, and Princeton laid aside their scholarly egos when they realized that, in an astonishing burst of technical one-upmanship, an unlettered blacksmith, a "shy, untutored genius," had hatched one of the nineteenth century's profoundest discoveries.[19]

From 1837 to 1843, Davenport strove to turn his patent into profits. He and a partner, furniture maker Ransom Cooke, formed America's first electric company in 1837 and issued stock, but their business manager embezzled most of the company's funds. Cooke pulled up his stake in the fledgling venture.

Another investor handed Davenport $3,000 in notes from an Ohio bank. Davenport spent only $10 of the stipend before the bank failed.

Through such deals as the sale of regional rights to his patent in New England, Davenport patched together funds for electrical experiments, many of which unfolded in a New York City workshop. Emily, as always, was his assistant. The experiments, however, quickly drained his purse.

Desperate to attract new investors by convincing them of his electrical motor's practical applications, he hooked up one of his devices to a printing press and published the world's first electrically produced journal. The venture soon collapsed from lack of funds.

In the fall of 1842, Thomas and Emily returned home to Brandon. The inventor "reluctantly" abandoned "hope of further assistance . . . and resumed my trade as a blacksmith . . . my only resource to gain a livelihood."[20] In 1843, galled by failure and worn out by his research, he suffered a physical collapse and never regained his health, although he lived to the age of forty-nine. He died on July 6, 1851, of a heart attack or stroke, his wife Emily at his bedside. She would outlive him by nearly three decades, but never remarried.

A few years before his death, Davenport had bitterly written: "I exhibited the wonderful power of my magnet and explained its object, which would no doubt eventually supersede steam. But this notion did not take."[21] He also lamented that "after struggling along . . . trying to convince my friends that the object of which I had so long been in pursuit was still worthy of their attention, I . . . gave up hope."[22]

Decades after Davenport's death, other men cashed in on the Vermont blacksmith's 1837 patent by refining his batteries into electric dynamos capable of producing a stream of current to power trolleys, trains, and other machines.

Thomas Davenport, the man who first opened the scientific portal to the age of electric power, the man whose name belongs with that of Thomas Edison and other acclaimed inventors, remains, to this day, a New England genius robbed of his historic and scientific laurels.

Despite a life of hardship and disillusionment, Davenport had "dreamed and accomplished." His nephew Walter Rice Davenport wrote a flowery yet appropriate paean to the inventor of the first practical electric motor:

> I sing of visions splendid
> That sorrows could not drown;
> Of words and deed heroic,
> And faith that would not down;
> Of one who made us famous
> And lived in Williamstown.[23]

A Class Act

On a warm, bright August morning in 1840, a man with long sideburns and a serious demeanor pressed his face against his camera's eyepiece and focused on his fellow alumni, the men of Yale University, class of 1810. As the photographer readied his exposure of these influential men in whiskers and stiff collars, he was about to make history: this would be America's premier class photo.

Although the photographer's name is an immortal one, his role in creating the first class photo has been overlooked, yet it has affected virtually every American from 1840 to today. If any American knew how to score firsts, artist and, later, inventor of the telegraph, Samuel F. B. Morse did. That he snapped the world's first class photograph stands unchallenged, but many historians believe that Morse also holds the honor of having taken America's first photos of any kind.

Before unveiling his electric telegraph apparatus to the prestigious Academy of Sciences in Paris in 1839, Morse studied the work and methods of Frenchman Louis Daguerre, who invented the photo-taking process that produced images called daguerreotypes. The amazed American scientist became inflamed with a desire to emulate and then to surpass the revolutionary discoveries of the Frenchman.

Morse penned his brother a letter that soon appeared in the *New York Observer* and provided Americans their first description of the photographic process. "No painting or engraving ever approached it," Morse wrote. "The effects of the lens upon the picture was in a great degree like that of the telescope in nature."[1]

Once home in New York City, Morse opened a daguerreotype studio and began to earn his nickname, the Father of American Photography. He was so eager to share his new passion with his friends and associates that in the summer of 1840 he lugged his monstrous, box-like camera, copper daguerreotype plates, and assorted chemicals to his thirtieth Yale reunion.

As his classmates arrived at the New Haven depot and headed to their collegiate stomping ground, they had no clue that Morse intended to immortalize them with his lens. When the class of 1810 had gathered, one alumnus wrote: "S. F. B. Morse stated that he had come with the necessary instrument and plates to take a Daguerreotype impression of the Class in group. . . . It was voted to attend to this business at 8 o'clock A.M. the next day."[2]

On the morning of August 18, 1840, the Yalies—clergymen, lawyers, doctors, and captains of commerce—assembled in "the yard north of the President's house" and stiffly posed in front of Morse's lens.[3] Into his camera, the inventor inserted a copper plate treated with silver and exposed to iodine fumes. Then he removed the lens cap. For several minutes, his subjects strained to stay still as Morse exposed the plate. When he finished two plates, or impressions, he hoped he had captured the collective image of the Yale class of 1810.

Morse did not know if the shoot had been successful until he treated the daguerreotype plate with mercury and hyposulfite of soda. Then the familiar visages of his classmates emerged from the chemical wash.

At the home of a man named C. A. Goodwin, Morse and his former schoolmates met on the evening of August 18, 1840; as the alumni scrutinized the neatly framed daguerreotype images, a pleased subject related: "The likenesses were most of them very distinct and good."[4] Morse had developed thirty-five copies of the photo from two impressions.

Samuel Morse's idea of a class photograph would become the commercial bread and butter of generations of photographers training their lenses on graduates, from grade school to university. In countless American albums and yearbooks linger nostalgic school-day images of the sort conceived by the same man who gave the nation the telegraph. For today's professional shutterbugs, Samuel F. B. Morse turned graduation into gold.

Before Kitty Hawk: Crazy Whitehead's Flight

⌒

Newspaperman Richard Howell gaped skyward, ears throbbing from a din pounding "like an elevator going down a shaft."[1] Two other men and a twelve-year-old boy also stared at the sky.

Suddenly the enormity of the truth seized them: the frail craft soaring fifty feet above them and churning above the whitecaps of the Atlantic was *flying*. The burly, mustachioed man who strained frantically at the machine's controls to keep the bat-winged contrap-

tion's two propellers whirling and its bamboo-ribbed fuselage from nose-diving into the sea below was making history's first propelled flight.

The nearby shore was not the sands of Kitty Hawk, North Carolina. Nor was the pilot Orville Wright. The date was not December 3, 1903. Instead, the beach rolled toward the Atlantic off Fairfield, Connecticut, and the man risking life and limb to reach for the clouds was Bridgeport resident Gustave Whitehead. The date was August 14, 1901—two years, four months, and three days *before* the Wright brothers flew into immortality.

So say the proponents of the Connecticut man's case: he, not the Wrights, was the first to fly. And to the fury of staunch Wright supporters, who regard Whitehead's saga as something between fantasy and heresy, a compelling circumstantial case on behalf of the Connecticut aviation pioneer exists, a case featuring alleged eyewitness testimony. In fact, Whitehead's claim cannot be conclusively disproven—no matter how vehemently the Wrights' proponents have labored to debunk his story.

Who was this man whose backers challenge one of history's most sacrosanct achievements, the legendary feat of the Wright brothers? His saga began far from the shores of Connecticut.

Gustave Weisskopf was born on January 1, 1874, in the Bavarian town of Leutershausen, the eldest of six children. His father was a foreman for a crew of railroad-bridge carpenters, and wherever there was work along Bavaria's rails, he could be found with his family in tow.

As a child, Gustave Weisskopf proved a dreamer, a boy with "his head in the clouds." For he was obsessed with birds and with dreams that a machine could allow man to fly. The boy was as likely to fashion a piece of schoolroom paper into a little glider as he was to write an assignment on that sheet. For him, a handkerchief was less useful applied to a runny nose than hurled heavenward in the guise of a tiny parachute.

Orphaned in his early teens after illnesses claimed his parents, apprenticed to a Bavarian locksmith, the youth ran off to sea. In his voyages aboard merchant ships, he somehow laid his hands on a copy of a book titled *Der Vogelflug als Grundlage der Fliegekunst (Bird Flight as the Basis of Aviation)*, by Otto Lilienthal, a designer and pilot of gliders. Weisskopf would later assert that in 1893 or 1894, he traveled to Lilienthal's home outside Berlin and studied aeronautics under his tutelage. But it was in New England, not Germany, that Weisskopf would settle and win both acclaim and notoriety.

In 1895 he arrived in Boston, a city not known for hospitality toward immigrants. Weisskopf nevertheless walked into the office of a highbrow scientific group, the Boston Aeronautical Society. The twenty-one-year-old German, whose bristling mustache, lantern-jawed visage, and muscular two-hundred-pound frame virtually screamed *tradesman,* captured the attention of the society's nabobs and intellectuals by informing them that he had studied with Lilienthal.

To anyone with even a remote interest in flight, the name commanded respect. The society's members listened to what the self-proclaimed student of Lilienthal offered: a guarantee that he could build a glider that would thrust the society into the forefront of American aviation. All Weisskopf needed, he claimed, was financial backing; he soon convinced the Boston gentlemen to write some bankdrafts.

Sometime in the summer of 1895, Weisskopf's backers and spectators gathered on the grounds of an estate at a steep summit of the Blue Hills, lying several miles from Boston and offering a spectacular view of the city. According to one of the onlookers, Harvard University Observatory Professor William H. Pickering, all eyes were on Weisskopf's creation, "a glider without a motor, and no wheels. . . . The machine was modeled somewhat after the type of Lilienthal's."[2]

Weisskopf had indeed patterned his glider after Lilienthal's—but with a major difference: Weisskopf had fashioned his craft "to provide forward progression by movement of its oar-like wings with the strength of his arms."[3]

The strength in Weisskopf's muscular arms bristled for anyone to see, but the scientists in the crowd suspected that those arms could not power the thirty-two-foot-long glider through the air for long, no matter how sound its design. Author Stella Randolph reasonably suggests that Weisskopf was striving to furnish more propulsion than wind alone to his glider. In short, he sought airborne emancipation from fickle gusts.

On that day in 1895, Weisskopf's creation and his first version of propelled flight never got off the ground. Albert Horn, the mechanic hired by the Boston Aeronautical Society to assist Weisskopf in constructing gliders, recorded the scene: "It was taken to the estate of one of the sponsors for a trial, which ended in no flight, which was surmised by all concerned, knowing mere manpower could not propel the machine."[4] Horn did toss one plaudit Weisskopf's way by noting that the glider "was very light and strongly made."[5]

Because of Weisskopf's failure, the financial well in Boston quickly dried up. He soon left for New York City, chastened but not beaten, vowing to return to New England.

Weisskopf's failure notwithstanding, Horn later asserted that the Boston Aeronautical Society had procured a return of sorts from the departed immigrant. "We [Weisskopf and Horn] also made a glider after the pattern of Lilienthal's with which Weisskopf managed to get off the ground for short distances."[6] Horn also would fire a personal jab at Weisskopf: "A lighter person would have done better as his weight must have been nearly two hundred pounds."[7] Weisskopf, however, would do better himself.

By late 1895 or early 1896, Weisskopf, who had Americanized his name to Gustave *Whitehead*, was shelling out most of his meager wages to have a local mechanic build a small engine to the German's specifications. Nothing stopped Whitehead from working on his drawings. Nothing—until he met a pretty young Hungarian woman named Louise Tuba, and married her in November 1897.

Despite his obsession with flight, Whitehead did not shirk his duties to his spouse and soon their children. He found work at a buggy factory in Buffalo, enduring what his wife described as "the hardest kind of work"[8] in order to put food on the table and to pay the rent. But no matter how arduous his job, he always came home at night eager to tackle his aeronautical designs, his engine, and assorted parts for the aircraft he intended to build.

The Whiteheads soon pulled up stakes in Buffalo and moved to Pittsburgh, where the inventor found work in a coal mine. There, in the dim subterranean light, coal dust blackening his face and filling his lungs, he toiled with pick and shovel for his family and dreamed of flying far above the shafts and tunnels of the mine.

Whitehead shared his vision with another immigrant miner, Louis Davarich. Intrigued that a fellow miner believed he could achieve motorized flight, a feat no trained scientist had managed, and wondering if Whitehead were crazy, Davarich convinced the inventor to show him the machine taking shape in a shed outside Whitehead's apartment.

One look at Whitehead's handiwork, and Davarich was hooked. Whitehead not only gained a true believer in Davarich, but also an invaluable assistant. Night after night the two men shaped and re-shaped silk, canvas, bamboo, and wood into an aircraft and experimented with steam engines to power it.

When word of what the two men were up to spread through the neighborhood, people treated the pair at first with quizzical stares; then, as Whitehead began experimenting with steam boilers that often blew up in the predawn hours, neighbors' bemusement turned to rage in the wake of broken windows and shattered nerves. According to

Mrs. Davarich, Pittsburgh soon became an uncomfortable place for the Davariches and the Whiteheads, especially after the two men allegedly crashed an air machine into a three-story building. Even Whitehead's future supporters labeled the mishap a "hop"—not a real flight. That, according to Whitehead's plans, would come in New England.

Realizing that he had worn out his welcome in Pittsburgh, accompanied by Davarich, Whitehead took his aerial show on the road to New England and turned up in Bridgeport, Connecticut. His long-suffering wife and children planned to join him as soon as he found a job.

At first Whitehead encountered rejection at factories and foundries all over Bridgeport. Thanks to a boy who had heard Whitehead asking in a tobacco and candy store about rooming houses, the struggling inventor found lodgings with a family of fellow Germans. The boy, eleven-year-old Junius Harworth, after glimpsing Whitehead's notebooks, model gliders, kites, and battered steam engine, attached himself to the inventor and would serve as his assistant and gofer in the thrilling and dangerous years ahead.

Whitehead's immediate future cleared when he finally found work driving a coal truck, a post infinitely preferable to digging the sooty stuff from the bowels of a mine. Soon his family joined him in a ground-floor flat at 241 Pine Street, and in their new neighborhood, inhabited mainly by German and Hungarian immigrants, the Whiteheads were accepted in a way they had never experienced in Buffalo and Pittsburgh. His wife later remarked that she always worried that their welcome would vanish as soon as her husband fired up his steam engine again. She need not have, for they would live in the Connecticut city for the rest of their lives.

Whitehead first repaired his engine, soldering its crushed contours into shape in the kitchen. To his wife's alarm, he then purchased a tank of compressed air to commence evening experiments in the alley behind the flat. Wary that his neighbors might turn on him following a few nocturnal explosions, Whitehead befriended an Irish policeman named Cronin, who shooed the curious or the angry away from the alley while experiments were underway. Luckily for the Whiteheads, their neighbors were intrigued rather than dismayed by the noisy experimentation of the man they affectionately dubbed Crazy Whitehead.

Word that Whitehead was building an aircraft of some sort lured many visitors to his flat. One of them, a well-heeled New York businessman named Miller, found his imagination inflamed by the idea of flight. After a few chats with Whitehead, he handed the inventor $300, offered to bankroll his experiments, and persuaded him to quit his day job and to devote himself full-time to finishing the plane and flying it. The inventor leaped at the offer.

Whitehead used Miller's money to construct an inventor's dream, a workshop, in the yard of the apartment house. At Whitehead's side, as always those days, Junius Harworth marveled as the laboratory rose from the lot. When finished, Whitehead's lab was thirty feet long, twelve feet wide, and capped by a slanted, tar-papered roof. Inside, he constructed a six-foot lathe, a drill press, and an Otto gas engine with a thirty-inch flywheel powered at first by dry cells and later a magneto. That the workshop, rather than the family's kitchen, served as home to the inventor's experiments pleased Louise Whitehead immeasurably.

Freed from the strictures of a day job, Whitehead plunged with ceaseless vigor into the task of crafting his plane from 1899 to the onset of the summer of 1901. With Davarich, young Harworth, and a new helper, Charles Galombosche, all ready to dash nearly two-and-a-half miles to Lyon and Grumman's Hardware Store every time their boss needed a part or a tool, Whitehead first built a propeller of white pine, its varnished blades tangible proof of the enterprise ahead.

Whitehead then commenced work on the plane's fuselage, or carriage. He built it in stages, out of necessity, as the workshop was too small to hold the bamboo-strutted, steel-reinforced, silk-covered contraption. Attached to the carriage were two curved wings that Whitehead had ingeniously designed to fold for easy storage.

In 1900 and 1901, Whitehead attempted to fly his plane from

Bridgeport's streets and from the nearby shores of Fairfield, but failed. He took from each setback new ideas that led him to constantly re-model and refine his plane, each failure a trying but necessary lesson.

One lesson to which Whitehead always adhered was that a key to understanding flight was birdwatching. Each Sunday, Whitehead, flanked by his helpers and curious children, trekked to Seaside Park to observe ocean birds in flight and to trap, tether, and "fly" them as he had done so many years ago in the parks of Bavarian nobles.

Whitehead's single-minded pursuit of flight never flagged, but at some point in 1900 or 1901, his financial backing did. His attempts to contact his scientific sugar daddy, Miller, went unanswered but not out of a sudden lack of faith in Whitehead by Miller: the man had died. The grim news forced Whitehead back onto his old treadmill of factory work by day and aeronautical labors by night. When he snatched some sleep was anyone's guess.

Not even winter's chill stymied the inventor, who rubbed his cal-loused hands near a diminutive laundry stove, then resumed shaping wood, metal, and fabric into his plane's wings and torso and ham-mering engine parts atop his anvil. The sounds of his grinding lathe and even the occasional pane-rattling explosion of an engine experi-ment gone awry inside the Pine Street shed failed to turn his neighbors against him. As many later said, they believed Crazy Whitehead was really on to something.

By the early summer of 1901, what Whitehead was on to appeared little short of revolutionary: he was achingly close to powered flight. Having abandoned steam power for internal combustion, he had mounted two twenty-horsepower, calcium carbide–fueled engines to a gull-winged monoplane, one engine on the carriage's floor to fur-nish lift, the other engine directly in front of the cockpit to power two forward propellers. Whitehead, his landmark engines weighing an astonishingly light seventy-five pounds apiece, knew that this air-machine marked a radical departure from all before it—and sensed that this aircraft was *the one.*

The people of Bridgeport were accustomed to the sights of

Whitehead soaring above Seaside Park in gliders and of his jarring hops and crashes in motorized aircraft. But when he rolled his newest machine, No. 21, out of his yard, tethered with a strong rope to a friend's automobile, and climbed into the cockpit, a larger throng than usual gathered.

One of the onlookers, Edward Prior, would later testify: "The motor on the plane started, and the plane appeared to be operating on its own power, *with a slack rope*, when it struck the tree. It dropped about forty feet. All of us rushed forward, expecting to find Mr. Whitehead dead, but he was unhurt."[9]

Like the mythic cat with nine lives, Whitehead had survived another brush with death unscathed. And if Prior's assertion about the slack rope was accurate, Whitehead knew that his plane had climbed about forty feet without the aid of the car and the rope.

Whitehead, according to many neighbors, conducted other tethered flights that summer. By August 1901, the true test of his genius, or his madness, loomed. He readied his monoplane for unfettered flight; as always with the valiant but reckless inventor, the imminent possibility of death failed to steal his nerve.

According to Whitehead's supporters, sometime during the warm, languid evening of August 14, 1901, on a sloping Fairfield tract called Lordship Manor, Whitehead squeezed himself into the cockpit of No. 21. The sandy shore between Bridgeport and Fairfield stretched just beyond the long field, and beyond the beach were the waters of the Atlantic, starlight, and the beacons of a few passing ships glinting across the distant whitecaps. Near the plane stood young Junius Harworth, two other assistants, and *Bridgeport Herald* editor Richard Howell, all waiting for the first rasps of the plane's engines.

Whitehead took a deep breath and nodded at the four spectators. He started the engine mounted on the carriage floor. Pops and sputters fueled by fifteen gallons of gasoline in a compact tank beneath the pilot echoed in the night air. The plane's bicycle wheels gripped the earth for a few moments; then the delicate craft shuddered and began to roll along the field. Whitehead switched on the forward engine, and the two propellers whirred to life. As the blades spun faster and faster, Whitehead waited for just the right moment to ease the crude throttle back. Suddenly the nose of the plane arched upward, and with a shiver the monoplane's wheels jerked free from the ground. Sluggishly, the plane continued to climb at about a six-degree angle.

The three men and the boy peered upward as Whitehead strained at the controls to nudge the plane forward. The engines' "chung, chung, chung" clattered "like an elevator going down a shaft," but unlike an elevator going down, Whitehead's craft was climbing.[10] At fifty feet above the ground he leveled off and soared toward the end of the field. He began cutting the plane's power, praying that he could hold the nose steady for his landing, realizing that the slightest lapse in judgment could be fatal.

On the ground the foursome dashed down a lolling incline in pursuit of the plane. Slowly, steadily, it descended. "She settled down from a height of about fifty feet in three minutes after the propellers stopped," Howell later recorded. "And she lighted on the ground on her four wheels so lightly that Whitehead was not jarred in the least,"[11]

That night, Louise Whitehead would recall, her husband charged into their bedroom and cried: "Mama, we went up!"[12]

His supporters believe that Whitehead's was the world's first successful flight—preceding Orville and Wilbur Wright's otherwise notable achievement at Kitty Hawk by more than two years. And according to Howell and Harworth, on that same summer day, Whitehead clambered back into No. 21 and rose "to a height of 200 feet off the ground or sea beach at Lordship Manor."[13] Harworth would assert: "The distance flown was approximately one mile and a half and lasted, to the best of my knowledge, for four minutes."[14]

The *Bridgeport Sunday Herald* of August 18, 1901, and the August 19, 1901, editions of the *New York Herald* and the *Boston Transcript* trumpeted the news that man had finally flown. And that man, the papers proclaimed, was a Bridgeport mechanic named Gustave Whitehead.

With the trademark personality of the inventor who is never satisfied with even successful experiments, Whitehead left the field of Lordship Manor with ideas for improving his plane's performance. He also intended to inform the scientific community of his reputed achievement.

Whitehead published a long, detailed letter in the April 1, 1902, issue of the *American Inventor*, a respected scientific journal, in which he described his alleged flights of No. 21 and his latest plane, No. 22. (Whitehead's debunkers have sneered at the fact that his account of his alleged flights appeared on April Fools' Day.) His new monoplane was thirty-two feet long with a wingspan of thirty-six feet and was covered with sheets of aluminum; unlike No. 21, whose ribs were bamboo, No. 22's frame featured sturdy steel tubing.

The most amazing aspect of Whitehead's letter lay not in its description of No. 22, but in his assertion that he had flown it already, on January 17, 1902. This time, he alleged, showcasing a flair for self-promotion, he had vastly improved his airborne performance, his August jaunts into the skies veritable baby steps compared to his most recent flights. He claimed that above the churning winter waves of the Atlantic, he had swooped at the controls of No. 22 for nearly two miles and had "settled in the water [at the beach's edge—not in deep water] without mishap to either machine or operator."[15]

If future critics of Whitehead found that claim implausible, his next would shove their blood pressure into the stratosphere. He alleged that his second flight that day covered nearly seven miles and reached two hundred feet. "The machine kept on steadily in crossing the wind at a height of about two hundred feet when it came into my mind to try steering around in a circle." Whitehead claimed, "As soon as I turned the rudder and drove one propeller faster than the other, the machine turned a bend and flew north with the wind at a frightful speed, but turned steadily around until I saw the starting place in the distance. I continued to turn but when near land again, I slowed up the propellers and sank gently down on an even keel in the water, she readily floating like a boat."[16]

Again, a witness supported the veracity of Whitehead's alleged flights. Anton Pruckner, a skilled mechanic and associate of Whitehead's, added: "I flew in this machine with Mr. Whitehead, and saw him make the flight across the Sound [the January flight] to which he refers."[17] For a while, it seemed that the twenty-eight-year-old Whitehead would parlay his allegations of successful flight into a financial windfall for his wife and children. Local businessmen eager to back his flight experiments showed up at the shed on Pine Street. Others impressed by Whitehead's engineering skills commissioned him to build motors for everything from airplanes to boats.

Unfortunately for Louise Whitehead and her children, their provider was a disaster as a businessman, a classic case of an inventor whose ingenuity in the workshop was matched only by his incompetency in money matters. Too often he accepted commissions to construct engines, gliders, and other machines and failed to deliver, sidetracked by his own flight experiments. Some of his customers, acutely aware that by suing him they would never recoup their losses, vented their wrath upon his reputation: how could the claims of such an unreliable man be believed?

One of his creditors, Lee S. Burridge, a man who reputedly paid Whitehead $5,000—a large sum for the era—in 1911 to build a helicopter to Burridge's own design, grew incensed when Whitehead's well-intentioned attempts to build an engine for the craft dragged on too long for the client's taste. Burridge sued Whitehead. In court, the inventor, serving as his own attorney, lost everything—his workshop, his gliders, his planes, his engines, even his tools—except the house he had bought on a Bridgeport hill for his family.

When Burridge's hirelings showed up at Whitehead's door and proceeded to empty his cluttered workshop, the inventor stood in front of a window inside his house. His hands clasped behind his broad back, he did not stir until his life's work had disappeared, hauled away by several trucks. According to his family, the optimism and the stubbornness that had been his personal trademarks began to wane on that day in 1911.

Whitehead continued to work on engines and on various aspects of flight. But with his earnings hardly covering the needs of his wife and six children, there would be no more projects so grandiose as those of his glory years, 1899 to 1910. Along with his bank account and his sullied reputation, the inventor's once-bullish health slowly declined. A growth behind his left eye led to its removal by a surgeon; Whitehead suffered from angina, which his doctor attributed to a massive blow to the inventor's chest from a piece of heavy machinery.

On October 10, 1927, the year of Lindbergh's daring flight across the Atlantic, a heart attack claimed Gustave Whitehead. He left his family their house and $8 and was buried in a pauper's grave, his name and his work soon forgotten by most beyond Bridgeport.

Whitehead's story did reach the ears of writer and historian Stella Randolph in the 1930s. Intrigued but skeptical, certain that the Wrights had reached the clouds first, she set out at first to disprove Whitehead's claim. She interviewed his wife, his children, his friends, his associates, his foes, and his neighbors from Boston to Bridgeport. To her amazement, many flatly stated, in sworn affidavits, that they had seen Whitehead fly in 1901 and 1902. In most cases, the details matched.

The Wrights' proponents have attacked all such testimony. They point out that no ironclad proof—photos of Whitehead in flight—exists. To date, every picture of Whitehead's planes shows them on the ground.

Conversely, Whitehead's supporters mount a compelling circumstantial case. No one can dispute that Whitehead's engines powered successful flights by others' planes in the early 1900s. And to ignore the testimony of dozens, including many who were not friends of Whitehead yet testified they had *seen* him fly in 1901 and 1902, asserts that men and women with no stake in Whitehead's work and life perpetrated a mass hoax in unison with complete strangers from different parts of the nation. Why, Whitehead's backers ask, in 1964 did one of his old Bridgeport neighbors, a woman named Savage who lay dying of cancer and had hardly known Whitehead, state that she had seen him fly in 1901 and 1902? What could the doomed woman have possibly gained from her statement, and why, at such a moment, would she lie?

Adding even more vitriol to the air war between the band of Whitehead stalwarts and the proponents of the Wrights is the recent discovery of a contract between the Wright brothers and 1920s Smithsonian officials, an agreement that the museum would never even hint that Whitehead might have flown first.

To the further anger of Whitehead's detractors, although Orville Wright pronounced that Whitehead's plane could not fly, many modern engineers have pored over the blueprints and the photos of No. 21 and No. 22 and believe that just the opposite of Wright's edict is true (see "Author's Note," p. 154).

Whitehead's critics cannot contradict his other firsts of flight. He was the first to design lightweight engines able to power a plane; he was the first to affix rubber tires to aircraft. His ingenious use of folding wings heralded their use on aircraft carriers in World War II. Aluminum propellers? Whitehead's brainstorm. Concrete runways? Whitehead again.

Of course, as long as no photo of Whitehead in flight surfaces, his case will remain compelling but circumstantial. Claims that several such photos appeared in an exhibit in New York City in 1902 have arisen, but if true, their whereabouts are a mystery. While Whitehead wrote that a photographer attempted to capture the alleged January 17, 1902, flights, overcast skies and the dilemma of getting a proper exposure of the moving plane had prevented "a time exposure" of the alleged flight.[18] Still, one cannot help but wonder if the photographer may have captured a few blurred, grainy images of Whitehead's No. 22 aloft.

Along with all the other insults that assailed the deceased inventor's reputation, there are the barbs of scientists who imply that a man of Whitehead's limited formal education could never have garnered the know-how necessary to solve the daunting technical problems of flight. Of course, this school of thought conveniently overlooks the Wright brothers' lack of college sheepskins and their plebeian trade:

bicycle making. And to further gut such academic snobbery, one can offer two words: *Thomas Edison.*

Even if Gustave Whitehead soared above the shoreline of Connecticut before the Wright brothers swooped above the sand dunes of Kitty Hawk, the Wrights will remain the first name in aviation's annals—and rightly so. Their flight was the one that opened the future of aviation.

Perhaps flight historian David C. Cooke summed up the Whitehead v. Wright brothers dilemma best: "His [Whitehead's] story appears to be sufficiently documented to deserve a place among the true pioneers. And unless the whole thing is a tissue of lies, he might well have been the first to fly."[19]

A picture would be worth a thousand words.

Author's Note: In December 1986, one of Whitehead's supporters, pilot and science teacher Andy Kosch, of Bridgeport, climbed into a replica of Whitehead's No. 21 and got it off the ground—easily. The plane sits at a local marina, Kosch's flight culminating nearly three decades of research by Connecticut historians, aeronautical engineers, pilots, and Colonel (Ret.) William O'Dwyer, U.S.A.F. Reserves.

And to Kosch, no skepticism about the Bridgeport inventor lingers. He said, "I have no doubt at all that Whitehead achieved powered flight in 1901."

The controversy of New England's claim to mankind's first flight rages on.

ROCKED

BY

SCANDAL

〜

The Massachusetts Bay Madam

It was a good thing that John Winthrop was long dead in 1672. If he had not been laid in his grave in 1649, Alice Thomas might have put him six feet under in 1672, for Thomas, "a common Baud,"[1] unveiled a New World twist to the world's oldest profession in the Puritans' promised land. Thomas—the Massachusetts Bay Madam—opened the first recorded brothel among the chosen people and catered to a wide range of Puritan party animals who would "go ask Alice."

Prostitution arrived in the thirteen colonies virtually with the first settlers to wade ashore, the trade taking its place alongside such pursuits as farming, fishing, and shipbuilding. Within sight of Boston in 1637, America's first record of a working girl referred to "this goodly creature of incontinency,"[2] who drank, danced, and plied her trade around a maypole with colonial rogue Thomas Morton and his band of Indians and ruffians in Quincy, Massachusetts. Myles Standish and a contingent of soldiers clad in steel helmets and cuirasses and wielding swords and muskets put a stop to the parties and packed Morton, the Lord of Misrule, back to England. The fate of the goodly creature went unrecorded.

If Winthrop, William Bradford, and the colony's other early leaders believed that sex for hire would vanish with the toppling of Morton's maypole, they were sadly mistaken. Adventurers, freebooters, and sailors setting foot in New England in the Puritans' wake lured prostitutes to service any man, Puritan and outsider alike, with a shilling or two in hand. To the ire and embarrassment of the Puritans, the bauds of Boston and their patrons soon earned renown throughout the colonies for their wantonness—try as local leaders did to arrest the women and encourage them to depart for Virginia. By 1660, cases of "fornication, adultery, and whoredom" had doubled from 1640s levels in the City upon a Hill.[3]

The women hauled before the Puritan General Court for prostitution were mainly, in today's parlance, freelancers. But in the early 1670s, a different sort of prostitute emerged among the Puritans. Her name was Alice Thomas, and she began plying an age-old tenet of her trade under the noses of her neighbors: in colonial annals, she was the first recorded madam. Even worse to Puritan sensibilities, she was not some refugee of London's red-light districts, but a fallen member of their own community.

Stereotypical visions of a garishly made-up woman strutting along Boston's wharves and trolling for drunken clients inside such watering holes as Noah's Ark and the Blue Anchor are easy to conjure. Such preconceptions aside, the truth is that the Massachusetts Bay Madam was a middle-aged widow and ran a small shop of some sort on Boston's North End waterfront, a colonial Sodom and Gomorrah compared to the gentrified South End.

Whatever legitimate wares Alice Thomas peddled in her establishment besides liquor and victuals, she eventually hawked merchandise of a different type: sexual favors—for a price. Thomas was not working alone. She employed other women, several of them maidservants seeking to save money to buy their way out of indentures, and turned her brothel into a going concern.

For a time, the Widow Thomas and her staff flourished, the local law looking the other way whenever complaints against the all-night revelry in her shop were lodged. This state of affairs later led some to speculate that the madam either paid some version of Puritan protection money or knew some of Boston's leading men—how well was anyone's guess.

In early 1672, Alice Thomas's profitable sex shop began unraveling because of a nasty divorce case that landed her brothel so squarely in the public eye that the authorities could no longer allow her operation to continue unchecked. The divorce war pitted wealthy merchant

Edward Naylor against his wife, Nanny Naylor, whose family, the Wheelwrights, was one of the richest and most powerful clans along Massachusetts Bay.

Nanny Naylor sued her husband for divorce on grounds of adultery. According to the irate Nanny and several other prominent Bostonians, the site of her husband's illicit assignations was the shop of Alice Thomas, where he allegedly partied away evenings in the embrace of a maidservant named Mary More. Before the General Court on February 2, 1671, proper Puritan John Anibal testified, "I have often seen Mary More and Mr. Naylor at the Widow Thomas's house together."[4]

Pressed by a judge as to how the witness had gathered his information, Anibal claimed he had followed Naylor to Thomas's house and had peeked through her windows to catch the adulterous couple in the act. He assured the court—emphatically—that he had merely *observed* the bacchanals and had never ventured across Thomas's doorstep. Thomas's counsel did not, as caustic defense attorneys of future eras would have, make the Puritan peeping Tom sweat under cross-examination.

Court records do not confirm that Nanny Naylor won her divorce, but the scandal refused to die. The Wheelwrights and their formidable friends would not let it, incensed at Thomas's role in the marriage's breakup; that the disgraced husband had cheated on his well-bred wife with a common maidservant fueled the Wheelwrights's relentless rage as much as Thomas's shop having provided the sinners a cozy little nest. Even Puritans who had tolerated the unsettling reality of sailors, servants, and other low souls guzzling strong spirits and indulged in the sale of sex fumed at Thomas's role in the dissolution of a respectable Puritan marriage. For the sins of an upscale patron, Alice Thomas would reap the proverbial whirlwind, a Puritan tempest.

The repercussions percolated slowly. In January 1672, nearly a year after the Naylor-More affair, the constables arrived at Thomas's door—one wonders if some of them had entered under more convivial circumstances on other occasions—and escorted the madam to the Town House, the site of the colony's courts. Inside the steeply gabled, three-story frame structure, its columned portico always mobbed with merchants checking posted listings of ships' arrivals and departures, the Widow Thomas stood before a magistrate and listened as charges were heaped upon her with the same rapidity as men had piled coins into the coffers of her sex shop. For emphasis, after cataloging the charges, the court denounced her as a "common Baud,"[5] a woman beckoning the men and boys of Boston's better families astray. That she had hardly twisted the arms of these proper Puritan men and their proper Puritan boys mattered little.

Immediately after her arraignment, Thomas was tossed into Boston Prison, the first such facility erected in New England. It was "a house of meager Looks and ill smells on Prison Lane," where men and women were penned up together in common cells. The jail was built in 1637, per John Winthrop's orders, as a series of criminal firsts in the colony were followed by ever-escalating repeat offenses.[6]

In the grim, dank repository for Puritan sinners, Alice Thomas languished with some of her patrons arrested on various charges. And if the town's clerics and other leaders expected her to repent of her sins, other pillars of the Puritan community, men such as Edward Naylor, knew that her confession, if extracted, threatened ruin for her customers.

Thomas's day in court arrived in late January 1672. She could do nothing as the jury heard the magistrates accuse her of five major crimes: "aiding and abetting theft by buying and concealing stolen goods; frequent secret and unreasonable entertainment in her house to lewd, lascivious and notorious persons of both sexes, giving them opportunity to commit carnal wickedness; selling drink on the Sabbath."[7]

Thomas, no matter how jaded or imperturbable, understood the gravity of the charges. Although the severe penalties for carnal crimes, except rape and incest, no longer included a death sentence, theft sometimes did, and she was charged with being a fence.

The jury came in with a guilty verdict. The judges pronounced a stiff sentence: they ordered Thomas to pay "threefold restitution" for fenced goods, a fine of fifty pounds for her assorted crimes, and court fees.[8]

The fines furnished the least of Thomas's woes. The judges commanded that she stand on the town gallows for one hour with a noose around her neck while the magistrates decided if she should hang for thievery. If she was spared, the constables would strip her to the waist in freezing weather, tie her to the back of an ox-drawn cart, and administer thirty-nine lashes to her bare back as the ox dragged the cart and its human cargo through the town's streets while crowds jeered her. Assuming that she would survive the ordeal, the judges ordered her to serve a sentence in the prison until October 1672. In a final indignity to the prisoner, the court ordered that she be forever banished from Boston after her jail term's end.

Several days after her trial, Alice Thomas stood for an hour with a noose fixed around her neck; no constable kicked the stool beneath her feet. She endured the thirty-nine lashes—pain enough to kill many a burly man—as the cart dragged her half-naked through the streets, vegetables raining down upon her. She was then taken back to the jail.

For the next six months or so, Thomas nursed her wounds in her cell, out of sight, if not out of mind, of her furious neighbors. Then, she was suddenly on Boston's streets again. The court, for unspecified reasons, had granted her "Liberty to bee abroad from Eight of the clocke in the morning till Six a clocke at night. She giving Sufficient Security to the Keeper to Return to Prison every night at the hour Appointed & to be a true prisoner & this Liberty to continue till the first day of the next Court of the County."[9]

Whether Thomas was allowed to participate in a colonial version of a work-release program or was merely allowed to get her personal affairs in order, the "Court of the County" sent her into exile in the fall of 1672. Her foes prayed that with her banishment, "the sin of Whoredom and Uncleaness" would leave with her.[10]

To discourage anyone else from committing this sin, the court, still rattled by Thomas's house of ill repute, enacted a law to eradicate "the bold and audacious presumption of some to erect a stews [brothel] . . . or whorehouse."[11] The Puritans, thanks to Alice Thomas, had passed the thirteen colonies' first law banning brothels.

Although many Puritans assumed it was Thomas's sexual improprieties that had ruined her, some of her neighbors knew that her most grievous crime had been her enraging the powerful Wheelwright clan. The Massachusetts Bay Madam, although the Wheelwrights demanded her client list, never ratted out her patrons. To the family's additional ire, she never admitted that she knew Edward Naylor.

Puritans believing they had seen the last of Alice Thomas faced a surprise in July 1676, for she suddenly reappeared on Boston's streets in the summer haze like an apparition sent to torment righteous people. She was no apparition. Thanks to the fortune she had made in her sex shop, she had bought her way back into the good graces of the colony's higher-ups; from 1673 to 1676 she had contributed cold, hard coin to Boston's construction of public buildings and a harbor seawall. In July 1676, her petition for cancellation of her exile won approval from the General Court.

The former Massachusetts Bay Madam avoided trouble following her reinstatement. Some of her onetime stewardesses continued to ply their illicit trade in the town's taverns and along its docks, but the women did so freelance. Their former boss, the woman who had dared to run the first known brothel under Puritan noses, had retired, shutting off her red lantern for good.

The Bishop and the Bricklayer

〜

At John Doyle's tavern in Sandwich, Massachusetts, on September 1, 1830, a crowd was gathering, a crowd of *Roman Catholics* in a Protestant town. Some of them had walked nearly twenty miles for an event that might have sent the Cape's first settlers, Pilgrims and Puritans, grabbing for muskets and torches. Many of the girls and women were dressed in ragged frieze skirts and shawls; most of the boys and men were clad in tattered breeches and coarse shirts. The growing band of mostly Irish Catholics outside the tavern was in Sandwich to dedicate a small Catholic church.

The procession surged away from the tavern and headed down Sandwich's main street. From all directions came the hostile, stunned stares of local Protestants, who earned equally venomous glares from the Catholics' ranks; but the sight receiving the most scrutiny from the Protestants was the portly middle-aged man leading the procession. He was dressed in the ornate ceremonial garb of a Catholic bishop, his flowing robes tangible symbols of the papist trappings rejected centuries ago by Massachusetts's first settlers and still loathsome to many Yankees of the nineteenth century. Longtime residents of Sandwich knew that the cleric was sending a message: the Catholic Church was elbowing for room in New England. For New Englanders raised to view Catholics with fear and suspicion, the message did not bode well.

Benedict Fenwick, the man in the bishop's raiment, was not cowed by the hatred twisting some onlookers' faces. His curly hair and broad, pleasant features belied the steely will and amazing abilities of the man whose diocese stretched across all of New England. Part missionary, part administrator, part parish priest, Fenwick would leave an indelible mark on friend and foe alike. For two decades, he *was* the Catholic Church in New England. And in 1834, a lone New Hampshire bricklayer, nicknamed Old R, nearly undid all of the bishop's work.

Fenwick's bloodlines were as Catholic as any American's could be in the early days of the nation. His ancestors had been among the first Catholics to carve out an enclave in Maryland, where they practiced their faith despite constant challenges from neighboring Protestant settlers. Fenwick was born in 1782 near Leonardtown, Maryland, one of Colonel Richard Fenwick and Dorothy Plowden Fenwick's ten children, but Benedict would spend most of his life in New England. He soon displayed the intellect of a gifted child, and when he was eleven, he was accepted at Georgetown College. His advanced courses did not challenge the boy, who garnered high scholastic honors. He became a teacher at the school, but the brilliant young man, so eminently equipped for success in whatever field he selected to pursue, chose a vocation that certainly pleased his family: in 1805, he decided to enter the Catholic priesthood and enrolled at the Supplican Seminary, in Baltimore.

When the Society of Jesus, the Jesuits, formerly banned in America, was legally allowed to reestablish itself in 1806, the young scholar immediately enrolled as a novitiate of the Jesuit chapter in Georgetown. He was attracted by the order's reputation for scholastic, as well as theological, excellence. For an aspiring young priest with dreams of missionary zeal and social impact, the Jesuits offered both—along with the promise of conflict with Americans furious that the order had been restored. By the time Fenwick was ordained on March 12, 1808, he had given every indication that he was strong enough in intellect and steady enough in nerve to meet the challenges to come.

For the next seventeen years, the ambitious priest rose through the Jesuits' ranks in a host of tough jobs: he helped establish a solid parish base throughout New York and South Carolina and served as president of Georgetown College, where he succeeded his brother the Reverend Enoch Fenwick. His superiors were well aware that Benedict Fenwick was a star on the rise among their order, a man eager to plunge into the toughest jobs facing a church clinging to a growing but still tenuous foothold on hostile soil.

On May 10, 1825, the toughest task any Catholic priest could face was handed to Fenwick: he was named bishop of Boston. Even the brilliant, capable new bishop momentarily wondered if he was up to the job, for his diocese was not only Boston, stronghold of entrenched Puritan beliefs, but also the entire breadth of New England, home to perhaps the most anti-Catholic citizens in the nation. Still, no matter his doubts, the forty-two-year-old cleric sensed he was the man for the job.

When Fenwick arrived in Boston, he entered a city where Puritans had banned priests and where nobody had dared hold a Catholic service until 1788. Many of the city's residents longed for the good old days; vociferous foes of anything that hinted of popery, they did all they could in speeches and in print to reinstate the restrictions. But, as Fenwick learned, in the midst of Boston's Protestant South End was a Catholic church, Holy Cross Cathedral. The church was to be the headquarters from which he would reach out to Catholics from Rhode Island to Connecticut to the wilds of Maine. His flock was clamoring for priests and churches.

As Fenwick began addressing his diocese's entreaties in 1825, he learned to his dismay that in all of New England there were only two or three serviceable churches. Even worse, he had but two or three priests at his disposal.

Plunging into the task of creating a true diocese, Fenwick lined up lay assistants and began personal instruction of candidates for the collar. In 1827, he ordained two of his pupils, one of whom, zealous James Fitton, would become an invaluable missionary, organizing parishes in even remote regions of New England and proving Fenwick an astute judge of men committed to the cloth.

With his organizational flair, which won even the admiration of foes, and with a bull-like physical constitution, the bishop tirelessly set up parishes throughout his diocese. And hand in hand with the salvation of his flock's souls, he espoused educating its children's minds. He established a Sunday school at Holy Cross Cathedral; soon he expanded it into a day school in the church's basement, staffing it with candidates for the priesthood and offering the children of indigent immigrants a chance to receive some shred of education.

Proper—and not so proper—Bostonians were aghast at the speed and resolve with which the papist bishop attempted to consolidate a true Catholic diocese amid the stately spires of New England. In various newspapers, they vented their fears of Roman plots, conniving priests, and dark religious rites within convent walls—all the hackneyed but thriving propaganda that had poisoned many minds in the Old and New Worlds. Printed diatribes against popery and such raised Catholics' fears, especially among Irish, church members who irrationally believed that *every* Protestant was out to get them. Hatred and fear, born in Europe's religious wars and still scorching papist and "Proddy" hearts alike, confronted Fenwick in every project he undertook.

Seeking a vehicle to rebut printed attacks against him and his flock and to preclude Protestant misunderstanding of his goals, Fenwick founded the *Catholic Sentinel,* a newspaper whose first issue reached his parishioners' hands on September 5, 1829. (His paper exists today as the *Pilot.*) In Bishop Fenwick, the hard-pressed, hungry Irish Catholics streaming into Boston had a leader who was kindhearted almost to a fault, but unafraid to tangle in print or face-to-face with Boston's most virulent anti-Catholic forces.

Highlighting Fenwick's willingness to mix it up with his foes was his purchase of a Charlestown tract called Ploughed Hill. He decided to move a seminary of Ursuline nuns founded in Boston in 1820 to the site; in 1827, workmen laid down their saws and hammers and gazed up at their finished handiwork, a fine brick structure standing three stories. The Ursuline nuns proudly named their new home Mount St. Benedict in honor of their bishop and opened a school for girls in the convent, a school whose reputation for academic excellence would ironically lead Brahmans to send their daughters there. Little did they or Fenwick suspect that the stately convent would become the flashpoint for the religious hatred of Boston.

To Bostonians who felt that one order of nuns in the city was one too many, Fenwick's bringing a chapter of the Sisters of Charity to town in 1832 further heightened religious tensions. The new order opened a free school for the education of girls from impoverished families and also founded St. Vincent's Orphan Asylum. The nuns' good works, intended to help the community at large, convinced many Protestants that the Sisters of Charity were an asset to civic leaders trying to deal with the city's climbing population and its accompanying social problems. But hard-core haters of anything papist continued to see Catholic schemes even in the nuns' charitable agenda.

Fenwick hardly confined his activities to Boston. He traveled to isolated corners of his diocese to reach Catholics starving for churches and priests of their own. He visited Maine's Passamaquoddy Indians, many of whom were Catholics, the descendants of seventeenth-century converts, and assured them that they were as important to him as any other Catholics in his diocese. He delivered a similar message to the Indians of Old Town.

Having traveled all over New England and having seen there large tracts of land offering space for new communities and new churches, Fenwick urged many among Boston's swelling horde of Irish immigrants to consider a fresh start in other parts of the region. Backing up his proposition with the church's coffers, he purchased acreage in Aroostook County, Maine, in 1834; the land became the Catholic colony of Benedicta.

Despite Fenwick's advice that some local Catholics consider moving to the wilderness of Maine and other New England states, many preferred to remain in or near Boston, undoubtedly feeling that strength in numbers—Boston's rising Catholic population numbered about 10,000 in 1800—was the best protection against bigotry. In the late summer of 1834, that bigotry exploded with such force that Boston's Catholics and Protestants were equally jarred. The focal point of the tensions was the Ursuline convent.

By 1834, Mount St. Benedict had been expanded by two large wings enclosing a well-tended courtyard. Perched atop its grassy, terraced hill overlooking Charlestown, the convent's school had become a magnet for the daughters of many powerful Protestants, girls bearing such proud Yankee names as Adams, Endicott, and Storer. In August 1834, forty-four girls were enrolled at the school, ranging from six to eighteen years of age; no more than ten of the pupils were Catholics. But to many people near the convent, the notion of nuns teaching Protestant girls, not to mention Adamses and Endicotts sitting alongside Maguires and O'Briens, was akin to madness. Some Americans actually believed that the nuns used sordid, secret methods of brainwashing the girls.

Most of the students came from Unitarian families dissatisfied with the teaching methods of traditional schools. The parents were confident that the Ursulines were not converting Protestant girls to Roman Catholics. But other locals, especially working-class Protestants in Charlestown, loathed the nunnery as a Catholic invasion of the neighborhood and swallowed whole virtually any outlandish rumor about what went on behind the convent's walls. Mother Superior Mary Edmond St. George, lulled in part into a misguided sense of security by the fact that some of the best Protestant families favored her school above all others in the area, did not help matters with her imperious demeanor.

Fenwick was certainly aware of signs of trouble in Charlestown long before the summer of 1834. On Thanksgiving of 1833, a Protestant man was killed in a fight with Catholics in Charlestown. Some historians sympathetic to the Irish assert that a gang of Protestant toughs had burst into Roger McGowan's tavern to break up a dance. As tables, chairs, and fists flew in every direction, the Protestant was killed. But other historians write that a gang of drunken Irish brawlers looking for trouble beat the unfortunate man to death. Several nights later a mob of at least five hundred enraged Protestants swarmed to McGowan's house. Local politicians pleaded with the mob to disperse, and a contingent of marines dashed from the Charlestown Navy Yard to the scene. Refusing to listen, bent on revenge, the mob surged past the marines and razed the tavernkeeper's house. A New Hampshire man named John Buzzell led the charge.

Even more alarming to Fenwick and his priests than the attack against McGowan was the charade enacted by a young Charlestown girl named Rebecca Theresa Reed. A poor, bright young woman, Reed had abandoned her Protestant upbringing to convert to Catholicism. Father Patrick Byrne, her instructor, pleaded with Mother Superior St. George to accept Reed for free at the convent school in the hope that she could become a teacher. St. George sensed something unnerving about the girl's personality, but at Byrne's insistence the nun stifled her better instincts and accepted Reed. After all, converting a

Charlestown Protestant to the Catholic fold was an immense coup for Byrne.

Reed was a disaster from the moment she walked through the main gate of the convent. She quickly rebelled at the routines of the school and the tenets of the religion, and she neglected her studies. Mother Superior St. George decided that if the girl did not straighten herself out within six months, she would be dismissed—permanently. Reed, however, had another idea: a dramatic escape.

On January 18, 1832, less than four months from her arrival at the convent, Reed clambered up and over the fence that surrounded the brick building. The nuns and students watched through windows as Reed dropped from sight, smiles of relief on the faces of both Catholic and Protestant pupils.

Reed had cut and bruised herself during her escape, but her wounds were nothing compared to the damage her mouth began to cause once she was on the loose in Charlestown and Boston. To all who would listen, she claimed that the nuns knelt before Fenwick as though he were some potentate or had cast some spell on them; the bishop and the mother superior, the girl alleged, had been plotting to kidnap her to Canada for God knew what purpose. The latter was the reason for her desperate escape, Reed said. To heighten the effect of her lies, she acted them out, sparking outrage in minds all too willing to accept her falsehoods as truth.

A number of Protestant politicians and clerics who respected Fenwick dismissed the girl's rantings as nonsense, but her vivid lies foreshadowed another escape from the convent, an event with ruinous results for Mount St. Benedict.

On the afternoon of July 28, 1834, one of the Ursulines, Sister Mary John, formerly Elizabeth Harrison, wandered disoriented from the convent and turned up at the door of nearby brickmaster Edward Cutter. The nun, in a highly agitated mental state, begged Cutter to take her to the home of John Cotting, a West Cambridge man who had sent his daughters to the convent school. For reasons unknown, Charlestown selectman John Runey and his wife, rather than Cutter, loaded the dazed nun into their rig and drove her to Cotting's house. Cotting wondered what he was supposed to do with Sister Mary John and why she had asked for him, but took her in and tried to calm her.

Meanwhile, the Runeys drove to the convent and told Mother Superior St. George of her nun's plight and whereabouts. Wondering why the selectman had conveyed Sister Mary John all the way to West Cambridge, St. George hastily sent word to Fenwick in his residence near Holy Cross. Fenwick knew he had to reach the distraught nun before the news of her bolting from the convent spread wild rumors through every Protestant household and watering hole, and sent bigots to the fence of the convent. Within an hour or two he was at Cotting's home, asking to see Sister Mary John. But she refused to let Fenwick speak with her. Wisely avoiding a scene that might worsen the already delicate matter, Fenwick returned to his rectory, his facile mind seeking a way to head off any fallacious rumors that the nun had fled from abuse within the convent.

After a long night, Fenwick sent the nun's brother, Thomas Harrison, to Cambridge to visit his sister on July 29, 1834, to try to convince her to see the worried bishop. Whatever Harrison said to her worked, for he not only calmed her down, to the relief of the Cottings, but also persuaded her to let Fenwick make his appeal to return her to the convent and sort out her problems inside the cloister and out of sight of prying anti-Catholic eyes. With the silken tongue his Irish parishioners admiringly labeled the "gift of gab," the bishop assured her that if she still wanted to leave her order in two or three weeks, nobody would stand in her way, and he soothed any misgivings the nun had about returning to the convent. By the afternoon, he had brought her back to Mount St. Benedict, where the other nuns stared with anxiety and relief at their wayward friend. Also waiting was Dr. Abraham Thompson, who proceeded to examine Sister Mary John. She bore little resemblance to the dazed, frightened woman of the previous day.

With Sister Mary John safely inside the convent, Fenwick prayed that whatever her decision about her future it would be made away from public scrutiny; however, the proverbial genie was out of its bottle. It took the form of incredible lies depicting a wild-eyed nun fleeing unspeakable evils within the convent, only to be dragged back against her will for further depredations at the hands of the baleful bishop and the cruel mother superior. Such tales ran rampant throughout the city, rekindling the fantasies of Rebecca Reed from 1832. Trouble was simmering, and Fenwick knew it.

On the weekend following Sister Mary John's escape, a handful of Charlestown brickworkers met at a school within eyeshot of the convent. They talked of torching the nunnery but formulated no plan of attack—yet.

Four days later, they held another meeting, a larger one, according to historian George Potter, who, among later scholars, suspected that Boston firemen were also present and were deeply involved in the stunning events that followed. Apparently, the would-be incendiaries had learned of Fenwick's reported assurances that Sister Mary John could leave the convent of her own free will by the third week of August. Cooler heads—such as there were among the men itching for a chance to teach the papists a lesson—momentarily held sway: the volatile band of workmen and street toughs allegedly agreed to hold back any assault upon the convent until Fenwick's two to three weeks were up and everyone saw whether the nun had departed Mount St. Benedict.

Street gossip of a possible attack against the convent reached Fenwick and the mother superior, the latter believing, as did Charlestown's selectmen, that the controversy would ebb and disappear. But on August 8, 1834, the *Boston Mercantile Journal* ran a glaringly irresponsible article hinting that Sister Mary John had been coerced into taking nun's vows and was, in effect, a prisoner at the convent. Other newspapers quickly jumped on the story and ran similar accounts in their Saturday editions. Outraged readers turned their eyes toward the hilltop nunnery.

Words flew frantically from Fenwick's pen within hours of the first inflammatory article. His dashed-off denial of all allegations of misdeeds inside the convent ran in the Saturday afternoon edition of the *Boston Transcript*. It promised all readers, Catholic and Protestant, a true and detailed account of the strange case of Sister Mary John. The embattled bishop, wishing he could have written an in-depth rebuttal that Saturday but forced to rush his attempt at damage control to meet the *Transcript*'s deadline, was desperately striving to defuse the anti-Catholic forces.

By 8 P.M. on August 11, 1834, hundreds of Protestant workmen had gathered in front of the convent's wrought-iron fence. Brick mason John R. Buzzell shoved his six-foot-six-inch frame to the main gate and bellowed for silence.

Renowned from Nashua to Boston for his boxing and wrestling skills and for his "fearful power," the twenty-nine-year-old Buzzell always bragged that he could beat up any Irishman and routinely challenged to fight three at once.[1] He had had few takers. He had boasted that he had showed Irishmen "how things were settled in this country."[2]

Brandishing a large club above his head, Buzzell had been spoiling for action since that morning, when another workman had told him that men were going "to take down the nunnery tonight."[3] Early that evening, a spokesman for the workers had visited Buzzell at his rooming house and had said, "You are just the man . . . to lead us."[4] Buzzell had eagerly agreed and rushed to the crowded gates of the convent.

At 9:30 P.M., Buzzell led the men up the circular path to Mount St. Benedict. Shouts of "down with the convent" echoed over the hillside.[5]

Mother Superior St. George confronted Buzzell at the front door. He demanded the release of Sister Mary John. She refused, and taunts rang out from the crowd. "She was," Buzzell later said, "the sauciest woman I ever heard talk."[6]

Buzzell and the crowd retreated, but did not disperse, milling around the fence instead. When Mother Superior St. George reappeared, this time at an open window, and loudly reproached the men, many of them drunk, the mob looked to Buzzell. Several men had torches.

The mother superior ordered the nuns and the boarding students to the convent's summerhouse, at the edge of the back courtyard. Then, before joining the others, she alone checked every room in the convent to make sure all the children had been led to the cottage.

Within an hour or two the mob's numbers swelled to nearly seven hundred, but no one approached the empty convent. Then, around 11:30 P.M., Buzzell dashed into the building with scores of others behind him. They toppled furniture and smashed it, and looted desks, bureaus, cabinets, and cupboards. A thousand dollars in boarding fees ended up in the pockets of workmen who rifled the mother superior's desk.

Dozens of men tossed Bibles and other books through windows. Snatching them from the nun's closets, several looters donned habits and danced obscenely. A man found one of Fenwick's robes hanging in a hall closet and masqueraded as the bishop for his laughing companions. Another group of vandals heaved three pianos and a harp through windows. The convent ransacked, the mob turned to Buzzell again. He grabbed a torch from another worker.

By 1 A.M., flames engulfed the convent, the chapel, the schoolhouse, Fenwick's lodge, the barn, and the stables.

At the foot of the convent's garden, Buzzell and company burst into the adjoining Catholic tombs, smashed them open, tore nameplates from coffins as souvenirs, and broke open a casket to expose a corpse. Another knot of workers found a chest of Communion wafers hurriedly hidden in a bush by one of the nuns, and tossed them all over the grounds. By dawn only charred, crumbling buildings covered the grounds. The city's firemen had stood by and done nothing. Fortunately, no one had harmed the nuns and students in the summerhouse.

Most Bostonians, even those who cared little for Catholics, were horrified. Brahman Harrison Gray Otis and other proper Bostonians vowed that "the Protestant citizens of Boston would unite with our

Catholic brethren in protecting their persons, their property, and their civil and religious rights."[7]

To his everlasting credit, Fenwick, distraught, calmed his parish. But he insisted on a trial of the miscreants. The local politicians gave him one.

Twelve ringleaders, including Buzzell, were tried on charges of burglary and arson. The accused strode into court on December 2, 1834, confident that fellow Yankees on the jury would never convict them.

Sixteen witnesses detailed Buzzell's role as the ringleader as well as the acts of wanton destruction all twelve defendants had committed on that fiery night. The prosecutors presented an airtight case.

The defense attorneys gutted the evidence against their clients by resorting to anti-Catholic, anti-Irish smear tactics that brought nods and sometimes laughter from the jurors.

Buzzell and his eleven henchmen strolled from the trial as free men. Near Boston Common, the courthouse filled with cheers from local workmen immediately after the verdict. Hundreds of Buzzell's supporters held a victory party during which liquor flowed. Buzzell held a press conference in which he ranted against Irish Catholics in particular and the Catholic church in general. This performance was his last public foray; he soon dropped from history's sight. Many of his friends claimed he headed home to New Hampshire.

For decades, Buzzell's generalship in the first and last burning of a New England convent remained a tinderbox of antipathy between New England's Catholics and Protestants. Bishop Fenwick labored twelve more years to bring at least an uneasy truce between the two faiths, but with scant success.

On August 11, 1846, Fenwick died of a heart problem; one historian later wrote that the cause was weariness. The bishop's death came on the twelfth anniversary of the convent blaze.

The *Pilot*, the newspaper Fenwick had founded, wrote that he had died "on the very day on which he had drank the bitterest chalice of affliction during the whole course of his apostolic labors."[8] John Buzzell, the six-foot-six-inch brick mason and brigand, had filled the chalice.

A Royal
Scandal

〜

In May 1887, Boston rolled out the red carpet for a royal visitor, one *The Boston Globe* called "the dusky Queen Kapiolani, mistress of the Sandwich Isles [Hawaii]."[1] From the moment the queen and her large retinue checked into the tony Parker House and hotel officials raised "the ensign of Hawaii"[2] atop the building's flagstaff, Mayor Hugh O'Brien, the city and state's legislators, and Boston's Brahmans fell all over themselves to impress her. "The most disgraceful affair in the history of junketing in this city" was unfolding, and the "royal scandal" would swirl about the mayor, a man who had risen far above his beginnings and had done so by prudent management of city funds.[3] Or at least until Queen Kapiolani swept into town.

Only about two-and-a-half years before the mistress of the Sandwich Isles settled into a Parker House suite, Hugh O'Brien had reveled in his own status as the toast of Boston. He had been sworn in as the city's first Irish-born mayor on January 5, 1885. To many Yankees and Brahmans, his ascent represented a once unthinkable development in a region notable for its antipathy toward Irish Catholics.

O'Brien's odyssey to the top of the heap in Boston politics began in 1832, when his parents emigrated from Ireland to Boston with their five-year-old son. He displayed a considerable intelligence early on, but was yanked from the public school system at twelve to work as an apprentice to a printer for the *Boston Courier*. A tradesman's future beckoned the youth, lucky that he could escape the low-paying and insecure street-sweeping or dockside work so many of his fellow Irish immigrants were forced to take. Young O'Brien, however, set his eyes on a far loftier future—one amid the rarefied circles of Yankee commerce.

Following his stint at the *Courier,* O'Brien took a slot at the private printing firm of Tuttle, Dennett, and Chisholm, on School Street, learning the ins and outs not only of printing, but also of publishing. Eventually he put both his knowledge and ambition to the test by publishing *Shipping and Commercial List*. His publication was a smash hit among merchants and financiers who depended in any way upon the flow of goods and business news across Boston's docks. The Irish Catholic had accomplished quite a feat in making himself indispensable to well-heeled Protestants whose Back Bay and Beacon Hill brownstones generally meant only one thing to immigrants of the old sod—backbreaking work as maids or handymen. Brahmans who mocked "Paddy, the hopeless, witty Irishman, given to drink and quick to tears and laughter, who loved nothing more than 'rows and ructions,' and Bridget, the chaste and prudent but comically ignorant serving girl," looked grudgingly at O'Brien in a different light.[4] Many upscale Bostonians began to view him as an anomaly—one of the good Irish.

O'Brien's business value to New England merchants and moguls notwithstanding, the question of how far the ambitious publisher could rise among the "Irish-hating ice-cicles of Yankeeland"[5] intrigued local Democratic leaders who ruled the city's Irish neighborhoods. In 1875, the forty-nine-year-old businessman won election to Boston's Board of Aldermen, and the watchful eyes of the Irish community noticed when, over the next seven years, even hard-boiled Yankees lauded his "conscientious hard work."[6]

As a self-made man embracing New England traditions of industriousness and self-discipline, O'Brien contradicted the vicious stereotypes of Paddy and Bridget espoused by Brahmans inside their boardrooms, clubs, and mansions, and by poor Yankee workmen on construction sites and in local watering holes. The Democrats of the Irish community first put O'Brien's political palatability to the test in late 1883 by nominating the publisher and alderman as the party's mayoral candidate.

In the weeks before voters hit the boxes, many Yankees recoiled against the notion of an Irish-born mayor. They attacked his character—but not with the ethnic ammunition many Bostonians expected. The *Boston Transcript*, the political conduit of conservative Protestants, did not assail O'Brien's birthplace or his papist religion, but raised allegations of his "junketeering" as an alderman.[7]

On election night, the Irish turned out in force for their candidate, a man who, in his financial outlook, shared more in common with his Protestant and Republican foe, Augustus Martin, than with fellow immigrants. O'Brien lost the election, but by a narrow margin.

A year later, the name Hugh O'Brien once again topped the Democratic mayoral ticket, and enough Yankee voters swallowed misgivings about the Irish-born candidate to help the immigrant poor sweep him into office. His campaign platform of lower taxes and his proven ability as an alderman to back that promise had been a fiscal siren's song too sweet for many Brahmans to resist.

Hugh O'Brien took the oath of office on January 5, 1885, heralding a new political era for Boston and for the region. He wasted little time in keeping his campaign promises of sound spending and lower taxes, worked to improve the city's parks and roads, and helped to lay the groundwork of the Boston Public Library, where even Paddy and Bridget would be allowed to read and study.

Off to such a promising start in the mayor's office, O'Brien won reelection in late 1886, and as the first few months of 1887 passed, his conservative hand on the proverbial tiller of the city's finances continued to earn him the trust of even the stodgiest Yankees. Trouble loomed for the mayor, however, trouble in the guise of a royal visitor accustomed to the finest accouterments money could buy. And the guest's first-class tastes would stir up a first-class financial mess.

Determined to prove that Boston's accommodations were fit for a luminary accustomed to the finer things, from London to New York, the Parker House, "on hospitality intent," spared "no expense . . . in preparing the rooms for their royal occupants."[8] As Queen Kapiolani moved about her suite, she found it crammed with flowers including a special arrangement—the Hawaiian words for "I Love You" emblazoned "in letters of red immortelles upon a bank of similax and ferns."

Local florists handed carte blanche by city officials in the decoration of the queen's suite had created "bowers of floral beauty"[9] in each room.

After the guests had rested a bit in the fragrant rooms and eaten breakfast, the church bells tolled across Boston. The queen and her coterie, all swathed in the most dignified and stylish modes of European dress, swept down the hotel's staircase, through the grand entrance, and into their carriages for a jaunt to their first Boston landmark, Trinity Church.

Inside the stately church, the customary eloquence of the Reverend Phillips Brooks vied with the sight of "the strange visitors" for the parishioners' attention, "the most fashionable set in town" straining for a glimpse of the ruler of the exotic islands. The scene repeated itself at a service at historic King's Chapel, where the queen and her retainers settled into "quaint, high-backed pews" and "formed the center of attraction for the staid churchgoers who cling to the church of their fathers."[10]

Following the service at King's Chapel, Kapiolani enjoyed one of the few lulls in her Boston sojourn, the "visitors . . . allowed to follow their own inclinations" before the "official courtesies" that would intrigue New Englanders for the next week.[11] The civic and financial fallout of the upcoming week would turn intrigue into outrage.

A reporter commented that, beginning with breakfast on Monday, May 9, 1887, the queen and her retinue were "not allowed much time to waste in idleness."[12] Over breakfast in her suite at the Parker House, she received civic dignitaries and assorted Brahmans, the region's moguls and mavens dressed tastefully and fashionably for their chat with the monarch. Since deferential bows and nods from the society set and dignified gestures from the queen were the chief forms of communication, those who had brief audiences with Kapiolani could only speculate about "her opinions concerning the very elaborate official courtesies of which she is the recipient."[13] A reporter wrote that he wanted "to chronicle her opinions," but could not because "the Hawaiian language is not generally understood in Boston."[14]

Shortly after the receiving line in the queen's suite receded, she was driven to the Old South Church. There, she stared at Revolutionary War artifacts, "manifesting great admiration for the heroes of 1776."[15]

The next stop on Kapiolani's itinerary was an official breakfast, if a noontime meal could truly be considered breakfast. Mayor O'Brien hosted the affair in special honor of the queen and Princess Lili-uokalani, the strains of an orchestra wafting above crowded tables, the fragrance of yet another elaborate floral exhibition filling the room. The gathering comprised Boston's glitterati, guests distinguished in municipal affairs, politics, literature, and society, "each gentleman ac-companied by a lady."[16] In one onlooker's assessment, the meal and the following reception were a smashing success.

The guest of honor capped off her whirlwind Monday with an evening at the theater—two theaters, the Boston and the Globe, to be exact—where, once again, surrounded by the city's high-born and highly placed, she attracted more attention than the on-stage action.

Although Queen Kapiolani would spend a week in town, the of-ficial high-water mark of her sojourn came on Tuesday, May 10, with her visit to the State House, where Senator Morse, of Canton, Mass-achusetts, was delivering a speech from the podium. Suddenly the sen-ate chamber's massive doors were flung open. Morse fell silent. Sergeant-at-Arms Adams, "in all the glory of his tall hat, ornamented with a rosette and carrying the official mace," marched into the main aisle and stopped.[17]

"Her Majesty, the Queen of the Sandwich Islands!" the Sergeant-at-Arms proclaimed.[18]

Senate President Boardman cracked his gavel, and every man in the chamber stood. Preceded up the aisle by Adams, Queen Kapi-olani strode between rows of Democrats and Republicans who gen-erally behaved in that room with far less decorum than they showed to the mistress of the Sandwich Isles. In turn, the monarch bowed gravely to the state's power brokers.

For the rest of Kapiolani's stay, her rounds of nonstop official breakfasts, lunches, dinners, receptions, and tours continued, as did nightly visits to the Boston and the Globe Theaters. By the time the queen's stay in Boston ended, everyone who was anyone had met her.

Within a few weeks of the queen's departure, the bills for her visit came due. Mayor O'Brien found himself confronted with a public-relations nightmare precluding business as usual. "Scandal Over the Bills for Queen Kapiolani's Entertainment"—this and other such headlines filled the newspapers in late May 1887.[19]

O'Brien, who had overcome previous allegations of his penchant for junketeering, scrambled to cover the first bills of the queen's tour—$18,000, a staggering amount given her week-long stay. Boston's citizens were outraged at the figure, but only the mayor and his staff knew that the reported $18,000 was just the beginning of the monarch's expenses. Many of the larger bills, including the hefty tab for the week's lodging and meals at the Parker House, had not been detected by the press; the mayor and his staff wanted to keep it that way.

The bills already revealed to the public ignited "the biggest kind of row."[20] Among them lay an invoice for $4,500 worth of flowers from the Galvin brothers. Crowed a reporter: "Even Councilman Whall, Chairman of the Entertainment Committee, blushed when this bill was presented."[21]

At first, O'Brien refused to pay the Galvins. When they threatened to stir up trouble for him, the mayor, too immersed in the financial furor that was escalating into a bona fide scandal, settled up to head off any "row [that] would have caused all the facts to become public property . . . [as] this would not do."[22] By paying the Galvins, "a sensation was spoiled."[23]

The Galvins's "sensation" was merely one of many for the mayor in the financial fallout from Kapiolani's visit. Thus began a cover-up. Creative bookkeeping noted in the press claimed that the Parker House had billed the city a suspiciously modest $2,800. In the frenzy of questionable accounting, politicians buried, relabeled, or paid outrageous bills privately. One of the most notorious invoices undisclosed to the public came from the Victoria Hotel, which had hosted an official reception for the queen and her retinue. About one hundred guests had attended the fete and had rung up a bar tab for more than one hundred gallons of assorted liquor. A reporter remarked that, by his estimate, each guest downed a *gallon* of spirits.

The scandal died slowly, Mayor O'Brien's reputation for efficiency allowing him in large part to weather the controversy. The furor did not derail the career of Boston's first Irish-born mayor, who would win reelection in 1887. But in the minds of some locals, Queen Kapiolani's sojourn left a black eye on the city's political visage. Most Bostonians agreed with a reporter who labeled the royal visit "the most disgraceful affair in the history of junketing in this city."[24]

Rebels
with
a
Cause

Henry Pelham:
Betrayed by Paul Revere?

Young artist Henry Pelham was enraged, spewing words upon paper on the morning of March 27, 1770. The target of his wrath had, in Pelham's view, forged one of Pelham's drawings, printed it, and was reaping eight pence per print. The image in question vividly depicted the Boston Massacre and was destined to become one of the most famous engravings in America's annals. It was also the first image of the coming Revolution.

Who had stolen Pelham's drawing? The artist charged *Paul Revere*.

Henry Pelham, in his early twenties in 1770, was half-brother to John Singleton Copley, renowned on both sides of the Atlantic as a portraitist; while never to match his relative's fame, Pelham was a gifted artist in his own right, skilled especially in miniatures and works on enamel. To art lovers of the day, Pelham's face—if not his work—was familiar, immortalized in Copley's 1766 painting *The Boy with the Squirrel,* in which the thoughtful young man was Henry Pelham. As captured on Copley's canvas, Pelham's high forehead; large, pensive eyes; and serious visage portrayed a boy whose mind was not rife with boyish thoughts but was gravely pondering concerns more fitting to a grown man. The boy's demeanor reflected an aspiring artist already aware of the long creative shadow of his half-brother. Despite Copley's growing fame, Pelham was devoted to him.

Pelham knew the value of a pound or pence. After the death of his father, Peter Pelham, in 1751, the boy's mother, Mary Pelham, had struggled to keep food in the cupboard. In their home at the corner of modern Exchange Crossing and Congress Streets, she ran a tobacco shop, and she counted on the budding talents of her boys—especially Copley—to lift the family to success and riches.

In March 1770, as Boston seethed with unrest against the British, twenty-one-year-old Pelham seized an opportunity to put his talent to a test that might have seemed heaven sent had it not been so gory. On the evening of March 5, 1770, redcoats' muskets roared on King Street in front of the brick walls of the Custom House, and colonists were pitched torn and bleeding onto snow-shrouded cobblestones. Never had an event so polarized and traumatized the town as the infamous Boston Massacre. Pelham encountered company in his determination to create a memorable drawing of the night when frightened redcoats unloaded their muskets into a mob of Rebels and innocent onlookers. Paul Revere, the skilled artisan and silversmith of Boston's North End, harbored the same idea.

In preparation for an engraving, Revere sketched the scene on paper in black and white, diagramming King Street, its intersecting lanes, the Town House, the Custom House, and other buildings surrounding the scene of the massacre. But the most graphic element of the sketch was its depiction of the dead: they were not only marked by initials— "A" for Crispus Attucks, "G" for Samuel Gray, "C" for James Caldwell, and another "G," for Samuel Maverick, a young apprentice of a man named Isaac Greenwood—but also shown lying twisted on King Street and Quaker Lane. (Another victim, Patrick Carr, his spine blown apart by a British ball, died on March 9, four days after he was hit.) Revere noted the British soldiers, standing in front of the Custom House, by a tight knot of circles with protruding lines representing the murderous muskets.

Scholars would later speculate that Revere's sketch was rendered within a day or so of the massacre. The graphic sketches hinted that the artist had actually seen the bodies on the streets, and since the handwriting on the image was apparently Revere's, the sketch would usually remain attributed to him.

Revere was soon at work on his engraving, which he intended to sell as prints on Boston's streets and in its shops. Many historians believe he hired Christopher Remick, a local artist, to hand-color the engravings. If so, Remick's liberal use of scarlet for the "lobsterbacks' " greatcoats and victims' blood presented a grisly and masterful bit of propaganda, underscoring that the red-coated British had stained Boston's cobblestones with colonial blood. The imagery was bold and powerful and during the trial of the British soldiers who had fired into the crowd, defense attorney and future Rebel John Adams urged the jurors to disregard the already controversial print as evidence because it distorted the facts.

As effective as the elements of Revere's engraving were, his scene misrepresented many aspects of the actual Boston Massacre. Crispus Attucks, a large, powerfully built Black man, was pictured as short—and White. In the print, several victims were sprawled bleeding on a snowless street beneath a blue sky; however, the massacre unfolded on a cold night across snow-topped King Street.

According to historians, Revere's greatest distortion was his treatment of the British soldiers. In his version, the redcoats stood in a neat firing line, their faces composed and bearing a cold, tight-lipped collective visage that was close to a sneer or even a smile. Their commander, Captain Preston, lurked behind his red-coated butchers with his sword raised, seemingly cheering them on as, swathed in clouds of powder smoke, the troops pumped musket balls into the stunned crowd.

Butchery was the theme of the engraving, and if viewers had any doubt about that, Revere dispelled them with a sign that rested above the redcoats' dark Monmouth caps, on the facade of the Custom House. The sign was emblazoned with the words "Butcher's Hall." No such sign hung from the brick walls of the Custom House, a fact every Bostonian knew but that many were willing to overlook in their rage at the British.

That anger escalated soon after the appearance of an advertisement in the *Boston Gazette:*

To be sold by Edes and Gill
(Price Eight Pence Lawful Money)
A Print Containing a Representation of the
late horrid Massacre in King Street

Revere's print had hit the streets stoking locals' hatred of the red-coats. Revere realized every artist's dream—his work had a resounding and immediate impact.

The image of "the late horrid massacre" also had a strong effect on another artist, Henry Pelham. Revere's drawing and the one Pelham had been laboring on looked nearly identical. The sight of the words "Engrav'd Printed & Sold by Paul Revere, Boston," on the print assailed Pelham's artistic pride.

On the morning of March 27, 1770, the day after Revere's advertisement had run, Henry Pelham picked up a quill and scratched out a letter to the silversmith. Outrage filled every line of the artist's missive:

Thursday morning, Boston, March 27, 1770

Sir

When I heard that you was cutting a plate of the late Murder, I thought it impossible, as I knew you was not capable of doing it unless you copied it from mine and as I thought I had entrusted it in the hands of a person who had more regard to the dictates of Honour and Justice than to take the undue advantage you have done of the confidence and Trust I reposed in you. But I find I was mistaken and after being at the great Trouble and Expence of making a design paying for paper printing etc. find myself in the most unevergenerous Manner deprived not only of a proposed Advantage but even of the expense I have been at, as truly as if You had plundered me on the Highway. If you are insensible of the Dishonour you have brought on yourself by this Act, the World will not be so. However I leave you to reflect upon and consider of one of the most dishonorable Action you could be guilty of.

H. Pelham

P.S. I sent by the Bearer of the prints I borrowed of you. My Mother desires you would send the hinges and part of the press, that you had from her.

Paul Revere, a thief? A man who betrayed another's trust?

According to Pelham's use of the word "entrusted," Revere had seen Pelham's drawing of the massacre; and it does not take a scholar or an art critic to grasp the similarities between the two drawings when placed side by side. In both renderings, the soldiers, the crowd, the perspective, and each artist's Crispus Attucks—erroneously drawn as White and short—are virtually identical.

Supporting Pelham's assertion that he had arranged for printing his drawing is a March 1770 bill requesting him to pay Daniel Rea, Jr., two pounds for paper and nearly four pounds for 575 prints.

In today's courts, Pelham's case might have been a winner—even though Revere could have asked Pelham to prove his drawing was done first. But in the eighteenth century, questions of copyright were murky; printers in England and America routinely ran off copies of works by artists and writers without the creators' permission and often with no mention of their names. Artists and authors whose work had been purloined had little or no legal recourse.

Although Pelham asserted that the world would revile Revere for his plundering Pelham's drawing, his words reflected the naïveté of a young artist smarting from a rookie's mistake in the bruising big leagues of eighteenth-century printing. Whether or not one chooses to believe Pelham's charges, Revere, nearly fifteen years older than Pelham, knew how to play the printer's game. He had beaten the younger man to a printing press. Pelham's friends sympathized with him; but most printers would have said with a shrug of their shoulders or an adjustment of a tri-cornered hat, "Let it be a lesson to you, lad."

Still determined to present his print to the town, Pelham brought his work to printers Edes & Gill & T. & J. Fleet. On April 9, 1770, Pelham's prints went on sale. Their pricetag was eight pence apiece—

the same amount Revere charged. Unlike Revere's print, however, Pelham's work bore no signature and proved a poor seller.

Revere and Pelham reached an uneasy truce in their professional relationship; however, the fact that Revere was still selling his Boston Massacre prints several years after the bloody event galled Pelham.

With the onset of the Revolutionary War in April 1775, Paul Revere mounted his horse and rode into legend. Henry Pelham's life took a decidedly different course; the young artist who had portrayed redcoats gunning down his neighbors was by the war's beginning a Tory convinced that the Rebel cause was madness. While riding to Philadelphia in 1775, he was surrounded by a mob of patriots in Springfield, Massachusetts, who screamed oaths and threats at him. He managed to gallop unscathed from Springfield, but realized that dark days stretched ahead for Loyalists in New England.

Once Massachusetts exploded in rebellion in 1776, Pelham did not linger long in Boston. He fled his birthplace and set sail for London to join his famous half-brother, Copley, portrait painter of nobility. Having such a noted relative opened doors in English society for Pelham, who taught art, astronomy, and geography, and turned out some engravings and miniatures.

Pelham had found a new life in the British Isles, but he also found tragedy. He married Catherine Butler, of Castle Crine, in Ireland, but she died bearing twin boys. In April 1789, he and Copley learned that their mother, Mary, had passed away in Boston. For Pelham, utterly devoted to the woman who had scraped to feed and house her boys, the death of Mary Pelham was a devastating blow that launched him into depression.

Henry Pelham returned to work as an agent to the Irish estates of Lord Landsdowne, overseeing a wide range of engineering projects and using his artist's skills to draft maps of Ireland destined to prove invaluable to future scholars. In 1806, while supervising the construction of a tower, Henry Pelham drowned in the waters of the River Kenmare—far from the banks of another river, the Charles, that "the boy with the squirrel" had known so well, far from the town where Pelham believed artistic acclaim had been snatched from him by a man named Revere.

Obscurity might have forever buried Pelham had his letter to Revere not turned up in the collection of the Massachusetts Historical Society. Many historians now refer to the familiar print of the Boston Massacre as the work of both Revere and Pelham.

History has not been as kind as it once was to Paul Revere. Hordes of critics have attempted to debunk his hallowed ride in favor of William Dawes's and to accuse Revere of stealing other artists' work, including that of famed American painter Benjamin Church. Revere did have his flaws, but he remains a remarkable player in the drama of a fledgling nation struggling for freedom. He is a chipped icon of our past, but nonetheless a worthy icon. And his critics should remember one thing: while his ride may not have proven the mythic stuff of Longfellow's poem, Revere *did* mount up on that fateful April night in 1775.

Still, Pelham's supporters might rewrite Longfellow's words thusly:

Listen my children and you shall hear,
of a *privateer* named Paul Revere.

A Comrade in Arms: Peter Salem

On June 17, 1775, behind battered earthworks, the Rebel poured the last traces of powder into his musket and rammed home his last ball. Bodies were strewn all around him, some in homespun colonial shirts stained with blood. Many more of the dead and wounded were clad in the scarlet coats and white cross-belts of George III's regulars.

Minuteman Peter Salem, a sturdy, twenty-eight-year-old laborer, steeled himself, as did the Rebels around him, for the climax of the battle. Although hundreds of redcoats lay sprawled on the grassy slope beneath the American fortifications, their groans and sobs drifting through the clouds of smoke, the British were forming columns again, for a third charge.

With the rattle of drums and the tramp of boots and buckled shoes, the red wave moved slowly up Breed's Hill, the burning roofs and steeples of Charlestown visible through the haze below them. Some colonists manning the redoubt stole a quick glimpse of their homes, some of them for the last time.

Closing the gap, the redcoats leveled their bayonets. Salem scanned the oncoming mass for a target, preferably an officer. According to many accounts, a Rebel officer had cried: "Don't fire until you see the whites of their eyes!" In repulsing the first two assaults, Salem and his comrades had obeyed that dictate.

With a collective howl the redcoats broke from a quick walk into a run and swarmed below the redoubts. The Rebels' muskets barked, and scores of British toppled. Still, they regrouped and kept coming up the slope.

Slowly, the patriots gave way, edging backward from their defenses. A British major allegedly cried: "The day is ours!"[1]

Salem's musket cracked, and its ball reportedly tore through the officer's head or chest.

As John Pitcairn crumpled to the ground, a hated symbol of British tyranny went down. Back in April 1775, Salem had stood with his fellow Minutemen at Concord and had seen Major Pitcairn order his redcoats to clear the town green of Rebels.

Peter Salem was not just any Minuteman. He was Black—a slave. And amid the carnage of the Battle of Bunker Hill, he and another man named Salem became America's first Black war heroes. Years later, painter John Trumbull would feature Peter Salem in a famed painting of the clash.

Peter Salem was born into slavery in 1748 or 1749 in Framingham, Massachusetts, the property of Dr. Jeremy Belknap. The slave's days were spent working on Belknap's small farm, running endless errands for the physician. Salem nonetheless paid attention to the growing dissension between colonists and the British. Even when he was sold to another Framingham man, Lawson Buckminster, Salem eyed the coming struggle as a potential means to a new life in a new order. Historian Sidney Kaplan writes: "When the embattled farmers fired the shot heard round the world, it is probable that in New England most Blacks saw their destiny, if only dimly, in the triumph of a democratic revolution that might somehow, in the shakeup of things, give substance to its slogans [of freedom for all]."[2]

When the Minutemen gathered at the North Bridge in Concord on April 19, 1775, Peter Salem stood with them, his musket primed. Freed to volunteer with Simon Edgel's company of Framingham Minutemen. Drilling shoulder-to-shoulder with Whites who owned slaves, Salem prepared for his chance to prove himself in any fight for freedom. After each drill ended, he returned to his slave's quarters.

As Salem slept in his shed on the evening of April 18, 1775, seven hundred redcoats began a roughly twenty-mile march from their Boston billets with orders to seize the Minutemen's stores of powder and shot in Concord. Rousted from sleep by the alarm of a rider, Salem grabbed his musket and powder horn, scrambled to his place in the ranks, and marched to Concord.

The redcoats reached Lexington early on the morning of April 19, 1775. On the village green, some seventy men—mainly tradesmen, merchants, and farmers—faced the neat columns of redcoats. Among the Minutemen stood several free Blacks: Pompey, from Braintree; Brookline resident Joshua Boylston's ex-slave Prince; Cuff Whitemore; and Cato Wood. A future Black minister named Lemuel Haynes also claimed a spot among the patriots, and of that day's clashes would write about "the inhuman Tragedy Perpetrated on the 19th of April 1775 by a Number of the British Troops . . . which Parricides and Ravages Are Shocking Displays of Ministerial & Tyrannic Vengeance."[3]

As the colonials on the green refused to disperse, Major Pitcairn shouted: "Lay down your arms, damn you! Why don't you lay down your arms?"

"The shot heard round the world" rang out—no one knows whether a redcoat or a Minuteman squeezed the trigger. Ragged volleys followed, eight colonists falling dead.

The rest fled from the green and dashed with other Minutemen to Concord. They joined with several hundred other colonists to drive the redcoats from the North Bridge and force them "to run with greatest precipitance."[4] Throughout that long, bloody April day, the first of the Revolution, Peter Salem fired at redcoats as he crouched behind stone walls, houses, and barns almost all the way to Boston. By nightfall, 270 redcoats were killed or wounded. The man that many Rebels condemned for having "caused the first effusion of blood" was Major Pitcairn.[5]

Along with his former master, Lieutenant Buckminster, Salem and several hundred other Rebels crawled across Charlestown Neck past British sentries some eight weeks later. General Artemas Ward had ordered the patriots to dig in on the steep slopes of Bunker Hill, but the troops mistakenly fortified Breed's Hill, a lower incline.

When an unseasonably hot day broke across Boston, British commander Thomas Gage went into a rage at the sight of the entrenched colonists. He summoned his officers and ordered them to prepare a direct frontal assault, rejecting the sound advice of General Henry Clinton to attack the Rebels from the rear as well.

As 2,500 regulars piled into longboats and were rowed to Morton's Hill, British warships opened up on the Rebels and were joined by batteries on Copp's Hill, in the North End. Salem and his comrades huddled behind their makeshift earthworks as the cannonballs tore up chunks of Breed's Hill and claimed a handful of men.

Finally, the bombardment lifted. Salem and the other patriots raised their heads and stared at a chilling scene. Dense columns of red-coats, their regimental colors nodding in the wan breeze, the sun glinting off neat rows of bayonets, advanced down Morton's Hill, crossed the small level meadow leading to Breed's Hill, and surged up the slope in perfect order toward the Rebel's redoubts. The British drums thumped louder. Several colonists wavered, then bolted down the back of the slope. From a warship in the harbor, British general "Gentleman Johnny" Burgoyne would write that the advancing redcoats furnished "one of the greatest scenes of war that can be conceived."[6] But he also would note that "a defeat [at Breed's Hill] was a final loss to the British Empire in America."[7]

As the first wave of regulars approached the bastion, the order to hold fire "until you see the whites of their eyes" echoed among Salem and the other colonists. Suddenly, a deafening roar burst from hundreds of colonial muskets. The muzzles' smoke shrouded the hill's summit. Then, through gaps in the smoke, the colonists saw the redcoats fleeing down the slope, leaving scores of dead and wounded behind them. A cheer burst from the breastworks.

The Rebels' shouts ebbed as the British reassembled their ranks and, once again with the rattle of drums, tramped up the hill in close order, officers marching with their swords leveled at the colonists. For a second time they neared the earthworks, and another jarring volley cracked from the massed patriots. The British lurched back to the bottom of the hill, leaving hundreds more still or writhing redcoats on the slope.

Some of the Rebels believed that the battle was over, a stunning victory against King George III's vaunted regulars. And with colonial powder horns and cartridge boxes nearly empty, there was great relief among the Rebels at the apparent end of the fray.

At the bottom of the hill, sergeant-majors and officers were swiping the flats of their swords at the men who had survived the two charges. Slowly, the scarlet columns reassembled. The drums boomed again, and regimental colors shredded by musket balls reappeared above the men's heads, many of them bare because the Rebels' volleys had knocked bearskin shakos and black, tri-cornered Monmouth hats from their owners.

The regulars moved forward for the third time. Panic washed across the colonists as the bayonets neared, the redcoated ranks trampling their dead and wounded as the distance to the redoubts waned. Scores of British slipped on the blood-stained grass, fell, and climbed right back into line.

Sporadic volleys flared from Rebels who were down to their last shots. All around Salem, patriots gave way as the British neared the redoubts with brandished bayonets. "Among the foremost of the leaders was the gallant Major Pitcairn, who exultantly cried 'the day is ours!' " a colonist would recall. "Salem, a black solider . . . shot him through and he fell."[8] Another Rebel would write that "a negro man . . . took aim at Major Pitcairne [*sic*], as he was rallying the dispersed British Troops, & shot him thro' the head."[9]

Moments later Salem joined his retreating comrades, his musket still in hand, and as British musket balls whizzed past, stumbled to safety.

Although the redcoats had chased the Rebels from their hilltop perch, the victory was truly Pyrrhic, the redcoats having suffered 228 dead and 828 wounded, a staggering casualty rate of 42 percent (10 percent is considered high by military experts).

As the man who reportedly killed the infamous Major Pitcairn, Salem merits consideration as the first Black hero among the manumitted slaves on the greens of Lexington and Concord and at the redoubts of Bunker Hill. Samuel Swett, one of the first to write about the Battle of Bunker Hill, claimed that "[Salem] was presented to Washington as having slain Pitcairn."

Painter John Trumbull had watched the carnage from Roxbury, across the harbor. The artist, at the least, heard of Salem's feat and would remember it eleven years later when he put brush to canvas in one of his most famous works, *The Battle of Bunker Hill*. In the lower right-hand corner of the canvas, Trumbull conferred artistic immortality upon Salem, depicting him in the midst of the melee as a handsome young man clad in a thick homespun shirt and clutching the musket with which he downed Pitcairn. The painter's image of Salem resembled the few references to his robust, pleasant visage, later prompting historian Sidney Kaplan to state that Trumbull "possibly met" Salem shortly after the battle.[10]

Although Peter Salem won acclaim for his famous musket and for his likeness in Trumbull's painting, other Black soldiers also served valiantly at Breed's Hill. Swett wrote that, like Salem, a Black youth named Cuff Whitemore "fought bravely in the redoubt."[11] "He had a ball through his hat . . . fought to the last, and when compelled to retreat, though wounded . . . he seized the sword [of a redcoat officer] slain in the redoubt . . . which in a few days he unromantically sold. He served faithfully through the war, with many hairbreadth 'scapes from sword and pestilence."[12]

Another of the Blacks who fired at the whites of the redcoats' eyes also bore the name Salem—Salem Poor. Like Peter Salem, the twenty-eight-year-old Poor was a free man, married, and even a member of Andover's Congregationalist church. He had enlisted in Colonel Benjamin Ames's company. In the aftermath of Breed's Hill, fourteen rebel officers who had fought there sent a remarkable petition to the Massachusetts General Court. The letter was the first battlefield citation for a Black soldier in the nation's annals, patriot hero Colonel William Prescott adding his name to the other officers' beseeching "the Reward due to so great and Distinguisht a Caracter" as Poor.[13]

The petition stated: "The Subscribers begg leave to Report to you Honble. House (Which Wee do in justice to the Caracter of so Brave a Man) that under Our Own observation, Wee declare that a Negro Man Called Salem Poor . . . in the late Battle of Charleston [*sic*], behaved like an Experienced Officer, as well as an Excellent Soldier, to Set forth Particulars of his Conduct would be Tedious, Wee Would Only begg leave to say in the Person of this sd. Negro Centers a Brave & gallant soldier."[14]

Aside from the officers' praise, Poor received no reward. He served nearly to the war's end, mustered out in 1780, a veteran of Valley Forge and many battles.

Before the war began, Salem Poor already possessed what Peter Salem and other Black soldiers craved: freedom. But, in spring 1775, when Peter Salem wanted to enlist in the patriots' ranks, his owner granted the slave liberty.

Peter Salem proved the kind of soldier Washington prized most, one who did not shoulder his musket and head home after three-months' enlistment. The ex-slave carried his acclaimed musket onto Saratoga, Stony Point, and other battlefields, firing it with the same deadly effect as he had at Breed's Hill. On March 1, 1780, he was mustered out of the army. No White soldier could charge that Salem had shirked his duty.

Salem headed back to Massachusetts and soon settled in Leicester to find that for freed Blacks, earning a living posed problems. He could find odd jobs from local farmers and tradesmen, but for a pittance. And when he married Katie Benson, a pretty ex-slave, his need to find a trade, as opposed to a job, increased.

In his years as a slave, Salem had learned the old New England skill of weaving cane into bushels, sewing baskets, and furniture. Now, he turned to the craft for a living and discovered no lack of customers among local housewives and shopkeepers. In a plank cabin he nailed up himself in Leicester, on a small lot purchased with his back pay from the Continental Army, he ran his own shop and visited many neighbors' homes to mend chairs.

Above his cabin's tiny fireplace, Salem had hung his musket, and whenever a customer commented on the relic, Salem would recount its vivid history. Local boys, especially, showed up at the ex-soldier's cabin with or without a basket that needed mending or an order for a new one and pleaded with Salem to tell his adventures again and again. He always obliged. When he passed the children's parents on the roads of Leicester and Framingham, they nodded respectfully to the man who had shot Major Pitcairn.

For thirty-five years, Salem and Katie, a paid domestic, made enough to keep up their cabin's repairs and to feed and clothe themselves decently. Although he loved children, the couple never had them. Several historians claim that the marriage was never a happy one.

Sometime before 1815, Katie died. Peter Salem toiled to keep his cane-weaving business going, but his own declining health forced him to give it up. Unable to earn money, too proud to beg, he left his cabin unlatched on a late fall day in 1815, walked to Framingham, and entered the poorhouse. In January 1816, Peter Salem died there in his sleep at the age of sixty-six or sixty-seven.

By 1855, even the measure of fame Salem had earned at the Battle of Bunker Hill had faded. A historian of the era noted that the most recent accounts and images of the battle contained "a significant but inglorious ommission"—Salem.[15]

The commemoration of the Bunker Hill Monument in the early 1880s revived public interest in the heroes of the legendary clash, and scholars grudgingly began to accord Peter Salem his historical due. In 1882, the citizens of Framingham erected a monument honoring Salem, further resurrecting his name. Today, John Trumbull's *The Battle of Bunker Hill,* with its vivid depiction of Salem, hangs in the rotunda of the Capitol, in Washington D.C. The Leicester cabin in which Salem lived was restored.

The Bunker Hill Monument, in Charlestown, Massachusetts, once displayed an even more tangible relic of the slave who won his freedom in the American War of Independence: in a glass case at the memorial lay his scarred musket. Today, its whereabouts are uncertain.

The Father
of the Coast Guard

⤳

On March 21, 1791, the scratch of two quills across paper sounded a historic moment in the annals of New Hampshire and the United States. As the ink of two signatures—President George

Washington's and Secretary of State Thomas Jefferson's—dried, the words above the names bestowed immortality on a middle-aged Portsmouth sea captain.

"Know ye," the document proclaimed, "that reposing special Trust and Confidence in the Integrity, Diligence, and good Conduct of Hopley Yeaton of New Hampshire, I [Washington] do appoint him Master of a Cutter in the Service of the United States."[1]

Captain Hopley Yeaton had become the first naval officer commissioned by a U.S. president. Yeaton's stellar performance in the Revenue Cutter Service, the forerunner of the U.S. Coast Guard, would justify Washington's faith in the New England mariner. Two centuries later, Yeaton's legacy looms large among the men and the women sworn to serve in the waters off America's shores.

Hopley Yeaton was born in either New Castle or Portsmouth in 1740. Although no traces of his youth survive for historians to ponder, they do know that he headed to sea as soon as he could. The snap of canvas sails in an ocean breeze, the tang of salt air in his lungs, the pitch of ships' decks beneath his feet—the age-old notes of the siren's song of the sea seduced the New Hampshire boy into a swashbuckling affair that would last his entire life.

One of the first recorded sightings of the young seaman took place on the altar of the South Church, in Portsmouth, where Yeaton married a local woman named Comfort Marshall in 1766. Three years later he purchased a Portsmouth mansion featuring a pillared archway, two large chimneys, and such classic touches as shuttered windows, a trio of gables, and bay windows on one side. The Deer Street home rang with the cries of the couple's first child, John, by the fall of that year, and six more followed over the next decade, two of whom died in infancy.

Only twenty-eight or twenty-nine when he bought the mansion, Hopley Yeaton could afford an upscale colonial lifestyle because Portsmouth's merchants trusted him to captain their ships, to ferry their goods to Europe and the West Indies, and to return with hefty profits, including a generous cut for the ship's master. According to a local shipowner, Yeaton not only possessed the hard-nosed leadership and navigational skills a successful ship's master required, but also an equally important component, luck.

Yeaton's luck extended beyond his knack for bringing his commands home, no matter how rough the voyage. In 1769, while master of the brig *Olive* on a long journey from Wales to Portsmouth, he struck up a friendship with two passengers, Joseph Whipple and fellow sea captain Thomas Thompson. They dined in the master's cabin, playing cards and sipping whiskey, which Yeaton did only in moderation. Both passengers would play key roles in Yeaton's career.

Yeaton also made another important connection in 1769, when he began to attend meetings at St. John's Masonic Lodge, in Portsmouth. He signed the order's bylaws and became a member on January 18, 1770; among his Masonic brothers were his former passenger Captain Thompson, who had helped initiate Yeaton into the lodge, and John Sullivan, a New Hampshire luminary also destined to shape Yeaton's seafaring future.

In the years following induction into St. John's Lodge, Yeaton had his pick of Portsmouth merchantmen plying trade routes to and from England and the West Indies. Aboard such ships as the *Olive,* the bark *White Oak,* and the *Britannica,* he added to his reputation for safe voyages and to his purse.

The sea captain's mettle faced new tests as the colonies and Great Britain edged closer to conflict between 1769 and 1775. Yeaton was elected commander of Portsmouth's Sons of Liberty; at the onset of the Revolutionary War, he advocated loading local Tories aboard ships and sailing the Loyalists to any British-held port. While marching a company of volunteers to join the fledgling Continental Army, he halted the recruits in front of the Earl of Halifax Tavern, a notorious meeting place for Portsmouth's Tories, and warned the inn's patrons that he would shatter any window in which a Tory's face appeared. The Loyalists fled out the tavern's back door.

Yeaton's thirst for action delighted his Masonic brother John Sullivan, a brigadier general in the Continental Army. Sullivan recommended the mariner for an infantry captain's commission. Although he never received the commission, Yeaton assembled a band of New Hampshire men during the war's first winter and marched them through the snow to Boston to join George Washington's ragtag troops.

Despite his determination to help the colonies' cause in any way possible, Yeaton knew that he could best serve his country at sea. His first wartime cruise came aboard the brig *Polly,* but his hopes for making a mark in the conflict were seemingly dashed when a Royal Navy squadron ambushed the brig in the Caribbean and captured the crew. To Yeaton's relief, an American warship hailing from Salem, Massachusetts, seized the vessel as it ferried him to a British prison, and spared him the ignominy of waiting for an exchange of captives, or of imprisonment for the rest of the war.

Before long Yeaton returned to Portsmouth and by September 1778 was serving as a commissioned third lieutenant aboard the Portsmouth-built frigate *Raleigh,* a warship that would furnish Yeaton with all the action he craved. Although a third lieutenant's rank seemed a step backward for a man who had been master of many vessels, Yeaton's patriotism overcame his ego.

Action hotter than any Yeaton could have imagined took place in late September 1778, when the *Raleigh* engaged in a clash against the H.M.S. *Experiment* and the H.M.S. *Unicorn,* bearing fifty and twenty-two guns respectively, in the waters off Maine. The running battle raged nearly sixty hours, the British warships in pursuit, their cannons pounding the *Raleigh* as the chase stretched toward Penobscot Bay.

As the outline of Wooden Ball Island loomed dead ahead, the American frigate, its sails and rigging shredded, listed to port. At least twenty-six sailors lay dead or wounded on decks slippery with blood and tangled with debris. Unwilling to give up his ship to the British and see the Union Jack fluttering above her, the *Raleigh*'s captain, Fighting John Barry, later dubbed the Father of the American Navy, ordered his crew to beach the frigate on a sandbar.

The moment the ship scraped to a halt, Yeaton and the rest clambered with their wounded over the gunwales and into longboats, and rowed for shallow inshore waters as the British vessels bore down on the stricken frigate. Yeaton, dreading the prospect of recapture by the British, proved luckier than he had been in the Caribbean: the British warships turned around as they realized a sandbar loomed ahead; Yeaton was among the eighty-five *Raleigh* crewmen who eluded their pursuers.

According to historian Gerald D. Foss, another key event in Yeaton's life came within three months of the moment he fled the *Raleigh*. In December 1776, Yeaton was ordered to run the British navy's blockade in a sloop carrying fifteen barrels crammed with 60,000 musket flints for George Washington's troops around New York City. Hugging the shore by day in his lithe, shallow-keeled craft, chancing deep waters teeming with British warships at night, he dodged the blockade and delivered the precious flints to Washington's beleaguered regiments. Yeaton's trip earned him his first meeting with Washington. The pair would meet again.

His mission to New York completed, Yeaton returned overland to Portsmouth and soon reported for duty aboard a new ship, the frigate *Deane*, a French vessel refitted in Portsmouth for service in the Continental Navy. Yeaton served on the *Deane* until 1781, fighting valiantly on missions stretching from France to the West Indies to the waters off the thirteen colonies. By 1779, Yeaton had won a promotion to the rank of first lieutenant; the captain's slot eluded him, despite the efforts of the *Deane's* captain, Samuel Nicholson, to procure the frustrated first lieutenant a warship from the Continental Congress. Government officials wrote Nicholson that the young American navy had too many deserving officers and too few ships. Yeaton stoically accepted this fate for the rest of the Revolution.

Having done more than his part to win freedom for the new nation, Yeaton returned to his mansion on Deer Street and to his wife and five children, and resumed his career as a captain of Portsmouth merchantmen.

On December 8, 1787, Yeaton stood on the quarterdeck of a vessel owned by his old friend John Sullivan and bound from Portsmouth to Philadelphia with a load of beef. A bank of dark clouds was rapidly closing from the northwest. As the first gusts of wind and slaps of rain hit the ship, Yeaton sent crewmen scurrying aloft to roll up the sails before the full force of the gale could tear them apart. The storm struck first.

With a deafening crack, one of the brig's two masts toppled to the main deck, and the wind ripped the canvas from the other mast's spars. Huge waves washed over the gunwales in a freezing rush of salt water and frothing spray. The brig careened in the wave's troughs, Yeaton's years of experience at the helm no help.

For nearly three months Yeaton's family anguished over his possible fate; finally they received word that he was safe in Bermuda, having somehow navigated the virtually useless hulk close enough to the islands to get his men ashore before the brig sank.

The loss of a vessel was an occupational hazard for any sea captain, but Yeaton's shipwreck did not harm his reputation among merchants. Shortly after the disaster, Sullivan offered his opinion of the Portsmouth captain: "I must add that Yeaton has always been esteemed one of the most fortunate & best sea Captains in this state."[2]

In June 1788, Yeaton suffered a far more devastating loss than that of his ship: his wife died in their home. Few friends and neighbors would have wagered that the sea captain would outlive his wife. Yeaton, too, was taken by surprise. Comfort's death sent him into seclusion for several months. But in September 1789, he remarried. His second wife was a Portsmouth woman named Elizabeth Gerrish. With several children still in need of a mother and with the mariner away at sea for long stretches, he could not have remained a widower much longer.

About a month after his wedding, Yeaton stood at the helm of a barge cruising the waters of Portsmouth Harbor. Although the trip was one he could have made with his eyes shut, the short jaunt was noteworthy. On the deck of the barge was a tall, commanding figure— President George Washington. Choosing among some of America's finest ship's masters, the town's officials had entrusted Yeaton to take the nation's leader on a tour of the harbor and its defenses.

At a ball in Washington's honor the next night, Yeaton had a further chance to speak with the president. Washington also led the new Mrs. Yeaton across the dance floor. One can only speculate about what her husband and the renowned soldier discussed during the tour and the ball, but on December 11, 1789, Yeaton penned Washington a letter outlining the mariner's desire to serve his nation in some capacity at sea.

On March 21, 1791, Washington appointed the New England salt the first captain of the fledgling Revenue Cutter Service. The first presidential naval commission in American history soon arrived at Deer Street. (The original commission was found in the attic of a Yeaton family member in the 1930s and is now in the Library of Congress.)

Yeaton's first command in the Revenue Service was the cutter *Scammel,* a Portsmouth-built vessel. Two masts, schooner-rigged, rose from the craft's deck; from bow to stern she measured about sixty feet, her weight eighty-one tons. Built to pursue speedy coastal smugglers, the *Scammel* was lightly armed with four swivel guns. Yeaton's crew, including three master's mates, totaled nine men; his salary, $30 a month, was a drastic comedown from the fees he earned commanding merchantmen, but a stipend the wealthy sea captain could easily afford. For Yeaton, money was not the issue. He now had the naval commission he had craved during the Revolution. Still, as his correspondence would show, he did not believe that $30 a month was enough for a captain.

As Yeaton and his cutter prowled the waters off New Hampshire and Maine throughout the 1790s, smugglers were not his only concern. From the onset of his tenure with the Revenue Service, he diligently lobbied Congress to increase salaries, to enlist more seamen, and to commission larger, better-armed cutters. His efforts succeeded; by the end of the eighteenth century, Revenue Service captains received $50 a month, and the salaries of Revenue Service crews rose. Congress had also commissioned cutters three times larger than the *Scammel* and bearing up to fourteen guns.

Although Yeaton was accustomed to battling cunning smugglers and tight-fisted politicians, he finally found himself overmatched in 1799. His opponent was President John Adams. According to Yeaton's grandson Enoch D. Yeaton, political clashes between Adams and the sea captain led the president to discharge him from the Revenue Service. This embittered Yeaton, who had served his nation so well. He returned to the life of a merchantman captain for the next few years.

Yeaton's enforced exile from the Revenue Service ended when President Thomas Jefferson, whose signature, beneath Washington's, had launched Yeaton's distinguished stint aboard the *Scammel,* issued the Portsmouth salt a second Revenue Service commission in August 1802. Yeaton's new command was the cutter *New Hampshire.* His orders were to patrol the waters between Portsmouth, New Hampshire, and Eastport, Maine.

From 1802 to 1809, Yeaton resumed his familiar struggles against smugglers and corrupt port officials. When he learned in the fall of 1809 that a sloop, the *Rhoda,* had sailed for York, Maine, after unloading a suspicious cargo in Portsmouth, he considered the matter business as usual while setting a course for the Maine port. He was wrong.

After the *New Hampshire* slipped into York Harbor, where the *Rhoda* swung from its anchor chain, Yeaton boarded the vessel and determined that the smuggler's cargo had been hauled overland and reloaded aboard the sloop. He quickly posted a four-man guard aboard the *Rhoda,* and sailed back to Portsmouth.

Yeaton's Masonic brother Joseph Whipple, the port collector of Portsmouth, sent Yeaton back to York with orders to seize the sloop. But by the time the *New Hampshire* returned, a mob of waterfront toughs had seized the *Rhoda* from Yeaton's men. The sloop had put out to sea before the return of the cutter.

The incident with the *Rhoda* galled the sea captain, and in December 1809, not long after the *Rhoda* affair, the seventy-year-old

Yeaton resigned from the Revenue Cutter Service and retired to a farm he had purchased in Lubec, Maine. From his farmhouse, he followed the rush of events pushing the United States into a second war with the nation's old foe, Great Britain. Despite his advancing years, Yeaton mulled his possible role in the oncoming conflict.

He never had the chance to fight the old enemy again. On May 12, 1812, the seventy-three-year-old sea captain died in his Lubec home.

Captain Hopley Yeaton had one more voyage, a trip that unfolded 163 years after his death. Yeaton's remains were removed in November 1974 from a hill behind his farmhouse and stored in a crypt at West Quoddy Head to await interment in a crypt in New London, Connecticut, home of the United States Coast Guard Academy. On August 19, 1975, after a dignified ceremony, the flag-covered coffin was carried by a Coast Guard honor guard aboard the bark *Eagle*. The sleek vessel sailed to New London, much of the journey fittingly through the same waters Yeaton had sailed throughout his lifetime.

On October 19, 1975, the academy's Hopley Yeaton Monument was dedicated in a moving service. The honor guard laid the body of America's first commissioned naval officer to rest in a marble crypt. The last voyage of the Portsmouth sea captain ended among cadets who would continue the proud traditions of patriotism embodied by the old seafarer.

The man whose name emblazons the landmark commission remains a revered figure in the annals of the Coast Guard. The sentiments of Rear Admiral James P. Stewart, U.S.C.G., reflect the true measure of Captain Hopley Yeaton: "He was always a leader."[3]

Another fitting epitaph adorned Yeaton's original gravestone in North Lubec, Maine:

NO JOYS DOMESTIC
NOR LOVE OF EASE
COULD COOL HIS PATRIOT ZEAL
IN WAR OR PEACE

RAGS

TO

RICHES

"Sir William, Arise"

〜

R oyal Londoners had never witnessed such a scene. In June 1687, a round-faced, genial-looking colonist knelt in front of the be-wigged James II, the long-faced Catholic king soon to lose his throne to his Protestant foes. As the monarch's court—ministers and ladies in silk, lace, and gems—watched, "the homely Colonial"[1] waited for the king to bestow upon him an honor many courtiers had yet to garner: British Knight of the Realm.

The kneeling American, William Phips, of Maine, would become the first native-born American so honored. And the reason for the honor lay in another first. Phips had risked life and limb to chase a fortune in gold and jewels; the colonist had achieved wealth as America's first undersea treasure hunter.

William Phips was one of twenty-six children born to James and Mary Phips, English colonists who settled in Maine along the Kennebec River. Their boy William was trained as a ship's carpenter but yearned for adventure. In 1683 he traveled to London and won an appointment with King Charles II, with a proposal to add gold to the royal treasury, the Exchequer. The Maine mariner's scheme proved too intriguing for the Crown to ignore—even though it was conceived by a rough-around-the-edges colonist. At Phips's interview with the king, the American did not kowtow at the sight of the royal court. Instead, the man from Maine spun a tale of treasure just waiting for someone bold enough to salvage it—a sunken ship laden with gold, silver, and gems. Of course, there were a few hitches to Phips's dreams of ocean booty: the vessel was a Spanish treasure ship resting in Spanish waters off the Bahamas, and England and Spain were mortal foes. Phips needed money—lots of it—to mount an expedition complete with a ponderous diving bell and scores of men, some of whom would certainly perish in the depths surrounding the wreck. If a squadron of Spanish warships was suddenly to arrive on the wreck site and discover an English salvage team, Phips and crew would end up in nooses or as slaves chained to the oars of Spanish galleys.

Despite the dangers and the high probability that any money invested by the Crown would be lost, the picture of glittering booty scattered on the ocean floor and the chance to tweak Spain's collective nose by stealing the loot from under it was too seductive for Charles to decline. The king outfitted Phips with an armed naval frigate and a crew, and dispatched the Maine adventurer to the warm waters of the Bahamas.

Phips returned to London in 1684—empty-handed. He discovered that his benefactor, Charles II, had died and another Stuart, James II, wore the crown. James displayed his opinion of Phips's dream by seizing the treasure hunter's ship.

Phips immediately sought new financiers in England and quickly sold the Duke of Albemarle and other noble investors on the idea of a second salvage operation, this venture to a Spanish treasure ship sunk by a hurricane off Hispaniola (now Haiti and the Dominican Republic). Phips and his new crew of salvagers set sail in 1686.

Phips's expedition eluded the Spanish in locating the wreck site. Braving brutal diving conditions and the ever-present threat of discovery by the enemy, Phips's wildest dreams materialized: his men emptied the sunken hulk of 300,000 pounds sterling in gold, jewels, and pieces of eight. A staggering fortune was stolen from Spain.

Phips's arrival in London in June 1687 resembled a Roman triumph. The adventurer received a bona fide hero's welcome replete with cheering crowds and fawning nobles. The man from Maine had delivered stunning profits to his investors and, of course, a required cut to the Exchequer even though the Crown had not financed him. Moreover, he had emerged a wealthy man from his own substantial share of the booty.

Phips's next audience with James II proved vastly different from the first. The daring colonist approached the throne and knelt before the king; then, in the age-old gesture of England's monarchs, James tapped Phips's shoulders with the flat of his sword.

"Sir William, arise," the king intoned. "It is my pleasure to create you a Knight of the Realm."[2]

James had ample reason to feel pleasure—the Crown's cut of the treasure snatched from England's mortal enemy rested at a hefty 10 percent.

America's first knight appeared unimpressed with the ceremony. To the Duke of Albemarle, the treasure hunter's friend and partner, Phips said: "I am at heart a Puritan. My place is in New England."[3] He soon returned to his homeland—a rich Puritan. And in New England he remained, serving stints as provost marshal and royal governor of Massachusetts before his death in 1695. The Puritan's path to colonial power was paved with the Spanish loot Sir William had stolen from the ocean's depths.

Wheel of Fortune — And Misfortune

⤳

On a frigid Pawtucket, Rhode Island, morning in 1790, a tall, fair-haired man stood along the banks of the Blackstone River in frustration. Ice choked the swift flow of the current below him and imprisoned the waterwheel of his business partner's fulling, or cloth, mill.

Other mills throughout New England faced the same problem on any given winter morning, but none of them had so much at stake as the Pawtucket man, twenty-two-year-old Samuel Slater. Unless he freed the wheel, one of America's most momentous technological experiments could not commence. And Slater's brainstorm already lagged behind schedule.

As Slater usually did when faced with a problem, he adopted a hands-on approach. Grabbing a pickax, he clambered down the river-bank and edged onto the frozen Blackstone. One misstep, one weak spot in the ice was liable to send him crashing into the water. Slater crawled to the imprisoned wheel and hacked away at the ice sur-rounding it. With a potential fortune invested in that wheel, his own safety mattered little to him at the moment.

As Slater continued chopping, the wheel shuddered, creaked, and, slowly at first, began to spin. Its momentum increased, and from the mill a clatter of wood and metal machinery hooked up to the water-wheel erupted. The din heartened the sodden, shivering Slater. Prov-ing that water could power his revolutionary machines, it heralded the birth of America's first modern cotton mill, and the onset of Amer-ica's Industrial Revolution. It had all come about because of the Rhode Island resident's astonishing feat of memory. British mill owners viewed it, however, as an unparalleled feat of thievery.

The man who committed to memory Britain's closely guarded se-crets of modern machinery, pirated its factory system, and transferred them to America was born on June 9, 1768, in Belper, England. The son of well-educated, solvent farmer and timber merchant William Slater and his wife, Elizabeth Fox Slater, Samuel grew up at Holly House, the family farm, amid well-tended fields, lush orchards, and the fast-flowing rivers of Derbyshire.

In school, Slater showed a flair for mathematics and science, but what stood out most about the farm lad was his photographic memory. A studious child who nonetheless developed into a sturdy, ruddy-complexioned youth, Slater early on displayed his evolving mix of mechanical and practical aptitude by crafting a buffed steel spindle that his mother could use to wind thread.

When not engaged in school or at chores, Slater loved to dash to a mill in Cromford, about a mile from Holly House. Powered by the Derwent River, the cotton mill comprised the world's first bona fide factory. Always finding a warm welcome from the plant's supervisor, his family's friend and neighbor Jedediah Strutt, Slater gaped for hours at the yarn-spinning machines of Sir Richard Arkwright. The brilliant noble had not only designed revolutionary machinery that used water power—not traditional human and animal labor—but also had consolidated under one roof every aspect of turning raw cotton into finished, durable thread.

In 1782, Arkwright's partner, Strutt, needing to hire a clerk for a new hosiery factory, in nearby Milford, visited his friend William Slater and offered to give the job to his eldest son. For any young man seeking an opportunity, a clerkship under Strutt's tutelage offered a foothold in England's burgeoning textile industry, in which Strutt was a mover and shaker. William Slater welcomed the offer for his son—but not the son Strutt had in mind. Slater urged his friend to hire fourteen-year-old Samuel, the youngest, because he "wrote well, was good at figures," and loved machines.[1] On the latter point Strutt required little convincing, having seen the boy bound into the Cromford factory on countless occasions to study the Arkwright machines. Samuel Slater got the job.

In a customary arrangement of the era, Slater moved into his boss's home, although it was only a short distance from Holly House. The boy, as his father had surmised, soon became an invaluable asset to Strutt, absorbing not only the intricacies of tally sheets, balances, and depreciations, but also the manner in which Strutt hired, fired, and managed his employees, many of them children prized for nimble fingers much better suited to detail work than those of adults.

A youngster on the rise, able to spend time with both his family and his mentor, Slater so impressed his boss that Strutt viewed him more as a favorite nephew than as an employee. Then, less than a year after Slater arrived at Milford, his life turned with the sudden death of his father. Scarcely having time to grieve, young Slater had to sort out a future independent of the help his father had always provided. Once again, Jedediah Strutt stepped in with an offer—part business, part personal. If Slater would sign on as an apprentice at the Milford plant, Strutt would groom him to run a mill from the ground floor up, freeing the youth from a pigeonholed career as a clerk. Slater quickly signed an indenture of 6½ years. At age twenty-one, he could choose his own course in the textile industry, trained by a man whose very name would ensure Slater a comfortable post in virtually any British mill.

Strutt, as always in his dealings with the Slaters, proved a man of his word and imparted his management techniques to his ward. The businessman and his family also treated Samuel as one of their own, never allowing loneliness to embitter him.

So obsessed with his surrogate father's mill did Slater become that six months or so would pass before he walked the scant mile to visit his mother at Holly House. On many a Sunday, his only day off, he spent hours with Arkwright's machines, poring over every detail of their wooden frames, the iron-teethed cards that pulled raw cotton into manageable strands, and the spinning mechanisms that turned the slivers into durable thread.

Strutt rewarded Slater's dedication by assigning him more and more responsibility in running the floor of the mill. As he approached his twenty-first birthday, Slater had risen to supervisor of Strutt's hosiery mill—no mean feat in an era when men of more mature years usually held such a critical post.

When the term of his indenture expired, Slater, whose rawboned, nearly six-foot frame complemented his keen intelligence, offered Strutt or any other textile magnate, in the parlance of the day, "a likely lad." Slater's physical and intellectual pedigree was easy for prospective employers to gauge. Indiscernible were the deep ambitions that simmered within him, however. Slater did not crave a comfortable position; he wanted a fortune.

In 1789, now free to pick and choose a living at an Arkwright factory, Slater confronted impediments to his dreams of wealth and influence. Arkwright's patents were expiring, easing his stranglehold on the British textile industry. Competitors would open their own mills with his milestone machinery. With more factories opening, Slater's knowledge of Arkwright's system would decrease in value as other mechanics assimilated the inventor's wizardry.

Slater now realized that he would not attain the wealth he wanted unless he could obtain enough financial backing to open his own mill, and in a climate of stiffening competition, there was no guarantee of huge profits. Even his mentor, Strutt, no longer viewed cotton spinning as a means to millions, only to a comfortable living.

As Slater pondered his future, he learned from a newspaper article that the Pennsylvania state legislature had awarded $100 to an American man who had built a textile machine primitive by British standards. The young mill supervisor began mulling what American entrepreneurs might pay for the secrets of the Arkwright method.

Slater, his ambition turning ever westward toward Britain's former colonies, took a key step in that direction when he convinced Strutt to appoint him overseer of the construction of a new Arkwright-Strutt cotton mill. As the riverside factory rose from its foundation, Slater memorized every aspect—from floor to ceiling. Most important, he committed to memory more assiduously than ever each inch of Arkwright's machines.

Slater had chosen an opportune moment to look toward America. From Maine to Georgia, shrewd entrepreneurs had long craved the secrets of Arkwright's designs. American efforts to smuggle scale models of Arkwright's carding and spinning frames in crates marked "glassware" or "farm implements" rarely, if ever, made it past sharp-eyed British customs agents on the docks or past the Royal Navy's search-and-seizure raids on America-bound vessels. So, too, had the Crown stopped smugglers from spiriting detailed plans of Arkwright's machines to the New World.

Frustrated Yankees strove to invent their own textile machines, but whenever put to the test, they yielded inferior thread. A wealthy Quaker merchant living in Providence, Rhode Island, had sunk a sizable chunk of cash into a locally made pair of spinning frames and a carding machine, but the hand-run devices had produced only a weak facsimile of British cotton yarn and were gathering dust in a tiny clothing mill at Pawtucket. Still, their owner, Moses Brown, had not completely abandoned his desire to found an American textile industry and to free the nation from dependence on British weaves. But he needed someone to unlock the mysteries of Arkwright's methods.

And a man who fit that criteria had decided to seek his fortune in America. Samuel Slater concealed his plans even from his family, for if word slipped out that he planned to emigrate, the authorities would seize him. Parliament's dictates that anyone knowledgeable of Arkwright's machines must remain in Britain would leave him imprisoned in England.

On the sun-splashed day of September 1, 1789, a young man in the plain garb of a Derbyshire farmer and with ruddy features to match strolled away from the manicured fields and orchards of Holly House. Slater told his family he was taking a sojourn from work to tour London. Actually, with each step on the road from Belper, he knew that if all went according to plan, he would never see Holly House or the banks of the Derwent again.

Days after his departure from Derbyshire, Slater stood in front of dockside customs agents. He passed inspection and boarded a ship. Slater had never considered smuggling drawings of Arkwright's machines aboard, his chances of slipping past customs with them slim; however, if he was going to convince American businessmen of his expertise, he needed his résumé—his expired indenture with Jedediah Strutt, the renowned partner of Arkwright himself. Hidden somewhere in Slater's clothing or meager baggage lay the papers that guaranteed him a cell if discovered. He had passed the dockside inspection, but still had to worry about a Royal Navy boarding party somewhere on the Atlantic crossing.

Neither the Royal Navy nor customs officials would ever have discovered the other contraband Slater carried to his berth in the ship: hidden in his memory lay every detail of Arkwright's water-powered machines, every inch of his cotton mills, and every aspect of the British factory system. The Derbyshire man was ferrying the Industrial Revolution to America, to a village in Rhode Island.

Sixty-six days after Slater stood at the gunwales and glimpsed England's shores receding behind him for the first and last time, his ship docked in New York City. His mother and family now knew of his daring scheme. Just prior to his embarkation, he had posted a letter to Holly House, his quill having detailed his grandiose ambitions.

Once ashore, Slater headed straight through the seaport's crowded streets to the New York Manufacturing Company, on Vesey Street, where the outfit produced linen yarn with antiquated, hand-operated machinery. His indenture landed him a job, but the owners cared little that their newest hire carried the blueprint for a modern mill in his head.

After several weeks in the employ of the New York factory, Slater was seeking out better opportunities. He met the captain of a packet ship on the New York to Providence run, and the New England salt told him of a wealthy Rhode Islander named Moses Brown. Brown was ostensibly retired from the textile business but was always on the lookout for profitable ventures, especially a means to open a modern cotton mill.

On December 2, 1789, Slater dipped his quill into a bottle of "goose-black" ink and composed a letter to Brown:

> Sir,—
>
> A few days ago I was informed that you wanted a manager of cotton spinning, etc. in which business I flatter myself that I can give the greatest satisfaction, in making machinery, making good yarn, either for stockings or twist, as any that is made in England; as I have had opportunity and an oversight of Sir Richard Arkwright's works, and in Mr. Strutt's mill upwards of eight years. If you are not provided for, [I] should be glad to serve you: though I am in the New York manufactory, and have been for three weeks since I arrived from England. But we have but one card, two machines, two spinning jennies, which I think are not worth using. My intention is to erect a perpetual [water-powered] card and spinning [the Arkwright patents]. If

214

you please to drop a line respecting the amount of encouragement you wish to give by favor of Captain Brown, you will much oblige, sir, your most obedient humble servant.

Samuel Slater[2]

Moses Brown wasted little time in replying to Slater's letter, the Quaker merchant's business instincts piqued by the immigrant's alleged knowledge of Arkwright's machinery and ties to Strutt. Brown acknowledged, in a letter, that he and his associates were "destitute of a person acquainted with water-frame spinning."[3]

If Slater's claims proved true, Brown was willing to pay him a lofty fee: all profits beyond any future mill's operating costs, investors' cuts, and normal depreciation. The Quaker offered Slater the chance to "have the credit as well as the advantage of perfecting the first water-mill in America."[4]

Brown was too smart to advance money to Slater sight unseen, but invited him to Rhode Island to pitch his claims face-to-face. Later in January 1790, Slater boarded a ship to Providence. Almost as soon as he set foot there he headed to the home of Moses Brown.

At first glance, the elderly Quaker merchant, peering through spectacles and clad in his faith's flat-brimmed hat, from which his long gray hair peeked, looked less like a shrewd businessman than a grandfather just back from a prayer meeting. Soon after Slater handed his indenture papers to the Quaker, the immigrant learned otherwise. Brown fired questions probing the extent of Slater's professed knowledge and about his work for Strutt. Slater's responses convinced Brown that the young man was the genuine article—and the possible means toward a textile fortune.

Brown ended the interview and led his visitor to a sleigh. Across the snowy streets of Providence and then a few miles out of town, Brown drove Slater along the banks of the Blackstone River to Pawtucket, a dozen or so workmen's cottages huddled near the icy water. The sleigh slid to a stop at a small wooden building on the Blackstone's banks. Attached to the structure, an old clothier's mill, was a water-wheel within sight of a bridge linking Rhode Island to Massachusetts.

The Quaker guided Slater into the ramshackle mill and allowed him to inspect Brown's filthy hand-operated carding machine and spinning frames.

"These will not do," Slater said. "They are good for nothing in their present condition, nor can they be made to answer."[5] He had expected to revamp and refine the equipment into facsimiles of Arkwright's inventions, not to build machines from scratch. Then Brown urged him to build America's first modern mill from the ground floor up, but Slater balked.

The wily Quaker shifted tactics. "Thee said thee could make machinery," Brown challenged. "Why not do it?"[6]

Slater, unnerved that his envisioned role as a plant manager had turned into a task far more daunting, still demurred. Brown, however, had tweaked the man's ego. They haggled over what the Quaker could reasonably expect if Slater took on the job, and finally agreed on two major conditions: Brown would hire a skilled mechanic capable of translating into wood and metal the Arkwright designs Slater had memorized; the hireling must be legally bonded never to reveal the work, never to copy it, and never to steal it. Slater feared that an ambitious man might transfer the precious technology as Slater himself had.

Assuaged by Brown's pledge to safeguard the young man's secrets, Slater not only relented, but also pledged, "If I don't make as good yarn as they do in England, I will have nothing for my services, but will throw the whole of what I have attempted over the bridge."[7]

Ever the canny negotiator, the Quaker took the young man at his word, agreeing to pay for nothing beyond the venture's start-up costs and Slater's room and board until the business was running.

Slater's partner and backer, taking care of two key aspects of the agreement literally under one roof, boarded Slater at the nearby cottage of Oziel Wilkinson, another Quaker and an ingenious ironmaster with the hands-on talent to keep up with Slater's mental prowess inside Wilkinson's small forge alongside the Blackstone. The ironmaker's skills in shaping shovels, scythes, ship's hardware, and other staples of New England looked promising for Slater's intentions, but the mill supervisor wondered if the artisan could work from blueprints.

In Wilkinson's forge and in his cottage, Slater soon learned that his landlord could handle the intricate designs rendered by the tenant. Slater also discovered something else in the ironmaster's home: in a classic case of love at first sight, Slater fell hard for Wilkinson's lovely daughter Hannah. Not only did her appearance draw Slater's interest, but also her keen intelligence, one, like her suitor's, with a decidedly inventive streak. Years later that streak materialized in her creation of a superior cotton sewing thread. Within two years of the day Slater first saw Hannah Wilkinson, they were married. First, however, he had a task to complete, one that could provide the necessary means to support a wife and a family in the wealth he desired.

Throughout the winter of 1790, Slater daily entered the clothier's mill, buffeted by the chill gusts surging from the Blackstone, and fussed with Brown's inferior machines to determine if any of their parts were serviceable. They were useless.

Slater and Wilkinson drew on Brown's purse to stockpile wood, iron, and other material in the mill and the forge. Before Wilkinson could heat his bellows and ready his tools for new machines, Slater faced one of his most imposing obstacles: to shape the parts necessary to mimic the Arkwright machines' revolutionary ability to function at varied speeds as water power drove them. Slater had to mine his memory for the mathematical tables without which the machines' measurements would be faulty. He recalled them all.

In April 1790, as spring's thaw ensured more comfortable working conditions inside the drafty mill, Slater guaranteed that he could build Brown two carding machines, a drawing and roving frame, and two spinning frames, all powered by the Blackstone. The two men forged a more lucrative deal for Slater: he would receive a salary of $1 per day, half-ownership of the machines, and half of the mill's net profits. Now, all Slater had to do was to build that mill and its machines.

From within the wooden walls of the clothier's mill and Wilkinson's forge, the din of hammers and the hiss of cooling metal emerged above the river as several months passed. Slater chalked his frames' designs on wood, and Sylvanus Brown, a local wheelwright, sawed and shaped them from oak and attached them to each other with wooden dowels.

For the frames' spindles, shafts, and rollers, Slater turned to Wilkinson's son David, also a gifted hand with iron. To create the metal cards that would cue the machines to the proper length and width of yarn, Slater hired Pliny Earle, of Leicester, Massachusetts.

Working sixteen or more hours a day in the summer heat of 1790 and into the fall, Slater and his artisans finished the promised machines. The trial run of his equipment, his memory, and Brown's financial outlay was finally at hand.

On an autumn day, Slater fed raw cotton for the first time into his carding machine, hand-cranked that day by a local Black workman because Slater was not yet ready to hook up his machines to the waterwheel. He wanted to see if his carding apparatus, the key component of the Arkwright system, worked.

As Slater's helper continued to crank, the machine dragged the cotton along tiny iron teeth intended to pull, straighten, and twist the fibers into long, thin slivers that the spinning machine would coax into yarn. Slater grimaced as the cotton bunched up and snarled on the teeth of the carding machine. If he had erred in his recollection of Arkwright's mathematical tables—available nowhere in America—the chances of success lay as figuratively tangled as the cotton on the apparatus.

According to the Wilkinsons, Slater later fought back tears as he agonized over the abortive test. "If I am frustrated in my carding machine," he said, "they will think me an imposter."[8]

His distress notwithstanding, Slater went back to work. He spent many sleepless nights poring over every detail of the machine. Finally, he suspected that the problem rested not with the machine itself, but with too much space between the cards' teeth.

Slater lugged the cards to Leicester in his saddlebags and discussed his theory with the cards' craftsman, Pliny Earle. Then the duo made a primal correction: they picked up a junked piece of grindstone, took the measure of the cards, and pounded the teeth closer together.

Slater rushed back to his Blackstone mill, arranged the revamped cards on the machine, and loaded cotton into it as the device was cranked. Tightening and straightening along the teeth, the rough cotton turned into slivers ready for spinning. Slater had no time to revel in his correction, for the most critical test, the one that would prove whether he could power his mill with the waters of the Blackstone, loomed next.

The test unfolded on that frigid morning in December 1790, Slater and his helpers having connected the machines to the waterwheel. For the first time in America, water power and Arkwright-style machines would spin raw cotton into yarn—American yarn. America's factory age had arrived, its cradle the fuller's mill on Quaker Lane.

To produce high-grade, durable yarn for his partners, who included not only Moses Brown, but also William Almy, Brown's son-in-law, and Smith Brown, the Quaker's cousin, Slater hired a workforce based on the British model—one composed of boys and girls with dexterous hands. Within a month, nine children were churning out yarn for clothes and stockings. Although a compassionate man, Slater had unwittingly brought the future horrors of child labor to New England and the nation.

Each morning in the winter of 1791, except Sundays, the children readied the machines as Slater chipped ice from the wheel, his clothing soaked, his teeth chattering. The efforts of that winter sapped his health for the rest of his life. His hirelings, seven to thirteen years old, came from families of local craftsmen and included ten-year-old Smith Wilkinson, Slater's future brother-in-law. Working twelve-hour shifts six days a week in winter and fourteen- to sixteen-hour shifts in spring and summer, the children plucked dirt, leaves, and pods from raw cotton and ran all of the machines, often swooning in the plant's stifling summer heat. Slater shuttered the windows to keep away prying eyes.

Slater grasped that child labor was the future of American industry. Despite the secretive nature that led him to shut the children inside the mill, he believed in the responsibility of plant owners to treat them well and to educate them. His partners would not necessarily agree, but as the fall of 1791 arrived, the small size of the cotton mill's workforce precluded many child labor abuses that would arise along the Blackstone.

The high-grade yarn that Slater's children were turning out led Moses Brown to send samples of the mill's output to Alexander Hamilton, secretary of the treasury, to win his support for an American textile industry rivaling England's. In 1791, Hamilton not only agreed to help, but lauded Slater's mill before Congress: "The manufactory at Providence has the merit of being the first in introducing into the United States the celebrated cotton mill."[9]

After ten months in business, the Almy, Brown & Slater Mill had sold enough yarn for nearly 8,000 yards of cloth woven by Americans. So efficiently were Slater's machines clattering and his wheel spinning that supply was outracing demand; more than 2,000 pounds of surplus was heaped inside the mill. Brown urged Slater to cut production until the partners located new markets for the inventory.

The Quaker dispatched agents to prospective buyers in Salem, Massachusetts; New York; Baltimore; and Philadelphia. Merchants grabbed every bit of the surplus. The mill owners reveled in the dilemma of demand outstripping supply. Once again, Moses Brown and Slater found a solution: in late 1791, they boarded up the mill and drew up plans for a new one, also to stand on the banks of the Blackstone.

With the temporary closing of the operation, Samuel Slater, his financial future bright, married the ironmaster's daughter. They settled in Pawtucket and over the years would have nine children.

Slater spent most of his first year of marriage overseeing the construction of his new mill, whose two stories and 43-by-29-foot dimensions featured a traditional post and beam design and resembled "an unpretentious New England meetinghouse—a demurely sober and comforting image."[10]

Once the new mill opened in 1793, the conditions for workers did not prove particularly comforting. As with the first mill, the owners hired the cheapest labor—children—at low wages of two to five shillings per week. Alexander Hamilton publicly voiced his approval of Slater's use of child labor.

Impoverished New England parents exhibited few qualms about showing up at Slater's plant with their children in response to such ads as one he placed in the October 11, 1794, *Providence Gazette*:

Four or five active Lads, about 15 years
of Age to serve as Apprentices in the Cotton Factory.

Slater also received such letters as that from a local woman who "observing your advertisements in the papers for Boys to work in your manufactory took the liberty of sending one boy by the name of Thomas Tippets, who I wish may answer your purposes as he is at present destitute of a home and very poor."[11]

Slater initially attempted to train the Thomas Tippets types as apprentices, adhering to long-standing New England tenets in which employees trained boys as artisans and mechanics. But Slater had a problem with the tradition: he refused to share his knowledge of the Arkwright patents with his workers, straining to keep a virtual monopoly for himself and his partners.

Although he shortchanged his youthful employees on issues of apprenticeship, Slater hired Brown University students to teach his charges reading, writing, and basic mathematics in his Sunday school, where the factory children also received lessons in obedience, honesty, temperance, punctuality, and deference. Slater's determination to educate his hirelings aggravated his partners, who begrudged every

221

cent allocated for books, other school supplies, the classroom's heat, and teachers' wages. Almy and Brown constantly held back payments for the Sunday school, infuriating Slater and forcing many cancellations of the children's lessons.

Despite Slater's ongoing efforts to pry the school's costs from his partners, he shared their balance-sheet concerns on most other dictates of New England's apprenticeship system. By 1796, even though the mill's profits continued to swell, Slater, the Browns, and Almy grumbled over the soaring costs for apprentices. To board a youth with a local family, Slater and his partners shelled out $1.44 to $2 a week, adding 32 cents to the bill whenever a family supplied an apprentice with medicine, clothes, or shoes. By 1796, Slater was hiring fewer apprentices and more contract workers, children who labored in the dusty, noisy mill by day and returned to their parents' homes at shift's end. Slater paid them only their hourly wages. But the contract labor posed another set of headaches for Slater: as cash-strapped families came and went throughout the region, child workers showed up for shifts one day and were gone the next. In July 1796, Slater found himself shorthanded because his contract children were picking whortleberries with their families for "cash on the bushel."

Multiplying Slater's work-floor woes were runaway apprentices fed up with sixteen-hour shifts, erratic school sessions, and Slater's refusal to teach them the tricks of the trade. For bright, strong youths denied the traditional New England brand of apprenticeship by Slater, cooped up in the heat or cold of the mill for most of their waking hours, work as farmhands or teamsters took on a new appeal. In 1797, Slater informed his partners that apprentice James Horton had bolted from the factory, a second youth had followed, and "another will go tomorrow—so on until they are all gone."[12]

With Almy, Brown & Slater's cotton yarn carving inroads into the British mills' American markets, the partners needed to consolidate their workforce. Slater eventually shed the commercial burdens of apprenticeship and tapped into the region's families by creating a labor system in which children were the breadwinners. Where he had once hired the children of local artisans, such as the Wilkinsons, he now drafted help from the families of unskilled laborers hard-pressed to find jobs in the stagnant economy of the 1790s.

Slater drove the children hard on the work floor, but also assumed a role of patriarchal concern for them. He punished bad behavior, still fought to educate them, and often sided with parents' concerns about conditions in the mill and late payment of wages. In January 1796, Slater wrote: "You [Almy and Brown] must not expect much yarn until I am better supplied with hands and money to pay them with—several are out of corn and I have not a single dollar to buy any for them."[13]

Three weeks later, he appealed again to his partners: "Please send a little money, if not I must unavoidably stop the mill after this week. . . . Can you imagine that upwards of 30 [children] can be supplied with necessary articles that cannot be gotten short of cash. . . . Or, do not you imagine anything about it? This is the 3rd and last time I mean to write until a new supply [of money] is arrived."[14]

Even when Slater goaded his partners into paying back wages, the problem continually resurfaced. Slater threatened to close the mill and sell the precious Arkwright-style machines because he could not "bear to have people [the workers' parents] come round me daily if sometimes hourly and saying I have no wood nor corn nor have not had any for several days."[15] In a letter to Brown and Almy, Slater harangued: "Can you expect my children to work if they have nothing to eat?"[16]

When the children's parents also confronted Slater about the effects of the mill's musty interior upon the children's eyesight, the lack of heat in winter, and the serious injuries some of the boys and girls suffered from the dangerous machines because Slater could not possibly watch everyone at once, he took up the parents' cause. Now a father himself, he admonished his partners that "the children are quivering this morning at seeing it snowy and cold and no stove [here]."[17] In December 1794, a severe injury suffered by one of his mill children led him to fire off another missive to his tightwad associates. "You call for yarn," Slater railed, "but think little about the means by which it is to be made such as children."[18]

In 1795, some of the children's parents, driven by the need for back wages and worried by the mill's dangers, threatened to pull their children from work until the issues were addressed. Slater listened, but Almy and Brown ignored the challenge, figuring that the strikers were easily replaceable. But Slater realized that if word spread that children were badly treated in the mill, even the most desperate families would refuse to answer the factory's ads. Almy and Brown stood firm in their refusal to deal with the irate parents.

In June 1795, three households yanked their children from Almy, Brown & Slater. Other families followed suit in September. Slater's partners still refused to negotiate with the parents.

The mill owners finally listened in October 1796, when so many children walked away from the carding and spinning machines that Slater was forced to shut down operations. With orders piling up at the Blackstone mill, with bad press about the plant's condition spreading throughout the region, the parents forced the bosses to the bargaining table.

Always the point man between the families and management, Slater, having grasped that bad relations bred dwindling profits, devised a commercial compact between the mill owners and the families. Refining his plan, which would earn the sobriquet the Rhode Island System throughout the 1790s, he incorporated the need for employers to refrain from usurpation of the parents' roles in raising and disciplining children; divided workers by age, sex, and marital status in response to moral issues raised by parents who were alarmed by unsupervised contact among boys and girls inside the mill; and gave the parents a say in how their children were trained, educated, and disciplined by management.

In another shrewd gambit to mollify parents beset by hard times, Slater promised to hire, whenever possible, his workers' fathers as the mill's teamsters, security staff, lawnkeepers, and assorted laborers—at adult wages. Not only would the fathers earn a living, but they would also keep an eye on conditions inside the plant.

The compromises' enlightenment notwithstanding, Slater and his partners still held the proverbial upper hand over their employees and their families. And by 1798, Slater realized that if he wanted to implement his Rhode Island System without opposition from his partners, he had to open his own mill.

Maintaining his interest in Almy, Brown & Slater, he formed a company with his father-in-law and brothers-in-law. They built their first factory in Pawtucket and expanded their cotton empire throughout New England. Smithfield, Rhode Island; East Webster, Massachusetts; Jewett City, Connecticut; Amoskeag Falls, New Hampshire; and the aptly named Slatersville, Rhode Island—these and other sites of Slater's mills not only earned him the riches he had dreamed of, but also entrenched the factory system in America. That system, however, relied increasingly on children and, later, women. Although Slater continued his attempts to deal fairly with his youthful workforce and their families, many mill owners sprouting in the textile competition throughout New England did not share Slater's decency. Despite his compassion, his system had unleashed the nightmare of child labor from the Blackstone to the banks of fast-flowing rivers in New England and the rest of the nation.

Slater had also put America on the industrial map for the first time. When he opened his landmark mill in 1790–91, America's manufacturers turned out goods worth slightly more than $20,000,000. The nation's two-million-pound cotton crop largely fed England's spinning frames. In 1835, thanks to Slater's system, America's Northern cotton mills spun nearly $50,000,000 of goods, fed by 80,000,000 or so pounds of cotton from Southern plantations. Slater had set in motion the industrial North, which would defeat the agrarian South during the Civil War.

Many of America's leaders fully understood the scope of the Rhode Island mill magnate's vision. In 1817, President James Monroe arrived at Slater's second factory, the Blackstone River concern, which was the nation's foremost cotton mill. Slater escorted Monroe through the facility and boasted that the spinning frame he had built from memory nearly three decades earlier still worked.

The success of that spinning frame and the wealth it spawned brought fame and financial comfort to Slater, but by 1830 his wife and kindred intellectual, Hannah, had been dead thirteen years. He suffered from the rheumatism that had their beginnings in his ice-chopping bouts with his Blackstone waterwheel and worsened with the passing years. Largely bedridden in his sixties, his once-fair hair gray and receded, Slater still commanded the respect of America's high and mighty. President Andrew Jackson, traveling through Rhode Island in 1832, took time from his itinerary to visit the textile mogul in his Pawtucket mansion.

Jackson called the gaunt, pain-wracked Slater the Father of American Manufacturers, and thanked him for having launched an industry that provided so many jobs for Americans.

"Yes, Sir," Slater said, "I suppose that I gave out the psalm, and they have been singing to the tune ever since."[19]

On April 21, 1835, the composer of that tune died of heart failure in his Pawtucket home. Slater left behind a personal fortune one of his partners calculated at $1,200,000 (an extraordinarily large sum even by 1990s' standards). Although various historians would hail Henri Lorillard, a Southern tobacco magnate, as America's first bona fide millionaire in 1843, Moses Brown's 1835 estimate of his partner's wealth stakes a strong claim to the commercial crown on Slater's behalf.

Today, on the banks of the Blackstone River, Samuel Slater's second mill, its facade redolent of an early New England meetinghouse, still stands. His water-powered carding and spinning machines bear eloquent testimony to the architect of America's factory age. Those dark wooden devices offer equally telling witness to one of the most outstanding feats of memory in America's annals and to the grim birth of child labor in the nation's factories.

THE POWER OF THE PRESS

New England's
First News Hounds

In 1688, a Cambridge, Massachusetts, printer carefully arranged his type, laid a large sheet of paper upon his press, and set the gears of his cumbersome apparatus into clattering motion. He had done so countless times over the past several decades inside his little print shop. But the sheet emerging from the rollers that day differed from any he had ever published.

When he lifted the sheet and scrutinized the bold black typeface, taking care not to smudge the inked characters, he made history. For his latest broadsheet, *The Present State of the New-English Affairs,* soon to hit the streets of Cambridge, Boston, and beyond, was America's first newspaper. So say Samuel Green's supporters, who believe that his broadsheet's battle cry "to prevent false reports" would inspire future generations of American publishers—some publishers, anyway.[1]

To many media historians, anointing Samuel Green the father of American journalism poses a tricky dilemma; two other colonial New Englanders hold a claim to the title. America's first news hound *was* indeed a printer who hailed from the banks of the Charles River. He was, however, a man with three faces—those of Samuel Green, Benjamin Harris, and John Campbell.

Of the three, Samuel Green arrived in Boston first, in 1633, when John Winthrop's town was less than three years old. Green settled across the Charles in Cambridge, and by the 1660s was running Harvard's printing press, the only press in New England before 1665. How he assumed the duties of the colony's first print shop is cloaked in mystery; he had never served an apprenticeship as an ink-stained wretch. In 1675, Green would write, "I was not [before] used to it [printing]."[2] Somehow he had convinced the overseers of Harvard College to let him run their precious press.

Much of the material he set into type was religious matter put out by the college, a training ground for Congregationalist ministers. His lack of formal training never inhibiting his work, he set the type for at least 275 books in the seventeenth century, not to mention countless broadsheets and assorted handbills. Green's most famous project was *Eliot's Indian Bible*, intended by its creator, the Reverend John Eliot, to bring Indians into the Christian fold by translating the Good Book from English into the local Indian tongue. On this venture Green had help, leaning on the layout and design aptitude of a recently arrived Londoner named Marmaduke Johnson.

When Green was not cranking up his press, setting type, and inking metal characters to be imprinted on blank sheets of paper, he was immersed in his family. His two marriages produced nineteen printer's devils. Luckily for his burgeoning brood, he was capable of putting food on a huge dinner table.

Green spent his precious few hours away from his shop and his family with Boston's militia, drilling on the grassy, rock-strewn expanse of Boston Common with his fellow recruits and showing off his martial prowess with the others on days of thanksgiving and on the few other holidays in the Puritan calendar. Green rose through the ranks and was appointed a captain at the age of seventy-five, the one achievement he cherished as much as bindings and inked pages crafted in his print shop.

Green's no-nonsense temperament led him to abhor any false reports that sent neighbors into a panic over threats—Indian uprisings; rumors of French, Spanish, or Dutch invasions; whispers of witchcraft—that were sometimes real, with the arguable exception of the latter. In 1689, a genuine crisis, the Andros affair, crashed across New England with the fury of an Atlantic gale, disturbing Green and other colonists.

The Andros affair had begun in the mid-1680s, when King James II of Great Britain revoked Massachusetts's charter, its right to govern itself. Next the monarch had appointed Sir Edmund Andros as the royal governor of all the colonies north and east of Pennsylvania.

From the moment Andros set foot on Boston's Town Dock in December 1686, clad in a costly scarlet coat and in lace finery reeking of London's decadent royal court, he imposed his will on the region. To the horror of the colonial Congregationalists, the new governor forced them to allow Anglican services in the South Meeting House. Of equal distress to the Puritans, he also forced them to prove the validity of land grants and deeds to his satisfaction; he could arbitrarily order New Englanders from homes and land held by families since the colony's founding.

The Puritans' simmering rage against Andros boiled over in the spring of 1689. News that the Catholic king, James II, had been overthrown by Holland's William of Orange and his wife, Protestant Mary, the deposed ruler's sister, spurred the Puritans to seize and imprison the stunned Andros and to proclaim their support for Britain's new lord and his lady. Yet the insurgents feared that their monarchs would not condone the removal of a royally appointed governor and would punish the Puritans.

Acutely aware of his neighbors' terror that their arrest of Andros could be judged treason by the Crown and that the mother country could dispatch red-coated regiments to occupy Boston, Green decided to allay rumors. He went to his press, rolled up his sleeves, and began laying out what some would view as America's first newspaper, others as an important handbill.

Green's broadsheet hit the streets and was carried by readers into the Town House, private homes, shops, and taverns such as the Rose and Crown, Noah's Ark, the Bunch of Grapes, and the Blue Anchor. Colonists anxious for any news at all about the possible repercussions of the Andros affair saw a headline that immediately conveyed the printer's intent: *The Present State of the New-English Affairs.* "This is Published to Prevent False Reports."[3]

When readers' eyes darted from the headline to the accompanying text, they soon learned that Green's treatment of the volatile issues of the Andros mess read straightforwardly and was based on reason rather than rumor and rant. The printer had arranged his words with the same precision with which his alter ego, the captain, drilled his militiamen on Boston Common. His printed columns were deployed to lead his readers to one conclusion: the colony would not be punished for the uprising against Governor Andros.

Green's first column offered such sources as a letter from Increase Mather, the president of Harvard and Andros's implacable foe, who had fled Boston one step ahead of Andros's soldiers in April 1688 to plead with James II for the restoration of Massachusetts's charter. The missive, dated September 3, 1689, relieved New Englanders. "His Majesty [William of Orange] . . . was well pleased with what was done in New England. . . . He signifies His Royal Approbation of what has been done at Boston," Mather had written.[4]

Green's second reassuring column featured an excerpt from a London newspaper seconding the new king's approval of the revolt against Andros and claiming that New Englanders' "Privileges and Religion" would soon be restored.[5]

The Cambridge printer's self-avowed mission to convince his readers that they were now safe from royal retribution reached fruition with another of Mather's letters run in the news sheet. "Sir Edmund Andross . . . and others, that have been Seized by the people of Boston, and shall be at the Receipt of these Commands, Detained there, under Confinement, be sent on Board the first Ship bound to England, to answer what may be objected against."[6] Mather's words revealed that Andros and his crowd would soon be on their way across the Atlantic—by order of the Crown. Even the dourest Puritans, those who viewed New England as perpetually under assault by the outside world, could lay aside their fears in regard to the Andros affair, thanks to Samuel Green and his printing press.

Green's effort to prevent false reports was not much to look at—a single, two-column sheet, folio style, 8" x 14½"—but his inked lines accomplished their purpose. For whether or not the news sheet was, as historians such as William Shillaber have lauded, America's first newspaper, Green's determination to prevent false reports heralded a tenet of responsible journalism.

231

. . .

A second New Englander who could lay claim to the title of America's first news hound was Benjamin Harris, a man famed Manchester publisher William Loeb might have admired. In several respects, Harris mirrored future journalists. He was willing and able to fire verbal darts at entrenched powers, a dangerous practice he honed in England and brought to New England. And in both the Old and the New Worlds, he would suffer censorship.

In London in the 1670s, Benjamin Harris owned a flourishing print business, churning out books and pamphlets inside his Bell Abbey shop. Many of his publications ruffled the egos of nobles and politicians. Catholics and Quakers loathed him, for he was a virulent foe of both faiths and constantly assailed them in print. His first stab at a newspaper came in 1679, when he issued *Domestick Intelligence or News both from City and Country,* a paper reflecting his own prejudices. In April 1681, the Crown suppressed his paper, but if the government believed it had muzzled Benjamin Harris, it was dead wrong.

Harris's determination to print the truth—as he saw it—had already led him in late 1679 to issue an inflammatory pamphlet he titled *Appeal from the Country to the City,* a harangue of the king and Parliament. In February 1680, he was hauled into a courtroom on charges of sedition. Chief Justice Scroggs, displaying little affinity for freedom of the press, slapped the printer with a staggering 500-pound fine and a stint in the stocks. Unable to pay up, Harris was dragged to a cell within the grim walls of London's King's Bench Prison and languished there until friends paid his fine in December 1680.

With the ascension of the Catholic James Stuart, James II, to the throne in 1685, the radically anti-papist Harris published *English Liberties,* a diatribe against Catholics. The government quickly impounded five thousand copies.

Another stint in jail looming, Harris chose to flee from London. John Dunton, an old friend living in Boston, convinced Harris that New England offered just the haven for the printer.

In the fall of 1686, Harris and his son, lugging piles of books, landed in Boston and soon set up a bookstore and print shop on the corner of High (now Washington) and Great (now State) Streets. His business took off, and the success of his first publication of *Tulley's Almanack* (see "All Roads Lead from Boston," p. 240) entrenched him as a player in the town's fledgling book trade.

For his new neighbors, Harris's shop became far more than a spot where they browsed through books and pamphlets. Townspeople gathered there to discuss politics, to gossip, and to socialize with each other and the printer.

Harris, an astute businessman as well as a zealot, began selling coffee, tea, and hot chocolate in his shop in August 1690, enhancing the business's convivial aura of books and conversation and becoming Boston's place to see and be seen—the London Coffee House.

The colonial café was soon far more than a gathering place for luminaries such as the Reverend Cotton Mather and for tradesmen. Harris welcomed Boston's women, banned from entering inns and taverns, to his establishment. Puritan housewives in their bonnets, petticoats, and capes could reach for the works of Anne Bradstreet, the Ipswich poetess, on Harris's shelves. For women whose customary sojourns about town consisted of stops at the market or of Sunday services at meetinghouses, Harris's shop offered an oasis where fragrant whiffs of coffee, tea, and chocolate wafted through stacked pamphlets and books.

Idyllic as his business appeared, Benjamin Harris craved to stir something besides tea and coffee in his adopted town. On September 25, 1690, he published *Publick Occurrences, Both Foreign and Domestick*. Printed on the press of Richard Pierce, Harris's creation ran across three sides of a folded sheet and contained two columns of newsprint per page. The paper was a manageable 7½" x 11".

Unlike his colonial predecessor, Samuel Green, Harris harbored a new aim for his paper: he intended to publish it monthly—"or if an glut of Occurrences happen,"[7] more frequently. To preserve total editorial control, Harris refused to run advertisements.

Most remarkable about the three-page paper were the concentration on colonial news rather than British events, and its vivid prose, the trademark of Harris's past publications.

Not long after New Englanders began browsing the paper at the London Coffee Shop, Harris discovered that his edgy news coverage was infuriating to several prominent Puritans. On September 25, 1690, Harris's dream of a news sheet chronicling the colonial scene fell victim to censorship when Governor Bradstreet, a son of the poetess, ordered the immediate suppression of *Publick Occurrences*. Massachusetts Chief Justice Samuel Sewall, a heavily jowled jurist who later lamented his pivotal role in the Salem witch hysteria, couched the censorship in legal terms, claiming that the newspaper had been squelched because it was not licensed. Among the most vociferous critics of Harris's work was one of the newsman's regular coffee shop customers—the Reverend Cotton Mather, who seconded Sewall's opinion that Harris's forceful style "gave much distaste" and "high resentment."[8]

And what were Harris's printed sins? They numbered such transgressions as the mere mention of Britain's Catholic foe, the king of France.

In 1694, Harris—banned in Boston—sailed back to England. His eight-year stint as a New Englander had been successful, his London Coffee House a smash. Although Puritan powers had quashed *Publick Occurrences*, Harris had published what many scholars would later deem America's first genuine newspaper, staking a claim for Harris as the colonies' first news hound.

Less than a decade after Harris's paper vanished beneath the censors' hands, the news bug struck another colonist. John Campbell, born in Scotland in 1653, had emigrated to Boston at about the same time that Harris was packing up his books and pamphlets to return to England. Campbell and his brother, Duncan, plunged into New England's literary world; Duncan attracted Bostonians' attention first when he opened a bookstore. Proper Puritan John Dunton, impressed by the ambitious immigrant, wrote: "I rambled to the Scotch bookseller, one Campbell. He is a brisk young fellow, that dresses All-a-mode, and sets himself off to the best advantage; and yet thrives apace. . . . He's an industrious Man."[9]

Duncan Campbell, using his charm and flair for fashion to his best advantage, wooed and won the hand of Susanna Porter, the daughter of a well-heeled Boston merchant. For an ambitious man on Boston's commercial stage, the marriage helped. And if the upwardly mobile Scot truly loved his new bride, so much the better. If he did not, this would not have been unusual in an era when marrying well often precluded marrying for love.

Having wedded a fitting bride for a man going places, Campbell made it his business not only to sell books to the right sort of locals, but also to ingratiate himself to Boston's movers and mavens. By cashing in on his social connections, Duncan Campbell wrangled an appointment to town postmaster in the late 1690s, a post he would hold until his death, in 1702. His brother, John, was appointed to replace him.

The post office, the clearinghouse for all sorts of information about his friends and future foes alike, offered a perfect venue for an aspiring news hound. Campbell began to plot a newspaper; of equal importance, he pondered how to keep the censors away from the venture.

On April 24, 1704, the first issue of Campbell's *Boston News-Letter* rolled off the printing press, and as the publisher held the 7½" x 12½" half-sheet paper, cognizant of Harris's ordeal at the hands of irate censors, he peered at his typeset columns to make sure that nothing he had written could peeve the Reverend Cotton Mather, Judge Samuel Sewall, or any other local bigwigs, men who did, in fact, sport big wigs.

Campbell's attention to the egos and sensibilities of the elite paid off. From 1704 to 1722, *Boston News-Letter* was a staple of literary life not only in Boston, but also throughout New England. News from abroad filled most of the paper's columns, Campbell filtering the dispatches so as not to offend his readers with anything critical of their town.

Hoping the paper would jam his cash box with shillings, Campbell grew frustrated as years passed and his circulation remained stagnant. In 1711, he complained that he was straining to sell more than 150 copies a month—although hordes of locals were only too eager to borrow a friend's copy. When all was said and done, virtually the entire town ended up reading *Boston News-Letter* and never had to pay a cent to stay informed.

His gripes aside, Campbell continued to print his little news sheet, ink running figuratively in his veins. So committed to keeping New Englanders abreast of key overseas doings was the transplanted Scot that when an unusually heavy load of news reached him through the British papers he grabbed from newly docked ships, he swallowed his better financial instincts and ran off a wide-sheet edition of his *News-Letter* rather than the usual, cheaper half sheet.

As Campbell's paper made its way from hand to hand, the publisher could derive some satisfaction whenever he chanced upon a dog-eared copy of *Boston News-Letter* in the hands of a neighbor who may have actually purchased the paper.

In 1718, when he was replaced as the town's distributor of mail, Campbell no longer had the first peek at British newspapers sent to the post office for the Mathers; the publisher still continued to compile dispatches for readers who had come to depend on *Boston News-Letter* for the colonial equivalent of all the news that's fit to print. He cranked out the paper for four years following the loss of his postal sinecure, reaching a high-water circulation of three hundred.

In 1722, Campbell stepped down from his perch as the region's sole newspaper publisher and turned over his ink-stained labor of love to Boston printer Bartholomew Green—a son of Samuel Green. The younger Green proved a fitting choice, having set the type of *Boston News-Letter* and run it off his press for several years.

On March 7, 1728, Bostonians read a sad notice: "On Monday evening last . . . about 8 a clock died here John Campbell, Esq. . , Aged 75 years, formerly Post Master of this Place, Publisher of the

Boston News-Letter for many years, and One of his Majesties Justices of the Peace for the County of Suffolk."

The obituary ran in the *Boston News-Letter*.

One can argue the merits of Samuel Green, Benjamin Harris, and John Campbell and never arrive at a definitive answer to the question of which man was the father of the American newspaper. But the legacy of all three New England news hounds lingers whenever 1990s publishers, editors, and reporters strive to prevent false reports.

You Can Look It Up

〜

In 1788, a unique event unfolded in both New England's and America's history: the publication of the first English-language dictionary printed in America. But it is not West Hartford's Noah Webster or his printer, Connecticut's Hudson & Goodwin, who deserves accolades for publishing the landmark work. The honor belongs to Worcester, Massachusetts, printer Isaiah Thomas.

Isaiah Thomas was born in Boston on January 19, 1749, and six years later was indentured to a printer. As he grew into a tall, strong young man with piercing eyes, Thomas came to love his trade and sought to emulate the success of his idol, a printer named Benjamin Franklin.

Little in Isaiah Thomas's early career and personal life suggested he would ever publish anything so sedate as America's first English-language dictionary. By 1775, his printing press had become the mouthpiece of Boston Rebels' cries for independence. His controversial newspaper, the *Massachusetts Spy,* vehemently denounced British policies and earned its publisher British condemnation as "the Snake of Sedition."[1] Thomas's critics, however, later charged that opportunism shaped his politics, an allegation fueled by the *Spy's* editorial shift to increasingly rebellious views as the Revolution loomed closer. "He had endless ambition, a certain pugnacity, and a Bermudan wife who was a scandal. Printing presses and books were his absorbing passion," wrote one historian.[2] But many of Thomas's contemporaries knew him as "a soft touch for anyone in trouble."[3]

To the utter embarrassment of the Rebel printer, his wife fell in love with a British officer and ran away with the redcoat to Newburyport in February 1775. Although Mary Dill Thomas "had a bastard [unknown to Isaiah Thomas] & she had been prostituted to the purposes of more than one," some historians have also pointed out that hot-tempered, obsessive Isaiah Thomas was not the easiest man to live with.[4] Despite the scandalous circumstances of the couple's divorce on May 27, 1777, Thomas continued to provide money to the woman who had given him a son and a daughter, and saw to the children's financial needs for the rest of his life and beyond.

Fearing arrest in the spring of 1775, when tensions between the British and the colonists exploded in warfare at Concord and Lexington, Thomas loaded his printing press into a horsecart and lugged the machine west. On April 20, 1775, he "rode down the wide and quiet street [Worcester's Main Street] on which in years to come he was to win fame even beyond his youthful dreams."[5] He printed his first Worcester edition of the *Spy* in the basement of Daniel Bigelow's house on Main Street in early May 1775.

The life of the printer took a welcome turn when he married a local widow, Mary Fowle, in May 1779. She provided Thomas the solid, happy union he had never truly known during his disastrous first marriage. Mary could calm down her husband during his bouts of temper.

Thomas's Worcester-based printing business became one of the young nation's foremost publishing houses in the years after the Revolution. By 1782, his book-printing and -selling operations covered more than two hundred feet on Main Street. Profits from the books pouring off his presses allowed him, in 1783, to build a Court Hill mansion that testified to his status as one of Worcester's leading citizens and America's first printing mogul.

Thomas's books, many of them notable for their elegant, costly printing style, covered topics ranging from medicine, science, and history to religion, grammar, and literature. In 1785, Thomas printed six dictionaries, but none of the English language.

The year 1788 was auspicious for the Worcester printer and his expanding empire. He opened several branch offices including one in Boston that evolved into America's leading printing house, Thomas and Andrews. But Thomas's most notable achievement of that year unfolded in his Main Street headquarters when he decided to print the *Royal Standard English Dictionary.*

The *Royal Standard English Dictionary,* compiled and written by William Perry, had first been published in Edinburgh, Scotland, in 1775 and was in its fourth printing by 1786. Thomas, no doubt aware of the lack of an English-language dictionary printed in America, got his hands on a British edition of the tome, spent months revising it, and sold his Americanized version of Perry's work for seven shillings a copy. He dedicated the dictionary to the American Academy of Arts and Sciences, in Worcester.

Thomas's edition of Perry's dictionary was 596 pages long and featured an appendix of "Scripture Proper Names." Thirty-eight lines filled each page, and the dictionary's entries, arranged in double columns, were followed in most cases by one-line definitions. By today's standards or those of Noah Webster several decades later, the dictionary was simplistic; however, for the first time in the nation's history, all Americans, from schoolchildren to professors, could look up the meanings and the spellings of troublesome or unfamiliar words in an English-language dictionary printed in America. Courtesy of Perry, Thomas not only filled one-room schoolhouses, colleges, and home libraries with the bulky book, but also added to his bank account.

In a stunt that would have sent today's writers and publishers scurrying to their lawyers' offices, Thomas printed the dictionary without the author's permission and never paid Perry a cent. Thomas's seemingly underhanded actions, however, constituted common business practices among eighteenth-century publishers on both sides of the Atlantic. When a book reached print, it became fair game for any printer, and most authors, painfully aware of the era's hazy copyright laws, chose not to waste their time and money in the pursuit of literary pirates, especially transatlantic publishers such as Thomas.

Ironically, a better dictionary than the one Thomas printed in Worcester existed in England. Dr. Samuel Johnson's *Dictionary of the English Language,* first published in 1755, was truly the landmark dictionary of its era, but the first American edition of Johnson's work did not appear until a heavily abridged version was printed in Philadelphia in 1805.

The first complete American edition of Johnson's dictionary came out in 1818, some thirty years after the *Royal Standard English Dictionary* rolled off Thomas's Worcester printing presses and turned up in countless corners of the original thirteen colonies.

Language purists can sing the praises of Johnson's dictionary, revere Noah Webster's deservedly immortal work, and overlook Thomas's feat—that *other* dictionary. But no one can deny an ironclad fact: Isaiah Thomas printed America's first English-language dictionary in his Worcester offices. You can look it up!

All Roads Lead from Boston

∽

M any of us have reached for a road map to guide us to scenic locales, but few people realize that road maps are a venerable

American tradition. In fact, America's first road map for public use was printed in Boston nearly three hundred years ago—although purists could assert that the map was more of a guide.

In 1698, renowned Boston printer Bartholomew Green published *An Almanack for the Year of Our Lord M DC XC VIII* and sold the book "at the Printing House at the South End of Town." The almanac, the work of local resident John Tulley, charted "time of Full Sea, or High Water, with an account of the Eclipses, Conjunctions, and other Configurations of the Celestial Bodies." Tulley hoped his calculations would "serve any part of New-England."

At the rear of his almanac, Tulley included "A Description of the High Ways, & Roads." He had just published the first road map for public use in America's history.

As any cartographer will quickly point out, Tulley's creation was not a chart or a drawing; instead, his map was a word map that listed towns, roads, and distances from Boston, and described the best route to New York. According to Tulley's figures, New York lay 278 miles from Boston.

The guide offered readers two main routes. "From Boston to Dedham 10 miles, thence to Whites 6, to Billings 7. . . . Or, from Dedham to Medfield 9, to Wrentham 10 . . . (which is the smoother Road) to Providence 15. . . ." Peddlers, farmers, merchants, tradesmen, and assorted colonists taking Tulley's advice passed through such spots as "Half-way-bout, 9 miles outside of New York." Travelers unfamiliar with the roads around Boston and hoping to avoid some of the rocks and ruts that broke wagon wheels and turned trips on colonial roads into time-consuming nightmares could heed Tulley's mention of the smoother road.

Tulley's map did not end at New York. His guide also presented the route from that city to Philadelphia. If New Englanders lost their way on the arduous trip to the Quaker town, they found such landmarks as Mid-stone-brook and Crosswick's Bridge, both on the newest road to Philadelphia, in *Tulley's Almanack*.

Later editions of the almanac not only listed roads and distances out of Boston, but also the names of local tavern keepers. Whenever a weary, hungry, thirsty traveler with a fistful of jingling coins in one hand and a dog-eared copy of *Tulley's Almanack* in the other showed up at a tavern, the proprietor owed thanks to the man whose ads led business to local inns' doorsteps.

The ABCs
and Recipes

F orty-eight pages of "geography, essays on morality, religion, manners, etc., familiar letters, dialogues, and select pieces of poetry"—the material reads like a textbook or a Sunday school primer.[1] But this table of contents comprised America's first children's magazine.

Published in January 1789, the first issue of the *Children's Magazine: Calculated for the Use of Families and Schools* rolled off the printing presses of Hartford, Connecticut, publishers Barzillai Hudson and George Goodwin. Their magazine mirrored eighteenth-century tenets of childrearing, the forty-eight pages crammed with lessons and missives designed to guide children away from sloth and other vices and to steer them toward responsible, industrious behavior.

Of games, puzzles, riddles, and whimsical illustrations that later generations of Americans would associate with children's magazines, there was nothing in Hudson and Goodwin's pages. Their religious and moral themes offered little fun—just more lessons that children of 1789 were required to memorize and to recite in their homes and their schoolhouses.

The Children's Magazine was not profitable for the Hartford printers. After four issues, the pair suspended publication in April 1789.

In 1826, another New Englander, the aptly named Lydia Maria Francis Child, followed Hudson and Goodwin's path with a bimonthly children's magazine titled *The Juvenile Miscellany.* While hardly the lighthearted stuff of future children's magazines such as *Jack and Jill, Highlights,* and *Cobblestone,* Child's work was not as preachy as the Connecticut publication. The *Juvenile Miscellany,* which ran poems and stories that appealed to children, became America's first successful children's magazine. From the first issue, 108 pages published by Putnam & Hunt, of Boston, in September 1826, to the final edition, in January 1829, Child succeeded where Goodwin and Hudson had missed, and heralded a lucrative niche for future publishers.

Hudson and Goodwin scarcely needed a successful children's magazine to reap a fortune. The publishers of the *Connecticut* (later *Hartford*) *Courant,* papermakers, and booksellers, the duo took a risk on a young writer in 1806. That writer's name was Noah Webster, and his book was *A Compendious Dictionary of the English Language.*

A decade earlier, in 1796, the Connecticut publishers of America's first children's magazine won another first: a cookbook written by an American, Amelia Simmons. Except that she was a New England housewife and a self-described orphan, her name is all that is known of her personal background. Her forty-seven-page work bore the grandiloquent title, *American Cookery, Or the Act of Dressing Viands, Fish, Poultry and Vegetables, and the Best Modes of Making Pastes, Puffs, Pies, Tarts, Puddings, Custards and Preserves, and All Kinds of Cakes from the Imperial Plumb to Plain Cake.*

Previously, American women had turned to British cookbooks such as *Compleat Housewife* (1742), but as Simmons proclaimed on her title page, *American Cookery* was the first cookbook "Adapted to This Country and All Grades of Life."[2]

With distinctly American recipes for "Johnny Cake," "Indian Pudding," "Pompkin [*sic*] Pudding," a butter "Christmas Cookey [*sic*]" and myriad other recipes from main courses to desserts, Simmons truly covered the gamut of a genuine American cuisine. At two shillings and three pence, her little cookbook—replete with household hints and shopping tips such as how to spot spoiled but cleverly disguised meat, fish, and produce—was a bargain. The book proved no risk for Hudson and Goodwin; Simmons paid the costs of printing her treatise. No one is certain who paid for the newspaper advertisements of America's first cookbook.

One fact is known, however. The enigmatic Amelia Simmons launched one of the most profitable staples of future American publishers.

America's first homegrown cookbook and the nation's first children's magazine testified to the prescience of Barzillai Hudson and George Goodwin, and to Hartford's status as the birthplace of those publishing landmarks.

HEROISM
OR
HORROR?

Hannah Duston's Hatchet

O n the evening of March 30, 1697, near the banks of the Merrimack and the Contoocook Rivers, a haggard thirty-nine-year-old woman rose from her spot in a sodden campsite and stood above twelve sleeping Indians, seven of them children. Hannah Duston clutched a hatchet.

Stealing into place near Duston were Mary Neff and teenager Samuel Leonardson. Both had hatchets.

What happened next would shroud Hannah Duston in controversy. For as her hatchet struck again and again, the blows would earn her very name equal measures of heroism and horror.

Two weeks earlier, on the morning of March 15, 1697, Hannah Duston lay in bed, convalescing from the birth of her twelfth child, six-day-old Martha. Midwife Mary Neff, Duston's aunt, hustled about her niece's brick home, a mile or so outside the frontier settlement of Haverhill, Massachusetts, tending to the household chores and to Duston's eleven other children, ranging in age from three to eighteen.

A mile or so from the house and the five others near it, Duston's husband, Thomas, inspected his fields, tramping through a sparse covering of snow as he pondered his upcoming spring planting, his horse nearby. He gripped a musket; with King William's War still raging and raids on English settlements by French and Indians still frequent, he could leave nothing to chance. The previous summer, as four neighbors picked beans outside Haverhill, a party of Indians had suddenly emerged from the surrounding forest and killed them.

Duston, trodding across the acreage where he would plant his beans and corn, had much to be grateful for despite the dangers of

246

frontier life. He and his family had come through another harsh winter healthy, and King William's War was winding down. In the twentieth year of his marriage, the farmer and brick mason was not rich, but had attained a comfortable lifestyle by colonial standards. His small but sturdy home, the symbol of his decades of hard work, lay within his sight as he studied his fields.

Suddenly Duston spied a movement in the woods flanking the settlement. Howls filled the air as ten Indians in feathers and war paint burst from the brush and charged toward him. He jumped into his saddle and galloped to his house, his pursuers closing fast. Another ten or more Indians rushed toward the other houses.

Duston reined in his horse at his door, dismounted, and rushed inside to Hannah's bed. Mary Neff grabbed the infant and fled out the door—straight into the onrushing Indians.

Hannah quickly convinced her husband to get the other children to safety at the fort a mile away and to leave her behind in her bed. With the Indians approaching the house and his wife adamant, Thomas Duston ran from the house, clambered back on his horse, and charged after his children, who were scurrying across the fields and meadows toward the garrison.

Several Indians broke away from the pack and chased Duston and his children. Shots whizzed over their heads. Duston, maneuvering his horse to use it as a shield for his children, stopped, aimed his flintlock, and dropped one of the pursuers.

The Indians gave up the chase and ran back to the settlement as the children and their father neared the fort.

At the settlement, the war party kicked down the doors of all six houses, killed twenty-seven settlers in a bloody melee of musketry and flashing tomahawks, and scalped the dead. Hannah Duston still lay in her bed as Indians burst into her home and ransacked it. They swarmed into her bedroom, yanked her from her bedcovers, and dragged her from the house; one shoe and her bedclothes were all she wore. On the way out, a warrior snatched a large piece of cloth from her loom.

Tethering thirteen captives, including Duston, her infant, and Neff, together with a rawhide lead, stuffing loot into parcels tied to the prisoners, the war party dragged them away from the settlement, across the fields, and into the woods. Behind the prisoners, flames enveloped the homes, a pall of smoke billowing above the crumbling frame and brick walls.

Shoving the captives forward, determined to put as much distance as possible between the raiders and the militia certain to follow, the Indians tomahawked several prisoners unable to maintain the pace across snowy thickets, freezing brooks, and rugged hills. Duston and Mary staggered along, keeping up with their captors.

A short way north of Haverhill, one of the Indians snatched Martha Duston from Mary Neff's grasp, "dashed out the Brains of the Infant against a Tree," and tossed the lifeless form into the snow.[1] The baby's cries had reportedly irritated the warrior.

Duston and Neff trudged on, able to mourn only in silence.

By nightfall, having covered twelve to fifteen miles and confident that they had lost any search party, the Indians camped, tying themselves to their captives.

The same routine filled the next two weeks. Shivering, reeling beneath the weight of the packs loaded with booty from the settlement, eating raw meat, acorns, and whatever other morsels the Indians threw them, the captives staggered some one hundred miles northward. The warrior who owned Duston and Neff spoke a smattering of English and informed them he had lived with the Reverend Rowlandson, of Lancaster, Massachusetts, for several years and had practiced the Protestant faith. But, finding the French more to his liking, he had converted to Catholicism and had rejected the land-grasping Puritans. The other men of the war party had also embraced the faith of the colonists' age-old foe.

Adding insult to injury, the Indians prayed three times a day; Duston and Neff's master mocked them by saying that if their God truly wanted to save them, he would do so, but that he did not seem inclined to answer their prayers.

Of all the Indian's comments to the women, the most frightening came with his revelation that when they reached their final destination, St. Francis, in Canada, "they must be Stript, Scourg'd, and run the Gauntlet through the whole army of Indians."[2]

On the fifteenth day of the trek, the war party split into two groups. One camped at a small, wooded island at the confluence of the Merrimack and Contoocook Rivers; the other, larger band headed farther upriver. Duston and Neff belonged to the former group.

Their master, with the two women on their rawhide lead, and another warrior beached their canoe alongside several others on the island's shore and joined three Indian women and their seven children at a nearby campsite. Historians would later speculate that the women and children were the warriors' families.

On the island, Duston and Neff encountered another face, that of a teenager, Samuel Leonardson, who had been seized by the Indians in a raid on Worcester a year and a half earlier. When Duston realized that the youth spoke the Indians' tongue, she began to devise a desperate plan to escape, or to die trying.

At Hannah's urging, Leonardson asked one of the warriors, Bampico, how he killed Englishmen quickly and quietly. Bampico put his finger to his temple and said that it was the ideal spot for a tomahawk's blow.

Just before or after the conversation, Hannah, Neff, and the boy somehow managed to steal and to hide several hatchets from their owners.

On the evening of March 30, 1697, the three captives waited until they were certain the Indians were asleep. Hannah gave a signal to Neff and Leonardson. All three climbed quietly to their feet, hatchets in hand, having sliced their rawhide leash or having been untied by captors who believed escape was impossible.

The trio moved in the wan light of the campfire to positions prearranged by Duston. She crouched above one of the slumbering men, aligned her hatchet with his temple, raised her arm, and slammed the blade down against his skull.

Again and again she swung the hatchet as she moved from victim to victim. Leonardson drove his hatchet into one of the Indians and stopped. Neff merely stood there, but Duston's blood-soaked blade continued to strike.

Duston had learned Bampico's lesson well, his corpse proof of that fact. Leonardson's one victim and the nine dispatched by Duston's hatchet lay dead or dying, but one of the Indian women scrambled to her feet though "bleeding from several wounds," grabbed a boy untouched by the hatchet, and bolted away from the camp with the child.[3] They did not stop running until they reached the other Indian camp.

Finally Duston's arm went slack. Ten bodies, nine of them her work, were sprawled at her feet. Six were children.

Several months later, after one of the captives of the other war party was released, he would describe the moment when the bloody, disheveled woman and the child dashed into the camp with their account of Duston's fury.

With the second war party nearby, Hannah quickly collected food from the campsite, ordered Neff and Leonardson to don Indian clothing, and scooped up one of the dead warriors' muskets. She still had her hatchet.

The three captives lugged the food and weapons to the canoes perched above the riverline, sank all but one, loaded it, climbed into the craft, and paddled downstream in waters swollen by melting snow and ice.

Before they had paddled far, Duston decided to return to the island; neither Neff nor Leonardson argued with her. Hannah had forgotten one last task.

When they beached the canoe, Neff and the youth remained on the shore. Duston ran back to the camp, picked up a knife from one of the slain men, and scalped the ten bodies. Looking around for something in which to wrap the trophies, she spied the piece of cloth the Indians had stolen from her own loom. She bundled the dripping scalps in the cloth and rushed back to the canoe. Once again they shoved the vessel onto the river and paddled downstream.

They headed home with their grisly package, one worth a small fortune; the General Court of Massachusetts was offering bounty for every Indian scalp taken in King William's War. No canoes full of vengeful warriors appeared as the island's shore vanished behind them. But ahead of them lay a hundred miles of hostile territory, riverbanks where any stop could be lethal.

Despite the bitter cold, the weather was fortunate for the three escapees; the overflowing Merrimack River pulled the canoe downstream, the paddlers' chief concerns to keep the craft steady and to bail water. Because the river ran so high in late March, "it is probable that she was not obliged to land, certainly not in the daytime."[4] One of their journey's foremost obstacles, the falls near the future site of Manchester, New Hampshire, was "sufficiently full to be passed in a canoe."[5]

After several days on the river, Duston, Neff, and Leonardson beached the canoe on the riverbank at Haverhill and stumbled toward the settlement. Duston, clutching the hatchet, the musket, and the ten scalps, viewed the charred remains of her home. Her neighbors and her family, having mourned her as dead, heard of her ordeal and her exploit—proven by the scalps.

Duston and her husband soon drew up a petition for the General Court to convert "her just slaughter of so many barbarians" into cash.[6] The couple traveled to Boston, where the Reverend Cotton Mather and Judge Samuel Sewall, the "hanging judge" of the Salem Witch Trials, feted Hannah as a genuine Puritan heroine. In his account of the killings, drawn from his conversation with Duston, Mather marveled at how she had "struck such Home Blows, upon the Heads of their Sleeping Oppressors, that e're they could any of them Struggle into any effectual Resistance, at the Feet of those poor Prisoners, they bowed, they fell; where they bowed, there they fell down Dead."[7]

In recounting his wife's deed for the General Court, Thomas Duston asked the magistrates to compensate him for "having lost his estate in the calamity."[8] Then, he offered the reeking scalps to the court.

With those trophies and the colony celebrating Hannah Duston as a heroine, the General Court wasted little time in rewarding her. On June 8, 1697, the magistrates proclaimed that "Thomas Durstan [*sic*] in behalf of his wife shall be allowed and paid out of the publick treasury twenty-five pounds, ten shillings and the young man named Samuel Lenerson [*sic*] concerned in the action the like sum of twelve pounds, ten shillings."[9] Mary Neff received the same cash bounty as the teenager, although she had not killed any of the Indians.

The Dustons used the money, a lofty sum, to buy more acreage in Haverhill and to rebuild their home and their lives. Accorded respect, almost awe, by her neighbors, Duston won fame throughout the other colonies after Mather's account of her was published in *Magnalia Christi Americana*. Governor Thomas Nicholson, of Maryland, sent her an engraved pewter tankard to commemorate her deed, and even men such as Judge Sewall turned deferential in her presence.

According to her contemporaries, Duston returned to her former life without a misstep. With Puritan piety, she spoke of her ordeal as a test from God, one she professed to welcome: "I am Thankful for Captivity, 'twas the Comfortablest Time that ever I had; in my Affliction, God made his Word Comfortable to me."[10]

Less than a year after her escape, Duston bore another daughter, her last child, Lydia. As the decades passed, grandchildren and great-grandchildren filled the lives of Duston and her husband, whose estate grew—courtesy of the ten scalps.

With the death of her husband in 1732, Hannah Duston moved in with her son Jonathan and his family, her name still commanding attention from her neighbors nearly thirty-five years after the moment she staggered up the riverbank with her grisly bundle. She died in early 1736 at the age of seventy-eight and was probably buried in Pentucket Cemetery, in Haverhill, though her headstone would not survive the centuries.

In death, Hannah Duston first reaped ongoing acclaim as a heroine of New England's frontier. She became the first American woman to have a statue erected in her honor, the monument raised on Boscawen, the New Hampshire island where she killed the nine Indians. Sculpted from Concord granite, the statue depicts Duston as a pretty, long-tressed colonial woman with a tomahawk in her right hand and a fistful of scalps in her left.

A hatchet thought to be the one shown in the statue rests in a case today at the Haverhill Historical Society with a knife taken from the body of Hannah's Indian master. Not far away, a boulder commemorates Hannah's last address, her son Jonathan's house. And in her hometown, a second statue honors Hannah; the image stands in the Grand Army of the Republic Park.

The feat that led to the building of those statues has become one of the darkest and most controversial episodes of colonial New England history. Duston, a bona fide heroine in her own day, an era in which atrocities were committed by settlers and Native Americans alike as the colonists brutally drove the tribes from their own lands, has not weathered the centuries well. On Boscawen, someone shot off the nose of Hannah's statue, and recently, Vermont and New Hampshire Indians branded her a monster and have urged the removal of her monument.

There is an inherent gap in modern attempts at psychoanalysis of the woman who saw her baby dashed against a tree and who, two weeks later, killed six sleeping Indian children and scalped them: although Hannah Duston herself imparted a graphic and pious account of her deeds to Cotton Mather, her actual state of mind when she brutalized her victims is a mystery. Lionized, demonized, and analyzed, she stands as America's first publicly acknowledged heroine. Her ordeal, and even her hatchet, remain for anyone to ponder.

Footnotes

MURDER IN THE NEW WORLD

1. *Records of the Governor and Company of the Massachusetts Bay in New England,* Dr. Nathaniel B. Shurtleff, ed., vol. 1, pp. 78, 79, and 81.
2. John Winthrop, "A Model of Christian Charity," in *The American Puritans,* Perry Miller, ed., p. 83.

DUEL IN THE SUN

1. Margaret Hodges, *Hopkins of the Mayflower,* p. 214.
2. George F. Willison, *Saints and Strangers,* p. 134.
3. "Goodmen" was a commonly used term for poorer Pilgrims.
4. William Bradford, *Of Plymouth Plantation,* Samuel Eliot Morison, ed., p. 75.
5. Ibid.
6. Mayflower Compact.
7. Bradford, p. 68.
8. The first name of Plymouth.
9. Bradford, p. 72.
10. Ibid., p. 77.
11. Ibid.
12. Willison, p. 141.
13. John A. Goodwin, *The Pilgrim Republic,* p. 161.
14. Alexander Young, *Chronicles of the Pilgrim Fathers,* p. 201.
15. Ibid.
16. Willison, p. 180.
17. Ibid., p. 438.
18. Young, p. 201.
19. Willison, p. 443; Bradford, p. 447.
20. Plymouth County Records; Eugene Aubrey Stratton, *Plymouth Colony, Its History and People, 1620–1691,* p. 284.
21. Ibid.
22. Ibid.

OUT OF ORDER: THOMAS LECHFORD, ESQ.

1. Thomas Lechford, *Note-Book,* pp. 67, 102, 127, 236, and 237.
2. Thomas G. Barnes, "Thomas Lechford," *Law in Colonial Massachusetts,* 1630–1800, p. 11.
3. John Winthrop's phrase describing Boston.
4. Massachusetts State Archives: "Disbarment Proceedings against Thomas Lechford."
5. Barnes, p. 13.
6. Ibid., p. 14.
7. Thomas Lechford, *Plain Dealing,* (section entitled "Proheme").
8. Barnes, p. 13.
9. Ibid., p. 14.
10. Ibid., p. 11.
11. Lechford, *Note-Book,* p. 48.
12. Ibid., p. 275.
13. Ibid., p. 47.
14. Walter Muir Whitehill, *Boston: A Topographical History,* p. 7.
15. Nathaniel Ward, "The Body of Liberties," Article 26 (Edwin Pow-

ers, *Crime and Punishment in Early Massachusetts, 1620–1692,* Appendix A, p. 536).

16. Darrett B. Rutman, *Winthrop's Boston,* p. 233.

17. Ibid., pp. 233–234; Barnes, p. 7.

18. Barnes, p. 7.

19. Whitehill, pp. 12–13.

20. Barnes, p. 21.

21. Lechford, *Note-Book,* p. 1.

22. Lechford, *Plain Dealing,* p. 69.

23. Lechford, *Note-Book,* pp. 67, 102, 127, 236, and 237; Barnes, p. 34.

24. Barnes, p. 34.

25. Barnes, p. 37; Lechford, *Plain Dealing,* p. 17.

26. Ibid.

27. Barnes, p. 26.

28. *Records of the Governor and Company of the Massachusetts Bay,* Nathaniel Shurtleff, ed., vol. 1, p. 270.

29. Edwin Powers, *Crime and Punishment,* p. 436; Lechford, *Note-Book,* p. 182.

30. Ibid.

31. Lechford, *Note-Book,* pp. 182–183; Barnes, p. 30.

32. Ibid.

33. Barnes, p. 30; Lechford, *Note-Book,* pp. 182–183.

34. Lechford, *Note-Book,* p. 182; Powers, p. 436.

35. Lechford, *Note-Book,* p. 23; Powers, p. 436.

36. Barnes, p. 29.

37. Lechford, *Plain Dealing,* p. 69; Powers, p. 436.

38. Barnes, p. 34.

39. Lechford, *Plain Dealing,* p. 77; Barnes, p. 35.

40. Shurtleff, vol. 1, p. 310; Powers, p. 436.

41. Lechford, *Plain Dealing,* p. 69; Powers, p. 436.

42. Lechford, *Plain Dealing,* pp. 28–30; Powers, p. 437.

43. Ibid.

44. Ibid.

45. Lechford, *Plain Dealing* (section titled "Proheme").

46. Barnes, p. 38.

THE MAINE MURDERESS

1. John Winthrop, *Winthrop's Journal,* vol. 2, James Kendall Hosmer, ed., p. 219.

2. An expression commonly used in the court records of colonial New England.

3. Winthrop, vol. 2, p. 218.

4. Winthrop, vol. 2, p. 219; Edwin Powers, *Crime and Punishment in Early Massachusetts, 1620–1692,* p. 288.

5. Powers, p. 288; *Records of the Court of Assistants,* vol. 2, John Noble, ed., p. 74.

6. Winthrop, vol. 2, p. 218.

7. John Gould, *There Goes Maine!* p. 32.

8. Ibid.

9. Neal W. Allen, Jr., "Maine Courts, Magistrates, and Lawyers," *Law in Colonial Massachusetts, 1630–1800,* p. 275.

10. Winthrop, p. 218.

11. Winthrop, p. 218; Powers, p. 288.

12. Ibid.

13. Ibid.

14. Ibid.

15. Ibid.
16. Ibid.
17. Ibid.
18. Ibid.
19. Powers, p. 287.
20. Winthrop, p. 219.

THE HARVARD HOODLUMS

1. John Winthrop, *Winthrop's Journal,* vol. 2, James Kendall Hosmer, ed., pp. 169–170.
2. Ibid., p. 170.

"JUST TO STAND ONE MINUTE . . . A FREE WOMAN"

1. Sidney Kaplan and Emma Nogrady Kaplan, *The Black Presence,* p. 216.
2. Harriet Martineau, *Retrospect of Western Travel,* vol. 2, p. 105.
3. Ibid.
4. Ibid.
5. Jon Swan, "The Slave Who Sued for Freedom," p. 52.
6. The Sheffield Declaration.
7. Theodore Sedgwick, Jr., *The Practicability of the Abolition of Slavery,* p. 15.
8. Swan, p. 59.
9. Ibid.
10. Sedgwick, p. 15.
11. Ibid.
12. Kaplan, p. 217.
13. Sedgwick, p. 15.
14. Ibid.
15. Ibid.
16. Swan, p. 52.
17. Ibid.
18. Ibid.
19. Sedgwick, p. 15.
20. Ibid.

21. Ibid.
22. Berkshire County Court Records.
23. Sedgwick, p. 16.
24. *Dictionary of American Biography,* vol. 8 , p. 469.
25. Ibid., p. 468.
26. Ibid.
27. Ibid.
28. Ibid., p. 469.
29. Swan, p. 54.
30. Ibid.
31. Ibid.
32. Ibid.
33. Martineau, p. 105.
34. Swan, p. 54.
35. Ibid.
36. Ibid. pp. 54–55.
37. Ibid., pp. 18–19.
38. Ibid., p. 54.
39. Ibid., p. 55.
40. Sedgwick, p. 17.
41. Ibid.
42. Ibid.
43. Ibid.
44. Ibid.
45. Ibid.
46. Ibid.
47. Martineau, pp. 106–109.
48. Swan, p. 55.
49. Sedgwick, p. 16.
50. Swan, p. 55.

A CONNECTICUT YANKEE AND OLD MAN ELOQUENT

1. *The Dictionary of American Biography,* vol. 1, p. 542.
2. John W. Barber, "A History of the *Amistad* Captives," p. 71.
3. Ibid.
4. *The New York Sun,* August 31, 1839.

5. Barber, p. 71.

6. *The New York Sun,* August 31, 1839.

7. Fred J. Cook, "The Slave Ship Rebellion," *American Heritage* (February 1955): p. 105.

8. Ibid.

9. Ibid.

10. Howard Jones, *Murder on the Amistad,* p. 172.

11. Cook, p. 106.

12. *The Argument of John Quincy Adams Before the Supreme Court of the United States, Appellants, vs. Cinque and Others, Africans, Captured in the Schooner* Amistad.

13. Ibid.

14. Ibid.

15. Ibid.

16. Ibid.

17. Leonard L. Richards, *The Life and Times of Congressman John Quincy Adams,* p. 137.

18. Ibid., p. 138.

19. Ibid.

20. *The Dictionary of American Biography,* vol. 1, p. 532.

21. Ibid.

THE GENTLE CRUSADER: SARAH HALE

1. Ralph Nading Hill, "Mr. Godey's Lady," *American Heritage* (October 1958): p. 20.

2. Helen Beal Woodward, *The Bold Woman,* p. 187.

3. Ibid., p. 188.

4. *Notable American Women,* Edward T. James, ed., p. 111. (Also, Sarah Hale, *The Genius of Oblivion*).

5. Sarah Hale, *Northwood* (1852 edition), preface.

6. Ibid., title page.

7. William R. Taylor, *Cavalier and Yankee,* p. 109.

8. Hale, *Northwood,* p. 235.

9. Ibid., p. 73.

10. Abraham Lincoln's famous term for slavery.

11. Taylor, p. 118.

12. Hale, p. 407.

13. Ibid., p. 401.

14. Taylor, p. 113.

15. Ibid., pp. 118–119.

16. Woodward, p. 191.

17. Ibid.

18. Hale, p. iv.

19. *Ladies' Magazine,* January 1828.

20. Taylor, p. 98.

21. Sarah Hale, *Godey's Lady's Book,* December 1877.

22. *Ladies' Magazine,* February 1832, p. 87.

23. Hill, p. 22.

24. *Ladies' Magazine,* January 1828.

25. Hale, *Godey's Lady's Book,* March 1854, p. 276.

26. Hale, *Godey's Lady's Book,* March 1852, p. 186.

27. Ibid.

28. Hill, p. 20.

29. Ibid., p. 101.

30. *Notable American Women,* p. 112.

31. Hale, *Godey's Lady's Book,* December 1877.

32. Hale, *Northwood* (1852), p. iv.

CALLING DR. LEE

1. Jean Hennelley Keith, "Ahead of Her Time," *Bostonia Magazine,* p. 60.

2. Ibid.

3. Frederick C. Waite, *History of the New England Female Medical College,* p. 88.
4. Ibid.
5. Mary Roth Walsh, *Doctors Wanted: No Women Need Apply,* p. 61.
6. *Boston Almanac & Directory,* 1872, p. 300.
7. Keith, p. 60.
8. Ibid.
9. Ibid.
10. Dr. Rebecca Lee Crumpler, *A Book of Medical Discourses in Two Parts* (title page).
11. Keith, p. 60.
12. Ibid.
13. Ibid.
14. Ibid.
15. Ibid.
16. Ibid.
17. Ibid.
18. Ibid.

FIRST CLASS ALL THE WAY

1. J. M. Fenster, "Palaces of the People," *American Heritage* (April 1994): p. 46.
2. Ibid.
3. Ibid.
4. Ibid., p. 45.
5. Ibid.
6. Ibid.
7. Ibid.

"THE MANSION OF HAPPINESS"—AMERICA'S FIRST BOARD GAME

1. The Mansion of Happiness, the gameboard's inscription.
2. Peter Andrews, "Games People Played," *American Heritage* (June 1972): p. 67.

THE LUNCH KING: WALTER SCOTT

1. *Providence Journal,* September 21, 1887.
2. *Providence Sunday Journal,* July 21, 1917.
3. Ibid.
4. Ibid.
5. Ibid.
6. Ibid.
7. Ibid.
8. Ibid.
9. *Providence Journal,* September 21, 1887.
10. *Providence Sunday Journal,* July 21, 1917.
11. Ibid.
12. Ibid.
13. Ibid.
14. Ibid.
15. Ibid.
16. Ibid.
17. Richard J. S. Gutman, *American Diner,* p. 12.

LILLIAN NORDICA: THE DOWN EAST DIVA

1. *The National Cyclopedia of American Biography,* vol. 9, p. 217 (quoted from a *New York Herald* review by H. E. Krehbiel).
2. Ira Glackens, *Yankee Diva,* p. 22. (*Yankee Diva,* by Ira Glackens, contains much of Lillian Nordica's considerable correspondence.)
3. Ibid.
4. Ibid.
5. Ibid., p. 31.
6. Ibid., p. 32.
7. *Notable American Women,* Edward T. James, ed., vol. 2, p. 634.

8. Glackens, p. 124.

9. Ibid., p. 152.

10. *Notable American Women*, vol. 2, p. 634.

11. Ibid.

12. *The National Cyclopedia of American Biography*, vol. 9, p. 217.

13. Notable American Women, vol. 2, p. 634.

14. *The National Cyclopedia of American Biography*, vol. 9, p. 217.

15. *Notable American Women*, vol. 2, p. 635.

16. Glackens, p. 274.

17. Ibid.

YOU SAID A MOUTHFUL

1. Clifton Daniel, *Chronicle of America*, p. 62.

CAPTAIN MOREY'S HORSE-LESS CARRIAGE

1. Richard P. Scharchburg, "First Liquid-Fuel Engine Made by N.H. Man in 1826," *Automotive News*, 1993.

2. Samuel Morey's Patent for "A Gas and Vapor Engine," April 1, 1826.

3. *The American Car Since 1775*, p. 25.

4. The Morey Patent.

5. Ibid.

6. *The Republican* (Springfield, MA), November 26, 1826.

7. Scharchburg.

8. Ibid.

9. Ibid.

10. Ibid.

11. The Morey Patent.

A SPARK OF GENIUS

1. Proceedings of the Vermont Historical Society, 1926–1928, p. 218.

2. Reverend Willard G. Davenport, "Inventor of the Electric Motor," p. 67; Bertha S. Dodge, *Tales of Vermont Ways and People*, p. 176.

3. Dodge, pp. 176–177.

4. Reverend Willard G. Davenport, p. 66.

5. Walter Rice Davenport, *Biography of Thomas Davenport*, p. 60.

6. T. Commerford Martin, "An Appreciation of Thomas Davenport" (An Address, Proceedings of the Vermont Historical Society, 1909–1910) p. 96.

7. Reverend Willard G. Davenport, p. 63.

8. Proceedings of the Vermont Historical Society, 1926–1927–1928, p. 211.

9. Ibid.

10. Proceedings of the Vermont Historical Society, 1909–1910, p. 97.

11. Dodge, p. 177.

12. Walter Davenport, p. 62.

13. Ibid.

14. Ibid.

15. Ibid.

16. Ibid.

17. Ibid.

18. Dodge, p. 180.

19. T. Commerford Martin, pp. 99–100.

20. Dodge, pp. 180–181.

21. Ibid., p. 179.

22. Ibid., p. 180.

23. Walter Davenport, p. 156.

A CLASS ACT

1. Beaumont Newhall, *The Daguerreotype in America*, p. 15.

2. Floyd Rinhart and Marion Rinhart, *The American Daguerreotype*, p. 38.

3. Ibid.
4. Ibid., p. 39.

BEFORE KITTY HAWK: CRAZY WHITEHEAD'S FLIGHT

1. Richard Howell, *Bridgeport (CT) Sunday Herald,* August, 18, 1901.
2. Boston Aeronautical Society Records.
3. Stella Randolph, *The Story of Gustave Whitehead,* p. 69.
4. Ibid.
5. Ibid.
6. Ibid.
7. Ibid.
8. Ibid., p. 70.
9. Affidavit of Edward Prior.
10. Howell.
11. Ibid.
12. Frank J. Delear, "First-Flight Controversy," p. 70.
13. Affidavit of Junius Harworth.
14. Ibid.
15. Gustave Whitehead, letter to *The American Inventor,* April 1, 1902.
16. Ibid.
17. Affidavit of Anton Pruckner.
18. Randolph, p. 113.
19. Cook, p. 103.

THE MASSACHUSETTS BAY MADAM

1. Suffolk (MA) County Court Records, vol. 29 (1672), pp. 82–83.
2. William Bradford, *Of Plymouth Plantation,* p. 204.
3. Edwin Powers, *Crime and Punishment in Early Massachusetts,* p. 172.
4. Suffolk County Court Records, pp. 82–83.

5. Ibid.
6. Ibid.
7. John Dunton, *Letters from New England,* p. 118.
8. Suffolk County Court Records, pp. 82–83.
9. Ibid., p. 126.
10. Edwin Powers, *Crime and Punishment in Early Massachusetts, 1620–1692,* p. 180.
11. Ibid.

THE BISHOP AND THE BRICKLAYER

1. George Potter, *To the Golden Door,* p. 290.
2. Ibid.
3. Ibid., p. 296.
4. Ibid.
5. Ibid., p. 297.
6. Ibid.
7. Ibid., p. 301.
8. *The Pilot,* August 15, 1846, p.1.

A ROYAL SCANDAL

1. *The New York Times,* May 9, 1887, p. 1.
2. Ibid.
3. Ibid., May 29, 1887, p. 3.
4. Thomas H. O'Connor, *The Boston Irish,* p. 132.
5. George Potter, *To the Golden Door,* p. 269.
6. O'Connor, p. 118.
7. Ibid., p. 120.
8. *Times,* May 9, 1887, p. 1.
9. Ibid.
10. Ibid.
11. Ibid.
12. Ibid., May 10, 1887, p.1.
13. Ibid.

14. Ibid.
15. Ibid.
16. Ibid.
17. Ibid., May 11, 1887, p. 1.
18. Ibid.
19. Ibid., May 29, 1887, p. 3.
20. Ibid.
21. Ibid.
22. Ibid.
23. Ibid.
24. Ibid.

A COMRADE IN ARMS: PETER SALEM

1. Sidney Kaplan and Emma Nogrady Kaplan, *The Black Presence,* p. 18.
2. Ibid., p. 15.
3. Ibid., p. 16.
4. Ibid.
5. Ibid., p. 18.
6. Clifton Daniel, ed., *Chronicles of America,* p. 147.
7. Ibid.
8. Kaplan, p. 18.
9. Ibid.
10. Ibid.
11. Ibid.
12. Ibid.
13. Ibid., p. 19.
14. Ibid. pp. 19–20.
15. Ibid., p. 18.

THE FATHER OF THE COAST GUARD

1. The Naval Commission of Hopley Yeaton, March 21, 1791, Library of Congress.
2. Letter from John Sullivan to Pickering & Hodson, of Philadelphia, March 5, 1788.

3. Dedication of Hopley Yeaton Monument, October 19, 1975.

"SIR WILLIAM, ARISE"

1. Alice Lounsberry, *Sir William Phips,* p. 148.
2. Ibid., pp. 152–153.
3. Ibid., p. 154.

WHEEL OF FORTUNE—AND MISFORTUNE

1. Arnold Welles, "The Factory System," p. 36.
2. Letter from Samuel Slater to Moses Brown, December 2, 1789.
3. Letter from Moses Brown to Samuel Slater, December 10, 1789.
4. Ibid.
5. Welles, p. 38; John Steele Gordon, "Technology Transfer," p. 20.
6. Ibid.
7. Welles, p. 38.
8. Ibid., p. 90.
9. Alexander Hamilton, Report on Manufactures to Congress, 1791; Welles, p. 90.
10. Barbara M. Tucker, *Samuel Slater and the Origins of the American Textile Industry, 1790–1860,* p. 72.
11. Letter from Sally Brown to Sarah Brown, November 14, 1794.
12. Letter from Samuel Slater to Almy and Brown, March 1797.
13. Letter from Samuel Slater to Almy and Brown, January 26, 1796.
14. Ibid., February 19, 1796.
15. Ibid.
16. Ibid.
17. Ibid., November 14, 1793.
18. Ibid., December 24, 1794.
19. Welles, p. 91.

NEW ENGLAND'S FIRST NEWS HOUNDS

1. *The Present State of the New-English Affairs,* 1689.
2. Letter by Samuel Green; *Dictionary of American Biography,* p. 555.
3. *The Present State of the New-English Affairs,* 1689.
4. Ibid.
5. Ibid.
6. Ibid.
7. *Publick Occurrences, Both Foreign and Domestick,* September 25, 1690.
8. The Diary of Samuel Sewall, pp. 332–333.
9. John Dunton, *Letters Written from New England,* p. 80.

YOU CAN LOOK IT UP

1. Richard C. Steele, *Isaiah Thomas,* p. 17.
2. Ibid.
3. Ibid., pp. 27–28.
4. Ibid., p. 13.
5. Ibid., p. 17.

THE ABCS AND RECIPES

1. Table of contents of the *Children's Magazine,* January 1789.
2. Amelia Simmons, *American Cookery,* title page.

HANNAH DUSTON'S HATCHET

1. Cotton Mather, *Magnalia Christi Americana.*
2. Ibid.
3. Ibid.
4. "Hannah Duston," *The National Cyclopedia of American Biography,* vol. 6, p. 103.
5. Ibid.
6. Mather.
7. Ibid.
8. The Petition of Thomas Duston to the General Court of Massachusetts, June 1697.
9. Proclamation of the General Court, June 8, 1697.
10. Mather

Bibliography

〜

The Adams Papers, Massachusetts Historical Society.

Almy & Brown Papers, Rhode Island Historical Society.

The American Car Since 1775. The Editors of Automobile Quarterly. New York: Automobile Quarterly, Inc., 1971.

Andrews, Peter. "Games People Played." *American Heritage,* June 1972, pp. 64–68, 69–78, 79, 104–105.

The Argument of John Quincy Adams Before the Supreme Court. New York: Negro Universities Press, 1969.

Baldwin, Simeon Eben. "Roger Baldwin." *Great American Lawyers,* Vol. 5, no. 3. 1908.

Banks, Charles Edward. *The English Ancestry and Homes of the Pilgrim Fathers.* Baltimore, MD: Genealogical Publishing Company, 1968.

Barber, John W. "A History of the *Amistad* Captives." New Haven Historical Society, 1841.

Barne, Thomas. "Thomas Lechford." *Law in Colonial Massachusetts, 1630–1800.* Boston: The Colonial Society of Massachusetts, 1984.

Barnes, V. F. "The Rise of William Phips." *New England Quarterly,* July 1928.

___."Phippus Maximus." *New England Quarterly,* October 1928.

Bartlett, Albert L. "The Story of Hannah Dustin." *Haverhill Evening Gazette,* August 30, 1933.

Baylies, Francis. *New Plymouth.* 2 vols. Boston: Hilliard, Gray, Little, and Wilkins, 1880.

Bradford, William. *William Bradford's History of Plymouth Plantation, 1606–1646.* New York: Barnes & Noble, 1946.

Browning, Frank, and John Gerassi. *The American Way of Crime.* New York: G. P. Putnam's Sons, 1980.

Carter, George Calvin. *Samuel Morey, the Edison of His Day.* Concord, NH: Rumford Press, 1945.

Chase, George Wingate. *The History of Haverhill, Massachusetts.* Haverhill: C. W. Chase, 1861.

The Children's Magazine, January to April 1789.

Commerford, Martin T. "An Appreciation of Thomas Davenport," Montpelier, VT: The Vermont Historical Society, 1929.

Cook, Fred J. "The Slave Ship Rebellion." *American Heritage* (February 1955): pp. 61–64; 104–106.

Cooke, David C. *Who Really Invented the Airplane?* New York: G. P. Putnam's Sons, 1964.

Coquillette, Daniel R., ed., *Law in Colonial Massachusetts, 1630–1800.* Boston: The Colonial Society of Massachusetts (Distributed by the University of Virginia Press) 1984.

Crumpler, Doctor Rebecca Lee. *A Book of Medical Discourses*. Boston: Cashman, Keating & Company, 1883.

Daniel, Clifton, ed. *Chronicles of America*. Mount Kisco, NY: Chronicle Publications, 1980.

Davenport, Walter Rice, D.D., *Biography of Thomas Davenport: "The Brandon Blacksmith," Inventor of the Electric Motor*. Montpelier, VT: The Vermont Historical Society, 1929.

Davenport, The Reverend Willard G. "Thomas Davenport, Inventor of the Electric Motor." Montpelier, VT: Proceedings of the Vermont Historical Society, 1896.

Delear, Frank J. "First-Flight Controversy," *Aviation History*, March 1996.

Dillon, Francis. *The Pilgrims*. Garden City, NY: Doubleday & Company, Inc., 1975.

Dobler, Lavina, and Edgar A. Toppin. *Pioneers and Patriots, The Lives of Six Negroes of the Revolutionary Era*. Garden City, NY: Doubleday & Company, Zenith Books, 1965.

Dodge, Bertha S. *Tales of Vermont Ways and People*. Mechanicsburg, PA: Stackpole Books, 1977.

Dunton, John. *Letters Written from New England*. Boston: The Prince Society, 1867.

Eliot, W. H. *A Description of the Tremont House, with Architectural Illustration*. Boston: Gray and Bowen, 1830.

Farrell, Jr., Gabriel. "Captain Morey." New Hampshire Historical Society collection, 1915.

Favors, John and Katherine. *John Quincy Adams and the* Amistad. Oakland, CA: Jonka Enterprises, 1974.

Fenster, J. M. "Palaces of the People." *American Heritage* (April 1994): pp. 46–58.

Foss, Gerald D. "Captain Hopley Yeaton." *The Royal Arch Mason* (Summer 1977); Portsmouth, Athenaeum Collections.

George, R. H. "The Treasure Trove of William Phips." *New England Quarterly* (June 1933).

Glackens, Ira. *Yankee Diva: Lillian Nordica and the Golden Days of Opera*. New York: Coleridge Press, 1963. (This biography includes much of Lillian Nordica's extensive correspondence.)

Godey's Lady's Book, 1837–1877.

Goodwin, John A. *The Pilgrim Republic*. Boston: Houghton Mifflin, 1960.

Goodwin, Katherine R. *Captain Samuel Morey: the Edison of His Day*. White River Junction, VT: Vermonter Press, 1931.

Gould, John. *There Goes Maine!* New York: W. W. Norton & Company, 1990.

Gordon, John Steele. "Technology Transfer." *American Heritage*, February 1990, pp. 18, 20.

Gutman, Richard J. S. *American Diner: Then and Now*. New York: Harper Perennial, 1993.

Hale, Sarah Josepha. *Northwood*, (second edition). New York: Long, 1852.

Hill, Ralph Nading. "Mr. Godey's Lady." *American Heritage*, October 1958, pp.

20–27; 97–101.

___. *Sidewalk Saga: A Chronicle of Steamboating*. New York: Rinehart, 1953.

Hodges, Margaret. *Hopkins of the* Mayflower: *Portrait of a Dissenter*. New York: Farrar, Straus and Giroux, 1972.

Hodgson, Alice Doan. "The John L. Sullivan & Samuel Morey Connection." *Towpath Topics*, Vol. 18, No. 2, (Middlesex Canal Association) April 1980.

Hoehling, Mary Duprey. *A Yankee in the White House: John Quincy Adams*. New York: J. Messner, Inc., 1963.

Hutchinson, William. *The History of the Colony of Massachusetts Bay from 1628 to 1691*. New York: Arno Press, 1972.

Ives, William. The Ives Papers. Salem: Peabody & Essex Institute collection.

James, Edward T., ed., *Notable American Women, 1607–1950, A Biographical Directory*. 3 vols. Cambridge, MA: The Belknap Press of Harvard University, 1971.

Jones, Howard. *Mutiny on the* Amistad. New York: Oxford University Press, 1987.

The Juvenile Miscellany, September 1826 to January 1829.

Kane, Joseph Nathan. *Famous First Facts*. New York: H. W. Wilson, 1980.

Kaplan, Sidney, and Emma Nogrady Kaplan. *The Black Presence in the Era of the American Revolution*. Amherst, MA: University of Massachusetts Press, 1989.

Karraker, Cyrus H. *The Hispaniola Treasure*. Philadelphia: University of Pennsylvania Press, 1934.

Keith, Jean Hennelley, "Ahead of Her Time," *Bostonia Magazine*, Summer 1995, p. 60.

Kulik, Gary; Roger Parks; and Theodore Z. Penn. *The New England Mill Village, 1790–1860*. Cambridge, MA: The MIT Press, 1982.

Ladies' Magazine, 1828–1836.

Lea, Gary R. "The Tragedy of Samuel Morey." *Vermont History* 31 (January 1964): p. 25.

Lechford, Thomas. "Note-Book, 1638–1641." American Antiquarian Society Collections.

___. *Plain Dealing: or, News from New England*. London, 1642. Boston Edition: J. K. Wiggin & William Parsons Lunt, 1867.

Lillian Nordica Collections, Farmington, Maine.

The List of American Patents.

Lounsberry, Alice. *Sir William Phips, Treasurer, Fisherman, and Governor of the Massachusetts Bay Colony*. New York: Charles Scribner's Sons, 1941.

Marble, Annie Russell. *From Apprentice to Patron: The Life Story of Isaiah Thomas*. New York: D. Appleton Company, 1935.

Martin, Christopher. *The* Amistad *Affair*. New York: Abelard-Schuman, 1970.

Martineau, Harriet. *Retrospect of Western Travel, Vol. 2*. London: Saunders and Otley, 1838.

Mather, Cotton. *Magnalia Christi Americana*. London, 1702.

Miller, Perry, ed. *The American Puritans: Their Prose and Poetry*. New York: Doubleday, 1956.

Morison, Samuel Eliot, ed. *Of Plymouth Plantation.* New York: Alfred A. Knopf, 1976.

Mowry, William Augustus. "Who Invented the American Steamboat?" New Hampshire Antiquarian Society of Collections, 1874.

The National Cyclopedia of American Biography. 63 vols. Clifton, NJ: James T. White & Company, 1984.

New England Quarterly.

Newhall, Beaumont. *The Daguerreotype in America.* New York: Dover Publications, 1961.

Nevins, Allan, ed. *The Diary of John Quincy Adams, 1794–1845.* New York: Longmans, Green, and Company, 1928.

Noble, John, and John F. Cronin, eds. *Records of the Court of Assistants of the Colony of the Massachusetts Bay, 1630–1692.* 3 vols. Boston: Published by the County of Suffolk, 1901, 1904, 1928.

O'Connor, Thomas H. *The Boston Irish.* Boston: Northeastern University Press, 1995.

Owens, William A. *Black Mutiny: The Revolt on the Schooner* Amistad. Boston: Pilgrim Press, 1968.

Peabody & Essex Museum, Salem, MA.

The Pelham Papers, Massachusetts Historical Society.

Perry, William. *The Royal Standard English Dictionary,* 1788.

Potter, George. *To the Golden Door.* Boston: Little, Brown and Company, 1960.

Powers, Edwin. *Crime and Punishment in Early Massachusetts, 1620–1692, a Documentary History.* Boston: Beacon Press, 1966.

The Present State of the New-English Affairs, 1689.

Providence Journal.

Quincy, Josiah. LL.D. *Memoir of the Life of John Quincy Adams.* Boston: Phillips, Sampson, and Company, 1859.

Randolph, Stella. *The Story of Gustave Whitehead: Before the Wrights Flew.* New York: G. P. Putnam's Sons, 1966.

Records of the Court of Assistants of the Colony of Massachusetts Bay, 1630–1692. Suffolk County Court Collections.

Richards, Leonard L. *The Life and Times of Congressman John Quincy Adams.* New York: Oxford Press, Inc., 1986.

Rinhart, Floyd, and Marion Rinhart. *The American Daguerreotype.* Athens, GA: University of Georgia Press, 1981.

Rollins, Charlemae Hill. *They Showed the Way: Forty American Negro Leaders.* New York: Thomas Y. Crowell Company, 1964.

Rutman, Darrett B. *Winthrop's Boston, Portrait of a Puritan Town, 1630–1649.* Chapel Hill, NC: University of North Carolina Press, 1965.

Scharchburg, Richard P. "First Liquid-Fuel Engine Made by N.H. Man in 1826." *Automotive News,* 1993.

Sedgwick, Theodore, Jr. *The Practicability of the Abolition of Slavery.* New York: J. Seymour, 1831.

Sewall, Samuel. *The Diary of Samuel Sewall, 1674–1729.* 2 vols. New York: Farrar, Straus, and Giroux, 1973.

The Sheffield Declaration, 1773.

Shipton, Clifford K. *Isaiah Thomas: Printer, Patriot, and Philanthropist, 1749–1831.* Rochester, NY: Hart Printing House, 1948.

Shurtleff, Dr. Nathaniel B., ed. *Records of the Governor and Company of the Massachusetts Bay in New England, 1628–1686.* 6 vols. Boston: The Press of William White, 1853–1854.

Simmons, Amelia. *American Cookery.* Hartford, CT: Hudson & Goodwin, 1796.

Slade, D. R. "Henry Pelham." *Colonial Society of Massachusetts Publications,* Vol. 5, 1902.

Steele, Richard C. *Isaiah Thomas.* Worcester Historical Museum, 1981.

Stratton, Eugene Aubrey. *Plymouth Colony, Its History & People, 1620–1691.* Salt Lake City, UT: Ancestry Publishing, 1986.

Swan, Jon. "The Slave Who Sued for Freedom," *American Heritage,* March 1990.

Taft, Robert. *Photography and the American Scene.* New York: MacMillan Company, 1938.

Taylor, William R. *Cavalier and Yankee: The Old South and American National Character.* Garden City, NY: Doubleday & Company, Inc., 1963.

Thompson, Mack. *Moses Brown: Reluctant Reformer.* Chapel Hill, NC: University of North Carolina Press, 1962.

Trimble, William. *High Frontier.* Pittsburgh: University of Pittsburgh Press, 1982.

Tucker, Barbara. *Samuel Slater and the Origins of the American Textile Industry, 1790–1860.* Ithaca, NY: Cornell University Press, 1984.

Tulley's Almanack. Boston Public Library Collections.

Venezia, Joyce A. "Connecticut Pair to Build Replica of First Plane." Associated Press, 1985.

Waite, Frederick C. *History of the New England Female Medical College, 1848–1875.* Boston: Boston University School of Medicine, 1950.

Walsh, Mary Roth. *"Doctors Wanted: No Women Need Apply": Sexual Barriers in the Medical Profession, 1835–1875.* New Haven and London: Yale University Press, 1977.

Weeks, Lyman Horace. *An Historical Digest of the Provincial Press, 1689–1783,* Vol. 1. Boston: The American Society, 1907.

Welles, Arnold. "The Father of Our Factory System." *American Heritage* (April 1958): pp. 34–39, 90–92.

White, G. S. Memoir of Samuel Slater, 1836. Rhode Island Historical Society.

Whitehill, Walter Muir. *Boston: A Topographical History.* Cambridge, MA: Belknap Press of Harvard University Press, 1968.

Willison, George F. *Saints and Strangers.* New York: Reynal & Hitchcock, 1945.

Winthrop, John. *Winthrop's Journal.* Vols. 1 and 2. Edited by James Kendall Hosmer. New York: Barnes & Noble, 1959.

Wintermantel, Ed. "Were We Wrong About the Wrights?" *The Pittsburgh Press,* November 30, 1969, p. 3.

Woolward, Helen Beal. *The Bold Women.* New York: Farrar, Straus and Young, 1953.

Young, Alexander. *Chronicles of the Pilgrim Fathers.* New York: DeCapo Press, 1971.
Zobel, Hiller B. The *Boston Massacre.* New York: W. W. Norton & Company, Inc. 1970.

The author is grateful for access to a range of archival material from the following repositories.

The American Antiquarian Society.
Boston Athenaeum.
Boston Public Library.
Bridgeport, CT, Historical Society.
Bridgeport, CT, Public Library.
Connecticut Historical Society.
Maine Historical Society.
Massachusetts State Archives.
Massachusetts Historical Society.
New Hampshire Historical Society.
New Haven (CT) Historical Society.
Portsmouth Athenaeum.
Providence (RI) Historical Society.
Providence Public Library.
Quincy, (MA) Historical Society.
Rhode Island Historical Society.
Slater Mill Historic Site, Pawtucket, RI.
Vermont Historical Society.

Index